DAILY LIVING IN THE TWELFTH CENTURY

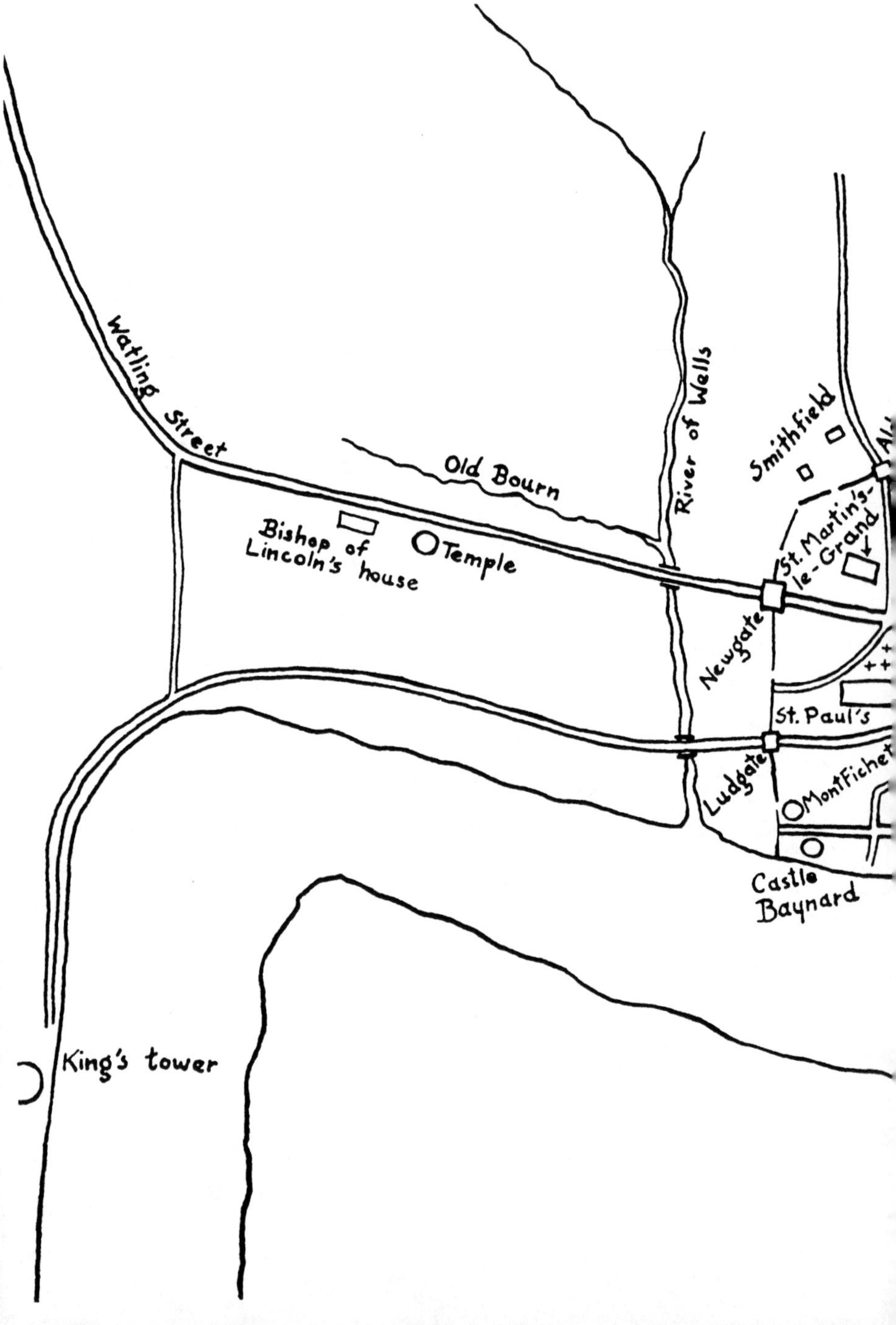
Watling Street
Old Bourn
River of Wells
Smithfield
St. Martin's-le-Grand
Bishop of Lincoln's house
Temple
Newgate
St. Paul's
Ludgate
Montfichet
Castle Baynard
King's tower

LONDON

in the year 1180

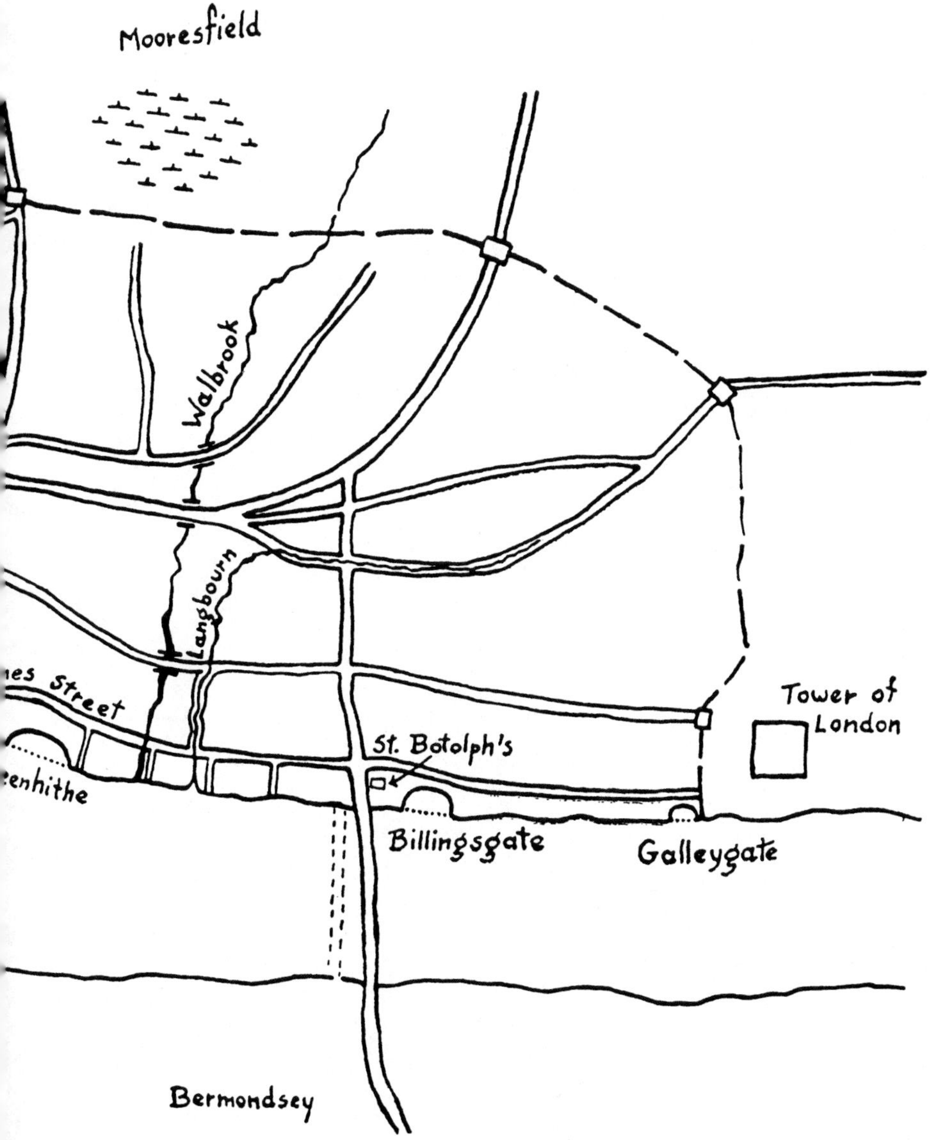

DAILY LIVING IN THE TWELFTH CENTURY ❦ Based on the Observations of Alexander Neckam in London and Paris

Urban Tigner Holmes, Jr., F.S.A.

THE UNIVERSITY OF WISCONSIN PRESS

The University of Wisconsin Press
2537 Daniels Street
Madison, Wisconsin 53718

3 Henrietta Street
London WC2E 8LU, England

Printed in the United States of America

ISBN 0-299-00854-1; LC 52-62000

look, following discovery and invention, accelerates the discarding of familiar objects and conventions.

I have used for this book sources written in Latin and French, and a few in English and Spanish, which date from 1150 to 1200; illustrations are taken from museum objects, sculptures, and manuscript illuminations of the same period. To follow this limitation strictly would necessitate the omission of the Bayeux Tapestry and the writings of Guibert de Nogent, Baudri de Bourgueil, and others, who are somewhat early, as well as the *Flamenca*, the *Livre des mestiers* of Estienne Boileau, John of Garland,[1] the *Blonde d'Oxford*, *Wistasce li moines*, certain fabliaux, and all the romances of Jehan Renart, which are a little late. But some of these sources give valuable details which are sketched only dimly in texts of the second half of the twelfth century. I have accordingly made limited use of some of these, with control. In one or two instances I have even used Renaissance evidence—for example, in examining the extant maps of London and Paris, and in citing Dr. Lister and Samuel Pepys on questions affecting sanitation and the procuring of water. These later pieces of evidence are useful in that they continue to reflect the ways of peoples living in a nonmechanized era. The reader may ask what is intended by "control." It means that detailed descriptions from outside the period can be used only where twelfth-century texts attest the existence of the object or practice, and where it is reasonable to expect no important variation in detail. Furthermore, if a procedure such as towing boats by horse up and down the Seine is attested for the eleventh century, and then again for the sixteenth, it is safe to assume that this was done in the twelfth. Even a few details of the method can be selected from the eleventh- and sixteenth-century accounts, especially where these agree. In discussing wooden houses, which then were common and which now have totally disappeared, I am somewhat at the mercy of the Bayeux Tapestry. I have tried, however, to rationalize a bit on the representations portrayed there.

The plan of accompanying Alexander Neckam on a journey to Paris from his home in Dunstable may smack a little of novelistic fiction. But the *De nominibus utensilium* is an interesting document, and the plan of following its author on a journey is a suitable way to use it. This is certainly in keeping with the mediaeval manner of description. The "describers," from John of Garland to Guillot de Paris and Walter of Bibblesworth, liked to have you accompany them as they moved about. I have incorporated into these pages an almost complete translation of the *De nominibus utensilium*, omitting a few moralizing and etymological sections. There are occasional places where the translation is not sure, and the reader should be warned that the Old French commentators who glossed the manuscripts used by Thomas Wright and others were not always certain of the meaning. At first I intended to add a critical text of the Latin original of the *De nominibus*, but this would be a separate study in itself as there are seventeen or more manuscripts.[2] I abandoned this plan and make page references to the edition printed by Thomas Wright. However, for my own use I have had a new text based upon a reading of the manuscript Worcester Q.50, folios 1–18. This was prepared for me by Miss Marion Greene. I have compared it with A. Scheler's transcription of Bruges MS 536, in *Jahrbuch für romanische und englische Literatur*, and with the Wright edition.[3] Variations in these have proved to be largely a matter of word order, with omissions and additions of a slight character.

It is my hope that this plan—concentrating upon smaller

areas of time in works dealing with early civilization—will be judged a success. The period 1325–75 would be an admirable subject for similar treatment, as would the first half of the fifteenth century.

This volume is not intended to be a compilation of secondary material. It is a personal interpretation based upon primary texts, upon archaeological evidence, and upon mediaeval iconography. I hope that I shall not be criticized for failing to include what is in So-and-so's book. No one should go through the notes seeking to find a synthesis of everything that has been said in the nineteenth and twentieth centuries about mediaeval life. Neither can this book be expected to offer the last shade of opinion on music, art, taxation, feudalism, and the development of political and civic institutions. Whole libraries have been devoted to these subjects. This volume is primarily a companion for literary studies, not an encyclopedia of mediaeval civilization.

This "loving attempt" to reconstruct the past would not have found much favor, I admit, with many mediaevals, who were on the side of the moderns:

> In every century its own hath been unpopular, and each age from the beginning hath preferred the past to itself, hence my times have despised me. . . . I give the name of modern period to the hundred years which have passed, and not to those which are to come, although they may have the right to the name, by reason of their nearness, since the past hath to do with narration and the future with divination.[4]

We take comfort in an observation made by Jehan de Meun: "For the present lasts so short a time, there is no count or measure of it";[5] and in this oft-quoted statement ascribed by John of Salisbury to Bernard de Chartres: "We are as dwarfs mounted on the shoulders of giants . . . we can see more and further than they . . . because we are raised and borne aloft upon that giant mass."[6] We are astounded today at the conceit which could cause John to believe that the men of his time could see further than Cicero or Seneca; but every age must have its own pride.

In gathering this material I have knocked at many doors. I owe much to Professor R. S. Rogers of Duke University, who has been my Latinist consultant, and to my friend and student Fr. Edwin D. Cuffe, S.J., who has shown an unerring eye in turning up valuable passages. For similar help I owe thanks to Miss Florence McCulloch. Several chapters in this book were read before the Mediaeval Institute at the University of Notre Dame in December, 1948. Sketches inset in the text were made by Dr. Hampton Hubbard, who, like so many surgeons, combines skill in the artist's media and skill with the scalpel. For clerical help I am indebted to the Carnegie Foundation for the Advancement of Teaching, which gave a small grant for this purpose. On one occasion I was allowed traveling expenses by the Smith Fund of the Graduate School of the University of North Carolina.

URBAN TIGNER HOLMES, JR.

Chapel Hill
April 17, 1951

The Chapters

The Illustrations

DAILY LIVING IN THE TWELFTH CENTURY

Chapter 1

Introduction

THE SECOND half of the twelfth century was a remarkable one for the development of intellectual maturity and literature.[1] At a date not far from 1150 some ingenious cleric, or clerics, adapted the form of the rhymed chronicle, making it retell the stories of Latin epic; thus the romance form was born. Just about the time Henry II of England was seeking to gobble up Toulouse (in 1159) another clever narrator put into verse form a brisk tale such as "men" like to tell: the fabliau came into being. Early in the 1170's someone else created the first branches of the *Roman de Renart*, a form of animal satire and adventure which has fascinated readers to the present day, when we read the stories of Uncle Remus by Joel Chandler Harris. A dozen years later, in the 1180's, Alain de Lille brought allegory to a new height in his *Anticlaudianus* (written in Latin), which prepared the way for the *Roman de la Rose* and centuries of allegorical poetry. During these years of artistic productivity, political history did not remain static; it was very exciting. Indeed, we are astonished that the literary material does not reflect in a more vivid way the events of western Europe. It is hard to detect parallels at all until after the Third Crusade (1189–91), when increased dislike for the Byzantines and some display of acquaintance with Byzantine and Oriental legends betray intimate and disastrous associations with the Holy Land. In the present book we are concerned with life as it was lived each day by an average man —the kind of man who had no use for war and intrigue, but who sought to lead a normal international routine with little concern for Eleanor of Aquitaine, the quarrel between Becket and the English king, the wars in Languedoc, and the struggles of Frederick Barbarossa in favor of his antipopes. There will be readers, however, who do not know this history and who will be impatient with our narrative of street and tavern unless they can perceive the colorful background of kings and emperors against which Alexander Neckam led his quiet life. For these readers we have designed the historical sketch which now follows.[2]

The political stage for western Europe in the second half of the century was being set early in 1152. On March 4 of that year, Frederick Barbarossa became king of Germany and united around him many feudal factions. On March 21, Eleanor of Aquitaine's marriage to Louis VII of France was declared invalid; in May she married the young Henry Plantagenet, eleven years her junior. By December, 1154, this Henry was king of England, Frederick had descended into Italy, and Louis had taken a new wife, Constance of Castile.

If we seek for one key figure in the politics of this period of fifty years, we find Eleanor of Aquitaine. She had borne two daughters to her first husband—Marie and Alix—but she had given no promise of being so maternal as she now proceeded to be in the eight years that followed her marriage to Henry. She gave birth to William (1153), Henry (1155), Matilda (1156), Richard (1157), Geoffrey (1158), and Eleanor (1161). One more child, John (1166), was seemingly an afterthought. These children, except for William, who died at the age of three, were to play an active part beside their mother in the years that followed. The first husband, Louis VII of France, had two daughters by his second wife. The elder, Marguerite, was permitted to fall into the hands of Henry II of England in 1158, at the age of seven months, when she was taken to England to become the future wife of the young Prince Henry. The second daughter, another Alix, suffered the same fate, to be the future bride of Prince Richard. Unfortunately this Alix, with her Spanish eyes, attracted King Henry so much, as she grew to some maturity, that he made her his mistress and thus increased the hatred between her father and himself.

Louis had opposed the seizure of Normandy by Henry Plantagenet, before the latter was king, but relations between the two remained quite cordial until 1157. Then it became more than evident, after a council held at Würzburg, that England and Germany were beginning a "squeeze play" against France. The reader must remember that, as king of England, Henry II was sovereign lord of England, Normandy, Anjou, and Aquitaine. He also had received feudal submission from the King of Scotland and the Duke of Brittany, and he was endeavoring to increase his power in Languedoc. The King of France was in name the feudal lord of the English king; but in fact he had immediate jurisdiction only over the valleys of the upper Seine and the upper Loire, that is, from Verdunois to Bourbonnais. The Count of Flanders, the Count of Champagne, and the Duke of Burgundy were his vassals, but they were shaky. Champagne and Burgundy were leaning towards Germany. When the powerful monarchs of England and Germany should unite against Louis, his position would be practically untenable. Frederick of Germany married Beatrix of Besançon in 1156 and held a diet in that city in 1157 which was attended by some of the supposed vassals of the French king. When Henry of England marched against Raymond VI of Toulouse, in June, 1159, it looked as though he would succeed in that direction. At this very time Thibaut of Blois sold out to the English, and Henry of Champagne threatened to acknowledge Frederick as his lord. At this climax Louis walled himself up in Toulouse with the threatened count. For some reason hard for us to comprehend the English king passed up the siege.

Louis at this juncture in his life was saved by the death of Pope Hadrian IV, in 1159. The properly elected pontiff, Alexander III, was supported by England; Germany set up an antipope, Victor IV. This controversy divided Henry from Frederick. The new pope, Alexander, came to Montpellier and remained in territory that was favorable to the English king until after 1162, the year when Frederick Barbarossa gave up trying to negotiate for recognition of Victor IV by Louis. The French king had been disposed to ignore Alexander because of the Pope's favorable attitude towards the treacherous behavior of Henry of England. Louis had married again in 1160—this time, a French lady, Adèle de Champagne, which immediately won him the support of the vassals of Champagne. In spite, Henry of England got the Pope's consent for the formal marriage of the little Princess Marguerite to Prince Henry, the bride being only three years of age. This permitted King Henry to collect her dowry, the Norman Vexin.

No sooner had the question of France's recognition of Pope Alexander been cleared away than another momentous event solidified this friendship. Henry of England had been aided and supported from the very first year of his reign by his chancellor, Thomas Becket. This cleric, in minor orders, had been unusually fond of expensive clothes and of warlike procedure. He had been very instrumental in furthering the attack on Toulouse in 1159, extracting money from the English clergy against their will. He had been left at Cahors, after the siege was raised, in charge of the English military. When the Archbishop of Canterbury died, in 1162, Henry conceived the "naughty plan" of making this worldly and venal cleric the first lord of the Church in England. He forced the election. But something happened to Thomas Becket. When he was ordained to the priesthood, and consecrated bishop on the following day, his outlook changed. He championed the cause of God and opposed every attempt of the King to weaken the Church. The rage of Henry can well be imagined. In 1164 the King obliged the Archbishop to come to Clarendon, where he was told to sign certain oaths. He refused. A few months later there was a convocation at Northampton. Deserted by nearly everyone on this occasion, Thomas was forced to withdraw secretly and flee the country. He found a refuge in France. From then until his return to England in 1170, Archbishop Thomas was protected by Louis. This enhanced the prestige of France beyond measure; but it brought war with England during those years. The Pope was resident at Sens from 1163 to 1165. A new antipope, Paschal III, was appointed by Frederick in 1164. During the interim 1167–70, English students were ordered home from Paris—an unusual event, which demonstrated how bitter feeling had grown over the Becket controversy.

Most of our readers are aware that Archbishop Thomas became reconciled with the King and returned to England, only to be murdered in his cathedral on December 29, 1170. For the next five years the tide ran against Henry II of England, except in Ireland. The conquest of that island had been contemplated in 1155 at the Council of Winchester, but it was not until 1171 that the campaign was undertaken. Henry went there in person. In 1173 came more trouble. Queen Eleanor had grown weary of her husband and had plotted with Louis, her former spouse, and her three eldest sons—Henry, Richard, and Geoffrey—to check the power of Henry. When the rebellion broke out, the sons fled to Paris. It took two years for Henry to suppress this revolt. As soon as he could lay hands on Eleanor, he put her into custody for the remainder of his life. Most of her imprisonment was at Salisbury (Old Sarum), where he enlarged the existing castle so as to keep her safe, in privacy. His daughter Eleanor was married to Alfonso VIII of Castile in 1170. In 1177 the youngest daughter, Joanna, was united to William II of Sicily. Thus it will be seen that when subjected to pressure the English king reached out in masterly fashion and increased his prestige, instead of allowing it to be lessened. In that same year Henry was asked to serve as mediator in a boundary dispute between Castile and Navarre.

So far we have said little of what was happening in the Iberian Peninsula. The two strong spots there were the east coast (Catalonia) and the west (Portugal). Old Affonso Henriques, first king of Portugal, had taken Beja from the Moors in 1159, and his territories now extended to all but the extreme southern portion of his coast. In Catalonia, Ramón Berenguer IV and his son Alfonso II had been equally fortunate. Sancho VI of Navarre had affianced his daughter, Berengaria, to Prince Richard of England. Since the English aid in the capture of Lisbon and Santarém in 1147, English merchants had been very active in Portugal. When Alfonso VII of Castile and León had died in 1157, he had divided his kingdom among his sons. His grandson,

Alfonso VIII, had succeeded to Castile in 1158 and, as we have noted, had become a son-in-law of the English king. But this Alfonso was not successful as a warrior. He made no permanent conquests against the Moors. At one time, in Toledo, he deserted his English wife for a Jewish lady. In expiation for this he turned his summer palace at Burgos, Las Huelgas, into a convent for Cistercian nuns, and this edifice became a sort of basilica where the royal family were buried. The first body was laid to rest there in 1181. Only recently (1949) these tombs have been opened. The prestige of England was immense in this region, but it was from France that most of the aid was forthcoming in driving back the Moors.

In 1177, Frederick Barbarossa came out on the losing side against the Pope and the Italian communes. A pestilence which attacked his army was of assistance in this. Frederick acknowledged Pope Alexander III in 1177, thus putting an end to the succession of antipopes. This was a bad year, also, for Louis. England now had all the political prestige, and Louis had only moral support. Fortunately, Alexander III came to his rescue and forced the English king to make peace. This is the year, or shortly thereafter, in which we begin the "homely" account of Alexander Neckam's voyage to Paris. It was a likely time for a young Englishman to travel abroad. Anywhere that he chose to go in western Europe he found the road open to him, a circumstance influenced by the dread memory of the alliances and the long arm of Henry II of England. Yet it was Paris that had the affection of everyone. England had power and wealth, but Paris had learning and moral prestige. English teachers loved to be in residence there; and no scholar who could possibly afford it failed to make his studies in dialectic and law in that center of the intellectual world. Only Montpellier and

Salerno in medicine, and Bologna in law, could rival or take precedence over Paris. We should mention, also, Orléans for studies in poetic and rhetoric, but these were not so popular.

Political events moved on rapidly after the death of Louis VII and the accession, in September, 1179, of his son Philip I (commonly called Augustus at a later date). Henry II of England was growing tired of war and campaigns. He suffered from arthritis and from a fistula. In a treaty made at Gisors he showed friendship to Philip, and there was no war between them until Philip made a savage attack on the old king's territory in May, 1187. Philip needed a breathing spell because his own chief vassals—the counts of Flanders, Blois, Chartres, Sancerre, and others, together with the Duke of Burgundy—made an alliance against him in May, 1181, which continued until July, 1186. The fighting was desultory and of the guerrilla type. Frederick Barbarossa favored Philip, although he did no actual fighting; Henry of England took the same attitude. Once these nobles had surrendered, the young French king turned his arms in the direction of Henry. Geoffrey of Brittany was encouraged to come to Paris, where he soon died from an accident. Then Richard made the same journey, angered by a letter written by his father in which his brother John was promised a large stretch of territory. Although a crusade was now preached to rescue Jerusalem, which had been captured by Saladin in 1187, King Philip, aided by Richard, proceeded to give old Henry no quarter. All of Maine, Anjou, and Touraine were overrun. Henry died in July, 1189, saddened by the defection of both Richard and John.

When Richard became king, he gathered together money by many dubious devices. He freed his mother Eleanor, of course, and made a pact with Philip whereby England regained nearly all the territory taken by Philip. This made Richard very unpopular in Paris. In June, 1190, both Richard and Philip departed for Sicily, whence they were to sail to the Holy Land. Frederick Barbarossa had already set out by the land route. Unfortunately, the German emperor stopped to bathe in the river Salef, in Cilicia, and was drowned on June 10. He was succeeded by his son Henry VI, who had married, in 1184, the heiress to the crown of Sicily and Naples—Constance de Hauteville. From the union of these two was born in 1196 the great Frederick II of thirteenth-century fame.

Philip and Richard had much bad blood between them in Sicily before their sailing. Once they were in Asia Minor, the feud continued. Philip left after little more than a year, and after a homeward voyage of four months was in France by December of 1191. In the meantime in England the government was carried on by Queen Eleanor and her youngest son, John. Most of our readers are familiar with the stories of Robin Hood, which were said to have happened at this time. The character of John is well represented in these. King Richard, when he arrived on the Dalmatian coast, was taken prisoner, and eventually, with the connivance of Philip and John, was held in the prisons of the Duke of Austria and of the Emperor Henry VI. Both John and Philip offered huge sums to the German to persuade him to retain Richard. In March, 1194, the English king was released for a sum exceeding 100,000 pounds sterling. Hostages had to be sent for the unpaid ransom. Richard was not long back in England before he was obliged to land in Normandy to hold back Philip. The errant brother John was forgiven. In view of the vast amounts of sterling sent to Germany, one wonders how the English treasury was able to pay so well its mercenaries in this fresh war against France. Three great mercenary captains were Algais, Louvart, and Mercadier. The war seesawed back and forth until 1197, when the leading vassals of the French king again deserted; the Count of Flanders was chief among these. Everything now began to go bad for the young French monarch. He was chased bodily in 1198 after his defeat at Courcelles. Like his father before him, he was saved only by intervention from the Pope, who sent Peter of Capua to negotiate a peace in January of 1199. Still another event of great moment followed on this. In July, 1199, Richard was besieging a rebel noble of Aquitaine when a crossbow bolt wounded him in the left shoulder. He died shortly after, of gangrene. This was at the Castle of Châlus in Limousin. Left now with only John as his chief adversary, Philip had a change of luck.

As we should expect, the economic situation of western Europe was constantly disturbed by these feuds and changes in balance of power. Our chief concern in this book is with France and England. In the course of our journey with Neckam we attempt to sketch lightly the economic picture, progressively, as it would come to the attention of a traveler or visitor. However, a general statement may be of assistance to some readers.

During the second half of the twelfth century, the baron in possession of his fief was the typical unit. A convenient portion of this estate was cultivated directly under the supervision of the lord's *maire*, or steward, by labor *corvées* of the lord's own serfs and by hired agricultural workers, or *hôtes*. This was the lord's demesne. The rest of the baron's holdings were sublet to peasant tenants and to the serfs, who were responsible to a steward. Such tenants supported themselves and sold their produce, paying an annual rent of some kind. A free peasant owed, in addition to his rent, tithes and extraordinary payments. A serf paid these in addition to further obligations imposed upon him by his status. He was required to labor a certain number of days on his lord's demesne. If he wished to marry his children off the estate, there was a tax; for the privilege of moving about there was still another payment. There was a general feeling of dissatisfaction towards the institution of serfdom. At this time many lords were manumitting their serfs, frequently in exchange for a large payment. The baron technically had the privilege of buying first, and of selling, the farm products of his peasants. He availed himself more often of the right to buy. The peasant brought his produce to the nearest market town on his lord's estate and offered it there for sale and barter. It was commonly forbidden to any speculator to go out into the country beforehand and buy up supplies. The produce must be offered to the purchasers at the market, within proper season. The farms of a given community were expected to supply the nearby towns and rural areas. A lord, however, might offer a surplus for sale in some more distant place.

Sufficient money was not minted to take care of day-by-day needs and purchases. This incommodity was aggravated by the absence of a banking system. Such coins as the twelfth-century man had were often hoarded in jars and chests and kept out of circulation. It will be understood, therefore, that in the small market towns much of the exchange of goods was made by barter. Furthermore, only small sums would be paid out in cash for wages. Most tradesmen worked for a certain amount of wine, grain, clothing, and meat, and for the use of a small piece of land. Conceivably the baron would owe rent and military assistance for his holdings to a bigger count, or duke. Theoretically the ultimate feudal lord might be the king. A baron who did not hold allegiance to a landlord above him was called an *aloués*. Military service of a kind was owed by every knight to the overlord of his county or shire, even when economically his lands were held as *alleux*.

In the towns, life was made difficult by conflicting and overlapping jurisdictions. The lord of the town, the bishop (if the town were a cathedral see), and the abbots of local monasteries had civil authority according to grants which had been made at various times. There were also the trade guilds, which had authority to define the hours of work, the number of apprentices, and the precise articles that could be made or sold. Fortunately, a community could absorb only a certain amount of household goods, textiles, and leather products. It was necessary to export, and this was done through the seasonal fairs. Champagne was a region easily accessible to French, German, Flemish, and English merchants. It supported a fair in March at Provins, and another during the summer at Troyes. The merchants were present for six weeks at each of these, although they required an initial eight days to unpack and spread their goods. Booths were assigned to each region, or to each town. Church authorities and feudal lords joined in the effort to make travel safe for these merchants who moved about. It was the surest way to stabilize commerce. At the fairs, textiles and leather goods were featured in succession, while ordinary goods were displayed continuously. Paris had three such fairs: the Lendit near Saint-Denis, the Foire Saint-Germain, and, earlier, the Foire de Saint-Lazare. A fair gave the appearance of a large open-air bazaar.

In southern France and Flanders, trade conditions were more favorable because of the prevalence of the "commune" system, under which the townspeople had immediate control over their own movements, judicial system, and financial responsibilities. The south was also favored by its proximity to Spain, Italy, and the commerce of the Mediterranean. Montpellier, for instance, was a great commercial capital as well as a medical center. In Flanders, the nearness of England, Germany, and the Scandinavian commercial centers gave similar advantage. It is not difficult to understand why the Count of Flanders was able to take such an independent position against the King of France; and we know why the county of Toulouse and adjacent areas were considered rich prizes by the rulers of France, England, and Germany.

The king of France and the king of England moved about like feudal barons, engaged in selfish pursuits, but there was a majesty associated with their office which no vassal could forget easily. John of Salisbury is our best authority on twelfth-century political theory.[3] When a king was crowned, he was anointed with oil by Holy Church. He was considered to be divinely chosen and ordained, and, at the same time, he had a personal responsibility to the people. He was an ecclesiastical-patriarchal type of king. The king, in a way, was the owner of all his subjects' goods and effects. In an extreme emergency, this was judged to be the case; in normal times, the king respected the private property of his people. The king was the state, and the community could not act for itself apart from the prince. A king might become a tyrant because of the sins of his people. After the people had repented, God would deliver them from the tyrant. John of Salisbury adds, however, that when a tyrant manifestly opposes the will of God he must be disposed of in some way by his people. At the very close of the twelfth century, political theorists inclined more to the belief that the *universitas* of barons in the kingdom could rightfully take justice into their own hands and rid the kingdom of a tyrant.

Although the king, by virtue of his anointing, was in a

special position with respect to divine right, it is true that the same concept of paternal authority was carried on down to lesser rulers—dukes, counts, and barons—until it included even the father of a family. The one in authority had a personal responsibility to administer justice to those subordinate to him. In return he should be accorded every evidence of respect. The reader of Chrétien's *Yvain* notices how when the King comes suddenly upon his knights they rise, and sit only at his command.[4] The same respect is accorded the Queen, but this is more a matter of personal courtesy.[5] On approaching an overlord in formal council, even when giving advice, it was customary to fall at his feet. But the lord, including the king, was obliged to consult his chief vassals on matters of justice and policy.

These were the times of Alexander Neckam, a schoolmaster who is unusually informative for his day.[6] He liked to make word lists and was quite ready to express his opinions. This renders him a most useful subject for our guided trip to London and Paris. He was born in 1157, we know, for he was the "milk brother" of Prince Richard. His education was acquired at the Benedictine abbey of St. Albans. He doubtless taught in the schools of Dunstable before making his memorable journey to Paris. As he was teaching publicly in Paris in 1180, we assume that he must have begun his study there at a slightly earlier date.[7] We have chosen the year 1177–78, when he was twenty years of age. He became a prominent figure on the Petit Pont. About 1186 he returned to Dunstable and continued to teach there. Later he became an Augustinian canon at Cirencester and was elected abbot in 1213. He died in 1217. Probably his *De nominibus utensilium*, which we translate, was a product of his stay in Paris. He adapted also the *Fables* of Avianus.

More serious works are his *De naturis rerum* and the metrical version of this, *De laudibus divine sapientiae*. Another work, the *Corrogationes Promethei*, has not been made accessible. There is a vocabulary by Neckam in MS 385 (605) of Caius College, Cambridge, of which C. H. Haskins has published a section.[8] This part, which Haskins calls *Sacerdos ad altarem*, lists the textbooks of the last decade of the twelfth century. Priscian and Donatus were the chief grammar authorities; both the *New* and the *Old Logic* were important for dialectic. Euclid and the Arabic summaries of Ptolemy were sources for mathematics and astronomy, alongside of Boethius. The Corpus Juris Civilis was cited for civil law; in canon law there were the *Decretum* of Gratian and the *Decretals* of Alexander III. Hippocrates and Galen, as well as Isaac and the *Pantegni*, were used for medicine. The *Sententiae* of Peter Lombard and the Bible were standard for theology. Latin classics which were mentioned include Cicero, Quintilian, Statius, Vergil, Horace, Lucan, Juvenal, Ovid, Sallust, Martial, Petronius, Quintus Curtius, Livy, Seneca, and Suetonius.

Chapter II

London

IN 1178 OR thereabout, Alexander Neckam, a young clerk teaching in the grammar schools at Dunstable, Bedfords, decided to go to Paris to continue his own studies. The little town of Dunstable was a village in the Chilton Hills, thirty-four miles to the northwest of London, situated at the juncture of two Roman roads—Watling Street and the Icknield. The town was governed by a priory of Augustinian canons regular, who exercised the function of lord of the borough. Alexander felt himself much drawn to these canons, so much so that later, after his return from France, he entered their community at Cirencester, becoming abbot in 1213. This decision of his has been given some explanation by modern critics, who reason that he should have entered the great Benedictine abbey of St. Albans, twenty miles nearer London, on Watling Street. He was a native of that town and had received his elementary education in that abbey. The story is told that the Abbot of St. Albans punned on his name (*Nequam*, "wicked," for Neckam) and offended him. It is sufficient to assume that Alexander had more active ties with the Augustinian canons as a result of his stay in Dunstable.[1]

In making his plans to go to Paris, he must surely have consulted with Abbot Simon of St. Albans. The Abbot had

Winchester Bible sheet (c. 1170), M 619, 1 fol. only
Courtesy Pierpont Morgan Library

David and Bath-sheba, illumination from M 638, fol. 41 v.
Courtesy Pierpont Morgan Library

been a close friend of the late St. Thomas Becket and was a great patron of letters. He had close associations with the Continent. The time was very auspicious for a journey to the French capital. On September 22, 1177, Henry II of England and Louis VII of France had sworn mutual peace and had agreed to take the cross together. In recent years the city of Paris had acquired a very suitable intellectual climate for students. The chief advisers to the French king were no longer feudal barons. To be sure, the health of the old king was bad, and everyone hoped that he would soon celebrate the coronation of his only son, young Philip Augustus. Count Richard of Aquitaine was the milk brother of Alexander. His recent exploits in France would have excited the imagination of the young teacher in Dunstable. Perhaps Abbot Simon gave money as well as advice. He is accused somewhat unkindly by Matthew Paris of being prodigal with money, of owing large sums to Jewish moneylenders, and of being nepotistic.[2]

The trip to London was an easy one along the somewhat battered Roman pavement of Watling Street. A traveler who rode seriously could average some thirty-five miles a day, making six miles an hour on his horse or mule. He would mount in the morning at six-thirty or seven, modern time, and would ride until the dinner hour at eleven. Usually he rested immediately after this meal. It would be nearly three o'clock, after *relevée*, before the traveler would once more mount his steed, and this time he would continue till nearly six o'clock. In the time-reckoning of the twelfth century we would say that the rider began his journey at *basse prime*, or at break of day, and went on till dinner at *haute tierce*. After *relevée* he continued till Vespers.[3]

Alexander was a cleric in lesser orders, or perhaps he had only the simple tonsure.[4] We will assume that his mount was a mule, borrowed for the occasion, to be left at the Augustinian priory of St. Bartholomew's in Smithfield, London.[5] The harness worn by such an animal was not unlike what we know today. The headstall was of cloth strips, or perhaps of leather. Like modern harness, the chin strap of this headpiece was slipped under the animal's chin and the metal bit was placed in his mouth. The upper strap looped over the ears. But, unlike what we see today, the headband continued around the head and was tied in the rear with long loose ends. Alexander describes the harness of a palfrey or mule, but his language is not very specific:

> Let the horse's back be covered with a canvas, afterwards with a sweat pad or cloth; next let a saddle be properly placed with the fringes of the sweat cloth hanging over the crupper. The stirrups should hang well. The saddle has a front bow or pommel and a cantle. . . . Folded clothing may be well placed in a saddlebag behind the cantle. A breast strap and the trappings for the use of someone riding should not be forgotten: halter and headstall, bit covered with bloody foam, reins, girths, buckles, cushion, padding . . . which I intentionally pass over. An attendant should carry a currycomb.[6]

We can do better than this, at eight hundred years' distance, by describing what we find in illuminations and sculptures of the time. The bit was always single, but double reins were attached to it. A *culière*, or crupper, passed under the horse's tail and fastened to the cantle of the saddle. The traveling pack was tied onto this. Over the seat of the saddle a third cloth was usually draped. This was called the *baudré*, and we are told that it was often of a rich brown material, well embroidered. It could be very long, almost touching the ground. The bows of the saddle were of wood and, more often than not, were ornamented with plates of ivory, hammered metal, or elaborately painted leather.[7] Supposedly such decoration should be added after purchase from the saddler, but John of Garland mentions the sale of painted saddles.[8] Precious stones could be soldered onto the surface of the pommel and cantle, producing, in our modern eyes, a very tawdry effect. Alexander refers to buckles on the saddle girths, usually two.[9] In the illuminated Bible page of the Morgan Library, the girths of Absalom's saddle seem to have hard knots at the end which slip into openings on the two straps hanging down from under the right side of the saddle. In brief, metal buckles existed, but it is evident that they were expensive enough to be avoided when possible. Metal pendants or little bells jangled from the *peitrel*, or breast strap, of the mount. Women had a sidesaddle (*sambue*), but whether they used it invariably is not clear.[10]

Alexander lists also the clothing that was best worn by a traveler:

> Let one who is about to ride have a *chape* with sleeves, of which the hood will not mind the weather,[11] and let him have boots, and spurs that he may prevent the horse from stumbling, jolting, turning, rearing, resisting, and may make him *bien amblant*, "possessed of a good gait," and easily manageable. Shoes should be well fastened with iron nails.

Most of the traveling at this date was done at a good walk. There are excellent examples of the twelfth-century spur in both Cluny and the British Museum. It had a single prong or prick, which could give the horse quite a wound if improperly used. The heavy shoe worn by a traveler might have a high top of soft leather, when it was called a boot (*huese* or *ocrea*). This is the type of footwear which Alexander has in mind. A peasant, however, might wear a heavy shoe of undressed leather (*revelins*) and drape his legs in baggy cloth which he would then bandage on with leather thongs. This arrangement also could be referred to as *ocreas*. Men of all classes often wrapped their legs with spiral puttees, which are visible to us in hunting scenes or on the legs of knights.[12] As a clerk in minor orders Alexander would have worn dark clothing, perhaps black, and his hair was cut shorter than was customary among the laity.[13] It was nonetheless a little shaggy about the neck and ears. A simple tonsure, or small shaven spot, was visible on the crown of his head. His face was more or less clean shaven. He could have worn a peaked felt hat, with a very narrow rolled brim, but it is not likely that he did. We will picture him as bareheaded.

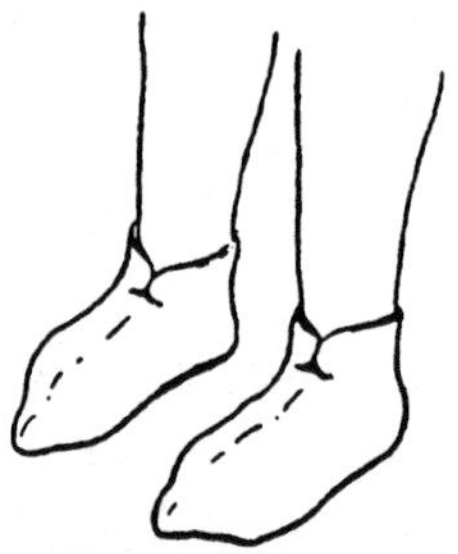

Although Alexander was traveling without a retinue, he must have made chance acquaintances along the road. When traveling on a walking mule there was ample time for companionship. For our story's sake we will assume that Alexander fell in with a Scot who likewise was on his way to London town. This man, like all his countrymen, wore "Scottish dress and had the manner of the Scot." He frequently shook his "staff as they shake the weapon which they call a *gaveloc* at those who mock them, shouting threatening words in the manner of the Scots." Alexander "closely examined his clothes and boots . . . and even the old shoes which he carried on his shoulders in the Scottish manner." We should like some details on these Scottish peculiarities of dress and manner, but Jocelin of Brakeland, whom we are quoting, gives nothing further. Englishmen were considered "cold of disposition" inwardly.[14]

As the two rode along they would be joined by others, and they would continue conversing in the "commun language" of England, the Anglo-Norman dialect of French.[15] This tongue was careless in its use of cases, and cultivated speakers were ashamed of this laxity; they yearned to improve their speech by a sojourn on the Continent.[16] Like most members of the clerical class, Alexander lapsed freely into Latin when he had complicated thoughts to express. Years of habit in the schools had brought this about. But the Norman speech was his mother tongue and he enjoyed speaking it with the "simple gent," and on occasion with brother clerics. Living in England as he did, Alexander could understand a little English, but the memories of it which remained from childhood, when he spoke it with his nurse and the kitchen knaves, had grown rusty. A few common words such as *welcomme* and *drinkhail* were used by everyone, often for comic effect. Alexander could barely understand the Scottish phrases and oaths with which the Scottish traveler frequently salted his remarks.

It was customary to travel in company for two reasons. First, there was the matter of protection from wild beasts and bad men. Both of these annoyances sometimes appeared out of the woods, which came down to the very edge of the road. The region to the north of London was rather heavily forested. A second reason was one of pride. Much importance was placed on external appearances. One of the greatest compliments that could be paid was to say that a man looked *fier*.[17] This meant that he looked every inch a man of quality. A person traveling by himself did not attract much attention, and his dignity could be slighted. We assume, therefore, that as Alexander rode along Watling Street he drew together with other voyagers.

On such an occasion it was customary to sing. "He came sitting on his horse, a song echoing to his voice; in the manner of travelers he thus shortened his journey."[18] If the company were friendly enough, they might exchange tales. The common types of song were the *virelai*, the *rondeau*, and the *rotrouenge*. Such verse forms had considerable repetition of melody and lines, which made it possible for all to join in. The *virelai* ran *AbbaA*, capital letters indicating repeated words or refrain. The *rondeau* had the form *ABaAabAB*. The repetition in the *rondeau* was so considerable that it lent itself admirably to group participation. The English members of Alexander's traveling party probably thought of singing in unison, but the Scotsman, if we are to believe Giraldus, would break forth into a free separate part in his quavering treble. Alexander, like Giraldus, would be astonished at the ease with which those who dwelt north of the Humber could chime in with a free organum, or second moving part. They learned to do this as children. If there had been Welshmen in the company, they would have added a third, and even a fourth part, but we will not burden our company with all those Celts. Welsh music was frequently not pleasant to English ears.[19]

Alexander's mule sometimes had to pick its way carefully over the worn Roman pavement, which was in frightful repair. Too often a neighboring farmer would have removed a few flat paving stones to build him a wall or the corner of his house. This kind of theft left a layer of rubble which was hard on an animal's feet. An occasional hole was deep enough to cause a broken neck. Along this road to London were scattered clearings, and a village or two. Groups of detached houses, usually of wood (unpainted), and rarely of small stones cemented together, stood along the road. Farmyards were seldom, if ever, contiguous to the houses. These yards were detached enclosures, walled with pales or tall wooden stakes, squared and sharpened at the top. Briars or other thorn branches were intertwined over the entire surface of such a fencing, to keep out intruders.[20] The yards were built sufficiently near to the house to allow the tenant to hear any disturbance among his chickens or his cattle. The houses themselves consisted of little more than a doorway and one window. The roof was thatched with straw or reeds. A large wooden shutter, hinged at the top, perhaps with leather thongs, was held open by a stick placed between it and the sill. Because of the constant wear of feet, each house was apt to have a depression in the unpaved ground before its door. This was too often filled with stagnant water.[21] Houses such as these were occupied by villeins and bordars (serfs).[22] Well-to-do peasant farmers would occupy manor houses of a kind set farther back from the highway.

As the road approached London the tillage lands seemed more prosperous and the traffic increased.[23] The site of London was low, lending itself to frequent flooding from the waters of the Thames. Only by building up an embankment was this avoided. Many springs and pools were in the vicinity. Two swift streams ran through London proper—the Walbrook and the Langbourn. As Alexander and his companions rode along, they were first made aware of their destination when Watling Street dipped a bit towards the Thames.[24] In the distance they caught their first glimpse of the big river and of the royal tower at Westminster, with its abbey church of St. Peter and clustering houses.[25] Alexander had been told there were interesting wall paintings in this royal tower, and he hoped someday to see them.[26] The Scotsman snorted a bit at this. He preferred to visit the palace of the English king at Woodstock, where during the reign of old King Henry there had been lions, leopards, and other strange beasts. Perhaps there were some still.[27] Then the road bent sharply to the left, and they were soon out of the forest, riding beside the Old Bourn, a little stream that appeared suddenly out of nowhere and flowed beside the road. Houses appeared, adjacent to pretty gardens. One house, on the right, was magnificent. Alexander, who had ridden there before, knew that it was the town house of the Bishop of Lincoln. Just a few paces farther along stood a large round tower of light-yellow stone, bleak and uninviting. There was much going and coming before its drawbridge gate. It was easy to tell from the dress of the inhabitants that this was the Temple, the stronghold of the Knights Templar. Many unsightly wooden buildings cluttered up the adjacent land. It was evident that the Templars had no room for expansion there. Someone said that the stone for their tower or donjon had been brought from Caen in Normandy.

A few more yards and the road prepared to drop down into a ravine. Our travelers gazed at a glorious sight which took the breath away from those who had not see it before. At the foot was a small river, the River of Wells, which flowed on into the Thames. Mill wheels were turning in it with a pleasant rumbling sound, and there were flocks of small boats gathered at each of the two bridges. One of these wooden bridges lay straight ahead, carrying Watling Street across the stream; the other was nearer the Thames and led across to Ludgate in the city's wall. The city lay at the crest of the opposite slope, several hundred yards beyond the ravine, but Old Bourn Hill was a little higher and our travelers got a sweeping view over the top of the massive wall into the teeming mass of chimneys and houses. The roar of many cries and jarring sounds now filled their ears. The guards on the *aleoir* or top of the wall, the throngs at the two gates, clamoring for admission through the narrow apertures—all were sights which held the travelers for a few minutes before they descended the slope to the bridge ahead, the stream of the Old Bourn rushing down the hill at their side. Alexander was not expecting to enter the city that night. He went up the road toward Newgate, but he took the lane to the left and skirted the wall to the open ground of Smithfield, the market site and jousting ground. Here, close to the wall, were the buildings of the Augustinian priory of St. Bartholomew's, built by the minstrel Rahere, on the spot where a gallows had stood some fifty years before. Rahere had caused the whole of Smithfield to be drained, leaving only one large pond, which was named the "Horsepool" as it served to water the horses at the fair and during the games. The priory served as a hostelry for travelers, and an auxiliary building was employed as a nursing home for the sick. The four canonesses and eight canons who were engaged in this work served under a master. The canonesses followed the rule of St. Benedict, and the canons obeyed that of St. Augustine. Men and women were kept strictly separate.[28] Alexander was undoubtedly known personally to the Prior from previous visits. Much advice, solicited and unsolicited, would be given him to help him make speed on his journey across the water.

The open area of Smithfield stretched wide, away from the buildings of St. Bartholomew's.[29] The smooth field, no longer marshy, supported a horse fair every Friday, except on special feast days. Crowds from the city, including many barons, flocked there to see the display of horseflesh. At one end were tethered the colts, elsewhere the palfreys, in another spot the *destriers* (war horses), and, in a place not so well favored, the pack animals, or *somiers*. Various races were run on these occasions. Stable boys did the riding, needing no saddle or any other harness except a headstall.

Horses were raced in threes or in pairs. Farm animals and farm supplies were also on sale at this market: plows, harrows, pigs, and cows. Oxen were on sale and so were mares intended for the carts and plows, often with foals trotting at their heels. Another class of merchants were offering furs, spices, swords, lances, and wines—all from distant climes. On afternoons, many of the clerics and young tradesmen would go out on this field to play ball. Each of the three schools flourishing in London would have its own ball, and the same was true of each guild of tradesmen. During Lent, on Sunday afternoons, the young men of the baronial class, and presumably some of the serjant class, would practice with lances and shields on that same area. The smaller boys had no iron heads on their lances. When the king was at Westminster or Bermondsey, the youths of the upper class went there, and Smithfield was left to the serjantry. All this sham fighting was done on horseback while relatives, also mounted, would stand by and watch. There was much prancing about and going in pursuit. During the summer, on the afternoon of holy days, there were field sports: jumping, stone throwing, javelin hurling, wrestling, and archery. On moonlight nights, groups of girls would hold caroles, or dancing, on this same smooth field. One might say there was never a dull moment there after dinner. The Friday market was a very important place for gathering and exchanging news of the day.[30]

On the morning following his arrival, Alexander may well have walked into London in the company of a canon, or perhaps with a servant of the priory. To ride on horseback would have been more comfortable, but progress through the crowded streets would have been slower. Aldersgate was just a few yards away and was less frequented than Newgate. A murage tax had to be paid by one entering the city, but the fee was not high.

London, like every other important walled town, teemed with people. The walls were some eighteen feet high. The gates were fitted with double swinging-doors of heavy oak, reinforced with iron.[31] Inside the walls, the houses were mostly of wood. Here and there appeared more prosperous ones of stone. These were seldom constructed from regular, hewn blocks of stone. Like the country houses, they were more often made of irregular quartz stones and flints, bonded together by cement. Some of the wooden houses had tile facings; some houses were obviously made with a sort of mud or stucco daubed over a wattle framework or lath. Alexander remarked, at a later date, that foolish people were not content with the practical details of a house. They must have useless ornamental decoration. This comment was highly justified in his day, the Romanesque era. "Gingerbready" is the word that would have come to us if we had beheld what Alexander saw on his visit to London. Stone houses had saw-tooth ornamentations, and elaborate moldings with small lozenges in the intersections, and criss-cross effects. Wooden houses, vastly in the majority, had the same sort of thing executed less skillfully.[32] Exterior decorative paneling such as we are accustomed to associate with Tudor architecture was extremely common. Many of the wooden structures had a little roof lift before the entrance. The beams supporting this could be topped by a heavy ornamental capital, imitating the opening of a flower or the head of a strange bird or animal. Some wooden piers which extended from the ground to the main roofs had this same type of capital. There were occasional wooden balconies, displaying tile and crossbeam decorations. Around windows and doors the casements were embellished with curlicues, not unlike what we find three centuries later in stone-decorated Gothic. Stone houses often showed the typical Norman chimney stack, that is, a conical cap pierced with smoke holes, rising from a cornice enriched with zigzag ornament.[33]

Nearly all the smaller houses were in solid rows, not detached, extending down the street. They housed tradesmen who manufactured their goods on their own front premises. The lower floor of such houses resembled a sort of booth with a low counter extending across the front. An opening in the counter gave passage in and out. This was the type of workshop used by knife maker, baker, armorer, or other tradesman. To one side there was a small spiral stair which led up to the main dwelling room. The stair well was a little tower which could be placed inside or outside the principal walls of the building. In these rows of houses it was surely inside. Upstairs was the *salle*, or main room, with ornamental windows facing on the street. There the wife of the household reigned supreme—during business hours, anyway. Houses will be described in more detail in a later chapter. We should notice that the floors of both shop and *salle* were strewn with rushes, green in summer, dry in winter.[34] The houses of wood were smeared with paint—most commonly red, blue, and black—which had a pitch and linseed base and gave constant promise of fires. It was hoped that by providing stone walls, to the height of sixteen feet, between adjacent houses this menace would be reduced.[35]

The street through which Alexander walked after passing the guard at Aldersgate was some ten feet across. It was a main thoroughfare, but not a principal street of the city. It led to Newgate Street and St. Paul's churchyard. Alexander would surely have been aware that the marvelous cathedral of St. Paul's was still under construction. Its tower was not yet erected. The stone used, like that of the Temple, was being transported from Normandy. After going around the

the moment, Alexander and his guide promised to return and strolled farther along the quays. They came to Coldharbor, and then to Oystergate, and St. Botolph's. At this last it was all they could do to buck the tide of people. They nearly turned back at once. Out in the middle of the river at this point, workmen were beginning to pave over the arches of the new stone bridge. The old wooden bridge, recently repaired, was discharging its passengers there before the church.[40] Billingsgate was just beyond. Wace describes this in brief: "In London, his best city, King Belin made a marvelous gate on the water which bears the ships. The gate was . . . set with marvelous skill; . . . over the gate he placed a tower exceedingly wide and high."[41] It can be judged from this that there was a gatehouse at the entrance to the basin, perhaps similar to one at Queenhithe. Fitzstephen was under the impression that a continuous wall had once enclosed the city on the water front but had been broken down by the water.[42] This wall may have existed at one time, but it is possible that gatehouses of a later date, guarding the entry to the more prominent wharfing spaces, might have created this impression of a once existent wall. Fitzstephen remarks that there was a large cookshop, a wonderful place, situated on the quays.[43] Whether it was on the Queenhithe side of the bridge or on the Billingsgate side we cannot be sure. I should make a guess that it was located close to the Vintners' quay. It was frequented by everyone in town. Cooked food was cheaper there than food "on the hoof." Vessels loaded with salt and, above all, with fish were tied up on all sides. Some were moored out in the river and had to be approached in small boats. Fitzstephen says that many foreign vessels, from the Scandinavian area as well as from the Mediterranean, were there. These were doubtless to be seen on the seaward side of the bridge, at Billingsgate or at Galleygate, near the city wall. By mooring there it was not necessary for these heavy ships to lower their rigging and masts. For a vessel to go through the piles of the wooden London Bridge at that time it was necessary to unstep the mast and handle by oars.

In the words of Wace we will picture what Alexander could have seen at the quays below the bridge:

There were the ships brought and the crews [*maisnees*] assembled. You would see many a ship made ready, ships touching each other, anchoring, drying out, and being floated, ships being repaired with pegs and nails, ropes being hauled, masts set up, gangplanks [*punz*] being thrust over the side, and ships loading. Lances were being straightened up and horses were pulling. Knights and men-at-arms were going on board, and the one would call to the other, some remaining and some leaving.[44]

Those vessels that were going under the bridge often had six men at the oars, three on a side. The vessels which were carrying horses were larger and were called *uissiers*. They had doors (*uis*) which opened in the side planking, making it possible to walk horses up the gangplank to the deck.[45] There were small merchant vessels called *sentines*, manned by only two seamen. Alexander had heard tell of one such boat which was operated by the owner—and a dog! The dog, he said, pulled the required ropes while the master steered.[46] This we cannot believe, but it is an indication of a kind of small vessel which Alexander must have seen. It is not easy to imagine all the boats which could have been on the Thames that day. There was a heavier type of craft which is clearly depicted in a bas-relief on the Campanile at Pisa.[47] This has a platform or castle constructed at the stern, with an open crow's-nest style of railing. There is another such castle at the bow. The *gouverneur* at the steering oar stands on the short deck forward of, and below, the aftercastle. A seaman is depicted on the aftercastle platform, bending forward, adjusting the yard of the mainmast on which the one sail is furled. Towards the bow is a second mast, canted well forward. It has a yard, and a fore-and-aft sail which looks like a lateen sail. This is set and is probably being used to keep the heavy vessel in the wind. Most of the boats seen by Alexander were of the lighter type, having one sail and no high castles—the kind which is represented somewhat crudely in the Bayeux Tapestry, and which was used for coastal and channel freighting. These had a transverse deck over the stern where the master sat at the steering oar and supervised the men working the lines and sail. A windlass would be placed on this deck, similar to the type used in building construction. It was a wheel on a frame, with spokes set into the hub. By spinning these spokes the sailor could tighten or loosen any line that was fastened to the axle of the wheel.

At this point there were other things to be observed besides ships. The huge white Tower of London stood on the left, outside the wall of the town. The exit from the wall toward the Tower was made by way of the Postern Gate. The Tower had not yet been incorporated into the wall, as it was in 1190, nor was the wide town ditch in existence which King John later had dug around the circumference of the wall. There was a vineyard planted between the town wall and the Tower, and a mill was on the riverbank just beyond.[48] As Alexander looked across the river, he became aware of the King's manor of Bermondsey. The manor lands extended from London Bridge as far as Rotherhithe. The fields were being tilled by villeins and bordars or cotters.[49] The road to Dover, considered to be a continuation of Watling Street, wound through these fields. The

Cluniac monastery of Saint Savior was visible where the Dover road turned more sharply to the left.

Alexander's companion may have told him, as they looked over the reaches of the Thames, perhaps from the wooden bridge, about the water tourney which was held on the river during Holy Week. A tree was set up in the river, and young men would stand at the prow of small boats being rowed swiftly down the stream and aim with a lance at the target on the tree. If a lance was broken on the target, the boy was hailed as a victor. If he missed, he was tossed into the water and then picked up by another boat that stood by. For this occasion the bridge and the balconies of houses facing the Thames were crowded with people. Perhaps at this point Alexander and his companion may have turned to thoughts of sliding on wintry ice. On Mooresfield, at the north side of the wall, there was still a marsh. When this was frozen in winter, young men would strap the shinbones of horses to the soles of their feet and slide rapidly along, aided by a pole shod with iron. Often the more mischievous boys would strike at each other with the pole as they shot past. There were many accidents. Ordinary sliding on the ice was also quite common. Still another sport was to seat someone on a cake of ice and pull him along.[50]

Remembering his agreement to call again at Dowgate, Alexander now turned back toward the western end of the city.

There is no evidence, one way or the other, that Thames Street was paved, with an old Roman pavement, but it surely was. Otherwise the mud would have been inevitable and the waterfront could not have been approached to any advantage. This was no low quarter of town, despite the crowds of seamen. In summer these sailors wore nothing but *braies*, or wide underdrawers, and possibly a snood cap, tied under the chin. Their hair was often long enough to curl at the back of the neck. Doubtless they had the usual part in the middle, affected by all classes and both sexes. The average man in the twelfth century did not shave more than once a week, and a short, dark stubble was the common thing. Many seamen wore true beards. On cooler days the seaman wore a coarse *gonne*, or frock, which he pulled up at the waist, over a belt, when he was obliged to step into the water.[51]

As we have said, this was not a low part of town. There was much wealth on display. In that time and age, wealth was shown by cloth heavy with gold and silver thread, brocades, and dark and cloudy gems, cut roughly into cabochon shape, which were encrusted on almost anything, from a helmet to the metal covering of a manuscript book. Silks and spices, which were imported at considerable effort and expense from the East, were another indication of *richesse*. When we consider that silks were transported by sea—sometimes by land—from China to India, from there to the Red Sea region by water, and finally down the Nile to the Mediterranean area, where they were picked up by Italian merchants, it is not hard to understand why their price advanced; and yet most well-to-do people had silken garments, and even silken sheets. Thames Street displayed much of this southern wealth, as well as the northern wealth of expensive furs.

There was something in the air of a mediaeval community such as London which we moderns are apt to forget. This thing was authority. There was unquestionably much mob violence and considerable injustice on all sides practiced everywhere daily. But even an outraged person felt awed by authority, whatever form it took. The *ribauz*, or good-for-nothings, were always on the edge of a crowd. They begged and plundered at the slightest provocation. They hung around outside the door of the banquet hall when a large feast was held. The king of England had three hundred bailiffs whose duty it was—though not all at one time—to keep these people back as food was moved from the kitchens to the hall, and to see that guests were not disturbed.[52] Frequently in twelfth-century romances a beautiful damsel is threatened with the awful fate of being turned over to the *ribauz*.[53] Nothing more horrible can be imagined. These people accompanied armies on their expeditions, helping in menial tasks and plundering what was left by the knights and other fighting men. And yet they were kept under control by authority. I imagine that the news that Walter Fitzrobert, lord of Baynard Castle, was coming down Thames Street would have caused such vagrants to scatter out of the way. In similar fashion the *gouverneur* of a seagoing vessel doubtless had a presence of authority as he moved along the quays. A twelfth-century mob could be unruly, but it was seldom completely lacking in discipline. Up the social ladder, the same observations could be made about the men-at-arms. The Count of Baynard, the Lord of MontFichet, the Constable of the Tower, and others of the King's immediate officers allowed their men a liberty which they could control if they wished. These men were bound by feudal oaths, or by villeinage. On the other hand, when the king was weak, as was Stephen, and again John, the serjants and knights of London must have been a plague to every merchant and every visitor. This is what Fitzstephen meant when he said that London was a fine city when it had a good governor.[54] Rebellion in twelfth-century England and France meant attachment to another overlord; it did not mean becoming a law unto oneself, unless the rebel chanced to be placed very high. When a prominent noble came to town, crowds of people of all classes would flock around him on the streets, anxious to see his dress and his equipment.[55]

It was not unsafe for a man such as Alexander Neckam to walk along the quays in the year 1178. He was only a clerk, and the occasional *ribaut* or man-at-arms who was looking for trouble did not make himself objectionable to a stray cleric. These young men dressed in black were under the jurisdiction of the Church, which, in the person of her bishops, was capable of avenging any outrage that might be visited upon her children by a layman, or king's man. Knowing this quite well, the students and other younger clergy often took full advantage of their position within a town. They roamed in groups, heading for the ball field without the walls on the afternoon of a holy day, but sometimes just looking for sport at the expense of others. A precept of the time was "Be wise with the wise, but relax and play the fool when you are with fools."[56] The mediaeval man loved a good laugh. He got this most often in ways that we would consider impolite or cruel. Running off with signs and other objects that were not fastened down, pitching unoffending creatures into the water, baiting an animal, mocking a man who had been the victim of misfortune—these were everyday sources of amusement. The streets of London, or of any other mediaeval town, showed a high percentage of mutilated and diseased people. The one-armed, the one-legged, the blind, the half-witted, and the just plain drunk were numerous. These unfortunates could furnish much amusement as they moved about awkwardly. The mockery was not often deep, and I dare say the victim sometimes joined in.

In a town where there was no sewerage, with *garde-robe*

pits or privies in the better houses only, it is to be expected that the natural functions were much in evidence. Walls were dirty, and unless there had been a recent rain, the roadway was smelly. The *odeur de merde* was never completely absent from anyone's nostrils. People were used to it; but we must not assume that nobody ever complained. There is a story told by Jacques de Vitry of a man whose job it was to clean out *garde-robe* pits. He did not mind this odor in which he worked all day, but his nostrils were badly offended by the smell of a snuffed candle.[57] The fastidious and very clean persons were rather few in the twelfth century, but they existed. In all ages, except perhaps in prehistoric ones, there have been three kinds of people: the fastidious, the nonfastidious, and those—greatest in number—who are neither one nor the other but conform more or less to circumstances. Today the fastidious are vastly in the majority in those levels of society which most university people frequent. In the twelfth century the proportions were different.

Alexander Neckam belonged to the majority group of his era and accepted smells and "sights" as a part of the daily scene. This time he paused to gaze at the Langbourn as it carried its share of filth into the Thames, but he made no comment other than that it was not so impressive a stream as its neighbor the Walbrook. At Dowgate, Alexander found a Norman shipmaster, or *eschipre*, who was free to talk with him. He was discouraged from taking ship in London. Such a vessel would require at least four or five days to get out of the Thames River and turn south into the Channel. There could be still longer delay then, while waiting for a wind. This compared most unfavorably with the short time at sea required to go from Dover to the nearest Picard port. The Seine itself was a tricky, tidal river which demanded that everyone on board should be a good sailor.[58] Shifting sandbanks meant poling off by all hands; the swift tides required sleepless vigilance and demanded that the ship be firmly anchored when the tide ebbed. All these disadvantages made the Seine a poor route for passenger service. Alexander was advised to follow one of the quick shuttle routes to Paris: two days by mule or palfrey to Dover, and then across to Calais, Wissant, or Boulogne. With a good wind a boat could make Wissant in nine hours, or Boulogne in thirteen. There then remained a four-day journey to Paris if the traveler landed at Boulogne. The stops en route were Hesdin, Corbie, and Clermont. One could take his own palfrey or mule across the Channel, but it would be more advantageous to buy a mount at the port in Picardy and sell it in Paris.

As Alexander and his companion moved back through the crowded streets, they may well have thought of the two afflictions which plagued this fair town of London—drunkenness and fires. Evidence of the drunkenness was plainly visible. On every crooked street within range of Alexander's eyes, there was one or more houses showing evidence of fire. In most cases the gutted dwelling was of wood and the adjacent structures were also charred and marked. Repair work was slow, as it is apt to be in a civilization where people are not too finicky. If the upstairs should burn, one could live for a while in the cellar. There was no organized fire-fighting. Interested neighbors and passers-by rushed to the water supply with buckets and other containers. Adjacent houses might be pulled down if the conflagration was severe.

The city was filled with street cries from dawn to dusk: some announcing the sale of wine in the taverns, others advertising apples, pears, plums, and quinces, peddled from baskets. The soap-and-needle sellers were among the noisiest.[59]

Turning left into Newgate Street, our travelers could have heard the collegiate church of St. Martin's-le-Grand, on their right, ringing the canonical hour, and listened as the peal was taken up by the bells of other churches, which were obliged to take their cue from St. Martin's-le-Grand.[60] The ringing occurred at Prime (approximately six in the morning), Terce, Sext, None, Vespers, Compline, Matins, and Lauds, all of which were a vague three hours apart—vague because a kind of daylight-saving time was observed. In summer the daylight intervals were longer, and the night hours were shorter; in winter the reverse was true.

Although the twelfth-century Londoner worked from dawn to dusk, he did not work at all on holy days. We should not grow too sentimental, therefore, over the long hours of labor that were required. There were a number of holy days in the course of an average month. Men of the baronial class spent much time hanging about the houses of the higher royal officials, such as the king's chancellor. When Thomas Becket held that office, he used to strew fresh reeds and grasses on his floors each day so that the crowds of court seekers would be able to sit on clean floors.[61] All the writers of the time, from Giraldus to Marie de France, are insistent that this court life was degrading. A roomful of barons must have presented a colorful sight, with much of the appearance of a menagerie.[62] Barons carried about with them hawks, falcons, pet monkeys, and parrots. Dogs were always present, gnawing bones, spoiling the rushes, and getting in the way. Alexander remarks that an occasional wolf was tamed and kept as a dog, although these animals were apt to return to their wild state as they grew older.

Newgate was an impressive place with its royal serjants on guard, and its bailiffs collecting taxes and local customs. There was perhaps an uneasy stir about the place, for it shared with the Tower of London employment as a king's prison.[63] Malefactors were not detained very long before they received "justice."[64] Common offenders were herded into a single room of the gatehouse, where they diced and made merry in other ways. Serious offenders, including political ones, might be lowered into holes resembling wells, where there was almost no light. In one of these foul-smelling holes, which were sometimes damp and wet, the prisoner lay wondering what fate would be his. Food was lowered to him: a jug of water, hard moldy bread, and perhaps a piece of bad meat. He dreaded the possibility of meeting with toads, snakes, and other creeping things, of which the mediaeval man was very much afraid.[65] The East Gate at Exeter, Devonshire, was connected with the castle, and possibly with the cathedral, by an underground passage entered by an opening outside the wall. We wonder whether such a subterranean system was ever employed in London.[66]

Alexander Neckam, after passing through Newgate, turned down the lane to the right and found himself once more at St. Bartholomew's in Smithfield. He now made plans for setting out within a day or two, possibly in the company of other guests at the hospice. He would be obliged to borrow another mount, to be left at Dover. To pass the time after supper, he may have engaged in a game of chess. He describes this game and the method of moving the men.[67] The board he used was larger than the one we are accustomed to. It could sit on two trestles like a table top, or it could be placed on the floor, while the players were seated on cushions, or on a rug.[68] The pieces were heavy and, if thrown with effective aim, they could inflict some damage. Alexander records that Reinald Fitz Aymon killed in this way the knight who was playing with him at Charlemagne's court, thereby starting a feud. This was a common source of feuds in the *chansons de geste*. Charlot, the son of Charlemagne, slew Ogier's son Baudouinet in this way, and the theme occurs in other epics.[69] From Alexander's description we know that the main points of the game in the twelfth century were similar to those we follow today, except that the queen moved like a bishop (*alphicus*)—that is, *gressum obliquans*. Sometimes the players sat at a game for an inordinate length of time: "Agolant sat down to a game of chess straightway and with him was the strong king Abilant. The games began around the hour of Prime, and they did not finish until None had passed."[70] But then these two players were pagan kings and could be expected to be extravagant. Alexander would be like the duke so primly described by Wace: "He cared only for suitable games—the sport of chess, the gain at draughts."[71]

Draughts (*dames* or *traiz*) was played with round pieces similar to our checker men. There is reason to believe that the game was close to modern checkers.[72] "Tables" was a kind of backgammon; it was played on a board, with dice.

Chapter III

The Journey and Paris

As THEY left the hospice in Smithfield, Alexander and those who rode with him looked much the same as they had on their arrival. They were perhaps gayer, stimulated by the sights of the great city and by the prospect of soon visiting the shrine at Canterbury. For some, also, there was the anticipation of seeing foreign shores. Much time would have been wasted in passing through the streets of the walled town and in crossing the wooden bridge and paying the tolls; so it is easy to believe that the party crossed the Thames by ferry, at the break of day. They would enter the boat somewhere between Baynard quay and Westminster and join the Dover road at Bermondsey. This road paralleled the course of the Thames for a considerable distance, traversing Deptford, Greenwich, Crayford, Dartford, Gravesend, and Rochester. Before reaching Deptford, however, the road passed over a causeway across a very broad ditch, now completely dry. Some of the company wondered at it. One of the number knew that this was the old *fossé as Danois* and that the Thames River had been turned into it only a few years before, in 1173, when the foundations for the new London Bridge were being set. There had been a sorry time for a number of months, as the port of London was almost dry. Two days of travel were required from London to Dover. The first night could have been spent at Sittingbourne, or perhaps at Faversham. On the second day, early in the afternoon, the travelers gazed down upon that lovely cathedral at Canterbury. The road crosses a ridge a few miles before reaching the town, and it was from this vantage point, as they turned out of a wooded stretch of road, that they suddenly espied the cathedral.

We may assume beyond question that the travelers stopped for an hour or so to visit the tomb of the Martyr. They found the cathedral town noisy with heavy construction work, but this was not rare in any large mediaeval community. The cathedral had suffered a fire four years before, in 1174. The choir was now being rebuilt and the nave lengthened. A terrible accident had occurred not long before Alexander's visit. Guillaume de Sens, the brilliant and dynamic architect from the Continent, had fallen from a rope and been badly crippled. The shrine of St. Thomas was still located in the crypt because of the construction work. The sarcophagus was surrounded by a wall pierced by openings, two on each side, through which the pilgrims could gaze while making their prayers.[1] Already many rich and rare gifts had been deposited at the shrine. Alexander purchased a tiny phial of lead, containing Canterbury water, to be hung around his neck. This was ordinary water to which an infinitesimally small quantity of the Saint's blood had been added.[2] Formerly the water had been sold in little wooden containers with—strange as it may seem—a mirror in the lid.[3] The wood persisted in leaking and a lead phial, sealed with wax, had been devised. Canterbury was not a restful scene at this time, with the workmen lifting heavy stones by pulley and hoist and the crowds of people stumbling over ropes. We are taking for granted that Alexander and his acquaintances left that afternoon and continued the journey toward Dover. The distance that remained was only seventeen miles, but leaving Canterbury as late as they did it was convenient to spend the night just short of their destination. As they rode they encountered many carts laden with fish. They would have seen more if they had been traveling north of London, instead of south, for Yarmouth was the great center of the herring trade.[4]

We wish we had an adequate picture of Dover in the late twelfth century. It was a very busy port at that time. At a later date, as one of the Cinq-Ports, it furnished, together with its associated towns, twenty-one ships for coastal protection.[5] As our protagonist approached the town, he noticed that it lay on low ground between two hills.[6] We will give these their modern names, Castle Hill and the Western Heights. A very small river, the Dour, flowed past the wall of Dover, emptying into the Channel below Castle Hill. Dover Harbor was located at that point where St. James and Russell streets now lie, at the eastern end of Snargate.[7] We assume that there was a mole or jetty, of Roman construction, extending out into the Channel sufficiently to protect the port from strong tide and wind. Some boats could be rowed a short distance into the Dour. Ships came into the port when the tide had risen enough, and they would go out when they had a good wind and an ebb tide. There was some circumventing of these channel ports, such as Dover, by merchant seamen. They found it almost as easy to anchor at high tide on a sandy stretch of coast outside of any harbor. There, when the ship was high and dry, they could load supplies and take on passengers, setting sail again when they had the wind and the tide in their favor. In this way Thomas Becket took ship not far from Sandwich, in 1164, avoiding the *portum publicum* and the inspection by the port guards.[8] Dover Harbor had ten guards at this time. A number of days could be wasted in waiting for a favorable wind. The Monge de Montaudo, though not referring to Dover, once expressed how dreary such a wait could be: "It annoys me much to be in port when it is very bad weather and rains heavily."[9]

On Castle Hill was the royal castle with its towers, curtain wall, and moat, recently constructed in fine stone by the King. The outer wall around this castle was still a palisade of wooden stakes, which was to be replaced with stone in the thirteenth century. In the midst of the wooden enclosure was a big Roman lighthouse, which was octagonal in shape from the external view. A signal fire was built each night on its summit platform. There were lookout windows on three sides of its main chamber. The ruins of another Roman lighthouse were visible on the Western Heights.[10]

Alexander may have spent a night or two, possibly a week, at the priory of St. Martin's-le-Grand on the Western Heights, which was under the jurisdiction of Christ Church Monastery in Canterbury. Its prior at the time was Warin, cellarer of Christ Church.[11] This hospice was far from sufficient to lodge the many travelers who stopped at Dover on the way to and from Canterbury. (A *maison dieu* was built to accommodate them early in the thirteenth century.)

To judge from the Bayeux Tapestry, a lookout balcony attached to a wooden building was in use, from which port authorities could observe the movements of ships.[12] This was obviously independent of the Roman lighthouse.

In the preceding chapter we gave the description of a busy harbor in the words of Wace. We now continue with his account of ships getting under way:

When they were all manned they had tide and a good wind. Then you would see the anchors raised, the pulling taut of stays, the tightening of shrouds, sailors climbing over the vessels to break out the sails and canvas. Some work at the windlass; others are at the luff [*lof*] and the halyards. The pilots are aft—the master steersmen, the finest—and each does his best at the steering oar. "*Avant le hel*" ["Hard on the helm"], and she goes to the left; "*Sus le hel*" ["Up on the helm"], and she goes to the right. In order to gather the wind into the sails they make the outer edges taut and fasten the boltropes. Some pull on the ratlines, and some shorten sail, in order to get the ship to proceed more slowly. They fasten clew lines and sheets, and make the ropes fast; they slacken the runners and lower the sails. They pull on bowlines . . . they make fast the brails to the mast, that the wind may not escape underneath.[13]

All of this makes good nautical sense today, except that the brails (lines which go from top to bottom of the sail, and which are distinctly visible in the bas-relief at Pisa) would not be fastened to the mast. The meaning of *lof* is obscure. Today the luff is the belly of the sail, and the meaning of its etymon in Norse—*lófe*—is "hollow of the hand."[14] But in twelfth-century texts the *lof* seems to have been a sort of pole which was applied to the lower edge of the sail; at any rate, it was something that could be manned: "Where shall we go and in what direction shall we turn the *lof?*"[15]

Here is another description, which tells of the provisioning of a vessel:

. . . the casks were piled on one another; salt meat, bread, wine, and grain . . . and chests and all aplenty, and fine arms and handsome shields [were there]. . . . The banners they had fastened to the castles [fore and aft]. . . . Eight full days passed before the fleet moved from there. The air was balmy and soft, so the ship could not move. At midnight the wind rose, strong and powerful, which struck the sails. Bauches cried, "Now, let's get to the ship quickly!"[16]

Alas, these expert descriptions of ships getting under way must be contrasted with Alexander's words. He was a poor seaman, and we are ready to believe that he was never on the sea except when making the Channel crossing:

If anyone wishes to fit out a ship let him have an asbestos stone, in order that the benefit of fire may not be lacking. If such a stone is once lit it is unquenchable. He should have a needle placed on a pivot; the needle will rotate and revolve until the point looks toward the east, and thus sailors understand where they should steer when the Little Bear constellation is hidden in the storm, although this constellation never sets because of the brevity of its circle.

It is necessary also to be supplied with grain and wine, also with arms and with an axe by which the mast can be cut down when a storm comes up, which is the greatest of evils, and so that the traps of pirates can be avoided. Side planking should be fastened with cords and nails, and, when fitted together, let them be daubed with pitch mixed with wax on the inside, or with paint [*unguentum*], and let them be smoothed on the outside, sparing the use of too much paint. Cross-weaving and wattling are required, in order that the swift and frequent jarrings may not unfasten or loosen the joints. It is needful to join the boards proportionately, with forecastle and aftercastle separated.

Let the mast be raised in a socket on the flooring . . . then let the sail be fastened to the mast, and have the cordage extend from side to side; . . . the lowest part of the sail is fastened to a spar carried crosswise. The swelling of the sail is its belly. Yard braces are needed; may these be placed almost "before the water" [*ante amnem*], of which the upper ends are called horns. The sail yard is at the peak of the mast and is called *carchesium.* The same yard is called *cheruca,* which means also "weather cock," which in French is named *cochet.* Let there be also openings through which oars can run, if rowing is required when a wind is lacking. . . . Let stays be extended, that is, very large ropes. Likewise let there be shrouds supporting the mast. . . . The oar has a blade and an arm; the end is called the blade. . . . Let the skipper have a transverse seat or thwart; . . . near this let there be a windlass that the lines may be bound more firmly and that the sail may be raised according to the shift of wind. . . . An anchor is needed. . . . Have a mallet—and note that the mallet is called *malleus*—by which the sailor gives signals to his comrades.[17]

The many omissions in the above translation are the punning etymologies of which Alexander was so fond, and which stud many of his writings. He was every inch the grammarian. His testimony about the compass is of especial value. Most compasses at this time consisted of a needle magnetized by contact with a lodestone, then thrust into a straw and placed to float in a saucer of water. It may have been that the compass deviation was such as to make the needle point east. Alexander noticed the windlass and the oars, but he was none too clear on the subject of the lines. It is possible that a hammer was struck against a metal plate when giving signals in a high wind. On the other hand, it may be that Alexander had in mind the hammer and anvil which the ancients used for giving rhythm to their oarsmen. In that event, he did not actually see such a hammer on his journey across the Channel. A metal hearth with a protecting shield against the wind was undoubtedly the type of cooking hearth used on these vessels. Our author confused this with the asbestos stone of mythical properties.

We are assuming that Alexander was notified one evening that his ship would sail at dawn. His identity was checked by the guardian of the port if the authorities in Dover had been alerted for any reason. In any case he was obliged to pay a small embarkation tax. The price of passage was not definitely set; the passenger bargained with the shipman.[18] Some years later Wistasce li moines offered five sous sterling for a crossing, and it is inferred that this was a little high. The Channel can be unpleasant, particularly in a small boat of very shallow draft. During the night hours when the wind was high, sailors would think they could hear sirens

Lookout from Dover, from the Bayeux Tapestry

Boisil on a bed, Add. MS 39943, fol. 21
Courtesy British Museum

"wailing, laughing, jeering, like insolent men in their cups."[19] Most of Alexander's journey was by broad daylight. After some thirteen hours of travel the boat approached the entrance to the Liane River and waited to enter with the tide into Boulogne Harbor.[20] How Alexander must have yearned to set his feet once more on solid ground.[21] The old Roman lighthouse, built under Caligula and repaired by order of Charlemagne, was high on a hill to the left. As twilight was descending over the mouth of the river, the beacon fire had already been lit. When sails were furled, the seamen manned the oars and brought the vessel where it could be tied to the quay.

Boulogne consisted of an upper and a lower city.[22] The lower was on the bank of the Liane, about a mile from where the river flowed into the Channel. It had a single street, connecting the quays. Another road led to the upper city, which was on a hill. We suggest that some sort of Roman jetty or mole protected the anchorage, and there may have been a wooden palisade around the lower city, which was crowded with seamen and hangers-on. This port belonged to the Countess of Boulogne who, in turn, was protected by the gallant Count Philip of Flanders (the patron of Chrétien de Troyes).[23] It was not English territory, so we can expect that some watch was made on travelers from England. Alexander had his letters with him in a leather box which hung around his neck on a cord. In the *Ipomedon*, one sees "a messenger come quickly who carried a box with letters."[24] From a box like this, Alexander would take his papers in order to satisfy the guard of his identity. There was a customs fee, which could be remitted as a sign of special favor.[25] Little attention would be paid to Alexander. The port of Boulogne had seen hundreds of young men pass through on their way to Paris and other schools.

They all looked somewhat alike. Alexander would inquire at the quay where he could find a suitable lodging.[26] Sumpter horses and mules, fitted with special saddles for carrying loads, would be standing about with their drivers. Our young clerk probably hired one to guide him toward his lodging and saw his few sacks of belongings piled upon the saddle.[27] Since he was intending to purchase a palfrey on the morrow, it is possible that he made inquiries about the horse fair. If the porter was anything like his brethren of later times, he doubtless undertook to sell a horse himself.

The next day was spent in making preparations.[28] People in the twelfth century had more time to kill than we do today. Arrangements were made to travel in a group. The stretch of road from Boulogne to Lyons (or Lugdunum) had been a principal highway in the time of the Romans. It passed through Montreuil and Hesdin (two and a half miles east of the existing town), across the Canche River to Doullens, and thence through Beauquesne and Pucheviller, across the Ancre River to Corbie, and on to Soissons, Reims, and Châlons. Corbie was an important junction. It had an abbey of importance which cared for both mind and body. Its library was distinguished, and so was the accommodation for travelers. From Corbie a slightly less important Roman road branched due south to Clermont and Paris.[29]

Travelers arriving in France were sure to appreciate highly the wine. In England *goudale*, or ale, was the common beverage, and a change was much desired. Englishmen, when they got together, practiced the silly custom of "Wassail! Drink-hail!" The first drinker would pick up a "mazer," or bowl of bird's-eye maple, filled with wine, salute his companion with a kiss, and cry "Wassail!" The other bestowed a kiss in turn and cried the other word. They both drank.[30] A great deal of humor was displayed in this, and it is easy to guess that a drinker's legs would not stand up under much of it. The people on the Continent observed this practice with awe and amusement, and were disposed to consider the English to be drunkards because of it. We will assume that the Englishmen at the hospice in Boulogne, if they found a suitable tavern, spent their evening in this manner. If Alexander paid the scot, he probably drew forth about three sous from the ten or more which he carried in the purse at his belt. This purse might have been of fine brocade.[31]

At this time all money in France and England was in silver pennies, or "deniers." A denier from the Paris mint of this date contained four cents' worth of silver according to the current United States price for silver. Higher values of money were made by weighing out scoopfuls of these deniers at the money-changer's. A "marc" was eight ounces, or two-thirds of a pound. This would be seven dollars in current United States money. A "livre" was a pound of twelve ounces—ten dollars. A "sou" was twelve deniers, or fifty cents. Occasionally a gold coin from Byzantium, southern Italy, or Spain passed from hand to hand. Its gold content was worth about five of our modern dollars. There was no fixed ratio between gold and silver in the twelfth century, but in 1199, in England, such a besanz was worth two shillings or sous—that is, about twenty-four silver deniers.[32] The equivalents in modern money given here are estimated from the weight of the metal and do not take into account the question of alloy. The purchasing value was a horse of a different color. In the first place, this varied with the type of purchases considered essential, standards of living, and the amount of actual money in circulation. We shall return to this problem at various points in the course of this book. An average purse carried about 125 deniers, or 10 sous. Larger sums would be carried by a traveler in a leather money belt strapped around his waist under the outer clothing. This could be a very heavy sum, perhaps reaching as high as sixty pounds (troy weight).

The Paris-bound travelers rose bright and early, we can be sure, and started on their way. On the first day they stopped for dinner at Montreuil. Much of the land was heavily forested. There were the Hardelot, the Forest de Boulogne, and the Forest de Hesdin. Our student traveler probably brought out his green-wax tablets on occasion and jotted down verses and accounts.[33] As in England, much time was passed with singing and the telling of tales. If the pace was sufficiently slow, someone may even have read aloud from a book. A road was a wonderful panorama in those days. Nothing was standardized. No detailed map existed—only itineraries or lists of towns were provided—so that a journey could offer something new and refreshing at every turn. There would be strange groups of people: parties of monks in unusual habits, ladies accompanied by knights or men-at-arms with magnificent equipment, itinerant traders and workmen, and jongleurs accompanied by a trained bear or a monkey. One might even stop for three or four hours and listen to a minstrel who was chanting away interestingly before a church or in a village street. There were awkward shepherds with their flocks, crowding the riders off the road. The unfortunate were continually in view, tapping the road with a cane, with mutilated limbs bound up, and here and there a silly stare meant a half-wit who could be counted on to offer a moment of amusement. No one was in a very great hurry, unless he were a messenger traveling for King or Church. Such messengers habitually halved the time of travel, but they often rode in the night. Temporary and permanent gallows were observed here and there. The stench was far from agreeable, but it was not considered very shocking. At night the travelers would make for the hospice which had been recommended to them at the previous stop. Perhaps they did not always eat at a cookshop in a town. They may have purchased enough to carry with them and consume beside the road—a capon, a *gasteau,* and a pot of wine with a *henap,* or wine cup.[34]

On the afternoon of the fourth day, after taking their dinner in Luzarches, the travelers became conscious of the approach to Saint-Denis, the venerable abbey which was just seven miles from the heart of Paris. The groups of monks, the pack horses with their leather bags strapped over their sides,[35] and even the many carts coming in from the side roads announced a well-populated area. The carts of the time were most frequently two-wheeled (rarely four) with high sides, giving a fencelike appearance. They were apt to be drawn by two animals and were employed for heavy hauling—casks of wine, household equipment, lances, mailed coats, and so on. A cart was despised, and no knight would consent to ride in such a vehicle, no matter how badly wounded he might be.[36] If he could not ride on horseback, he was conveyed on a litter stretched between two horses. Ladies, as well as sick persons, occasionally traveled in this way. Carts were slow and cumbersome and were relegated to cart roads, off the main track. Here is Alexander's own description of such a vehicle and its driver:

A carter about to drive his cart should wear a *chape* with a fur-lined hood, or a frock with sleeves so that his hands may project from them at will. If he is driving mules or horses let him touch their ears with a flexible rod, which is the origin of the word *auriga*. . . . [There he is etymologizing again!] He should wear boots on his legs in order not to be disturbed by thickets or muddy places. [This must mean bound leggings, not leather boots.] When the horses go up a hill or small mountain the weight of the cart will be on the forward part; but when descending a slope it is necessary to make a decision: let the horses be unyoked and one draw the cart forward while the other fastened to the rear of the wagon shall retard the motion of the vehicle, laboring with bended knee. See also that the driver hold the pin of the shaft at the rope with a firm hand. If the horse has a collar on back and neck let it be covered with felt. I omit mention here of yoke, harness, cloths, canvas, since I have mentioned them elsewhere. . . .

Let us talk about the same cart in another way. The wheels are joined by an axletree, each on a different side. The axletree at the extremities is encircled in a hub. The axle pins should be firmly fixed. In the hub spokes are fitted, radiating out to the fellies [forming the rim of the wheel]; at the ends of the spokes are the *stelliones*, that is, "tracks" or *orbite*. These make the tracks deeper. Let the outer rim of the wheel be furnished with an iron shoe in order that it may not be disturbed by the hindrance of small stones and other objects, or by unevenness. Boards should be set on a framework as the body of the cart with sticks inserted into holes on the planks which go crosswise, which are the side pieces of the wagon. . . . I have mentioned the pins of the shaft. Let our cart be equipped, lifting us up to Heaven like the chariot of Elijah.[37]

The significant point in this description of a cart is the rather obscure mention of *stelliones*, or *orbite*. We take it these these were projecting edges of some kind, on the outer edge of the wheel, which prevented it from sinking too deep into the mud. Perhaps they were the triangular broadening out of the spokes which are seen in mediaeval illustrations of carts.

At Saint-Denis, the town that had grown up around the abbey was surrounded by a circular stone wall and a "vallum," or dry ditch. It was not necessary to pass through this area. A traveler could skirt the wall until he came again to the paved Roman road. There was now a choice of two routes for one who was going to Paris. There was the Roman road, which we shall now call the Route Saint-Martin, and a parallel route still unpaved, the Chaussée de Saint-Lazare. This Chaussée was now the more important of the two. The two roads ran parallel toward Paris, some two hundred yards apart. Milestones were set on these roads. Between the town of Saint-Denis and the Church of Saint-Laurent no building was allowed by royal decree. This edict was being obeyed along the Route Saint-Martin and technically the other road was affected by the same order, but there it was not being obeyed. For some three miles after Saint-Denis the Roman road was bordered by vineyards and plowed fields, but the unpaved Chaussée was experiencing a small building boom.[38]

The group in which Alexander rode chose to travel along the paved route. After going a pleasant three miles, they noted the little settlement of Clignancourt on the right. The Chaussée ran through this. Another road led off from Clignancourt, ascending the hill of Montmartre. All this was quite visible to our travelers because they were surrounded by more or less open fields. Montmartre rose in the distance, above the surrounding countryside. It seemed to rise in three tiers. There were vineyards on the slope, but near the summit were some visible ruins (an old Roman temple) and the recently erected buildings of a convent.[39] Women travelers of distinction frequently stopped there and enjoyed the unique view of Paris which was possible from that point. One saw a "turreted city surrounded by great walls."[40] At the foot of Montmartre was the Martyrologium, a small chapel that marked the spot where St. Denis was martyred.[41] Between this and the city's suburb on the right bank of the Seine, there lay a stretch of fields and vineyards where a considerable body of men could be quartered in tents. It was there that the king of France marshaled his knights and men-at-arms when receiving a distinguished visitor such as the king of England.[42] There was a general lowering of the terrain as the road swept past Montmartre toward the city. Travelers usually stopped and "took a look." Straight ahead, four miles away, was the stockade or wooden palisade which protected the right bank.[43] The two parallel roads led to this enclosure. The paved one entered at what seemed to be a stone gate, close by a church which was pointed out as being Saint-Merri. There the ground rose a little, at the Monceau Saint-Merri. The unpaved road headed toward the great bridge; the stockade also ended at that spot. It was evident, even at that distance, that the chief activity of the suburb was concentrated there. People were pouring out of the stockade and into the turreted gate which admitted to the bridge; still other people were going the other way. As the visitor's gaze drew back again along that road, he saw a small church surrounded by tiny crosses that were barely visible. This was the Church of the Holy Innocents, and the crosses marked what was now the principal burial ground of the city. This cemetery was still an open field, and there were indications that it was marshy in spots.[44] A road led off to the right from the cemetery, running parallel to the river. This was the road to Clichy—a town farther down the Seine—which cut off sixteen miles of tedious sailing on the snakelike river for anyone who chose to land his cargo there. As a river port, Clichy had the advantage of not being directly under the watchful eye of the *marchands de l'eau* of the city of Paris. Many carts and pack animals, loaded with goods, were moving back and forth along the Clichy road. The observer finally tired of watching all this movement, and following the Chaussée back toward Montmartre, he did not fail to see the leper hospital of Saint-Lazare over towards his right. This was opposite Saint-Laurent, which was just ahead. The two hundred yards or so which separated the two was now bare of any occupancy, but it lodged the Fair of Saint-Lazare for a week each May.[45] The famous Lendit, or Fair of Saint-Denis, was held farther back along the road, nearer to the town of Saint-Denis. The Lendit was celebrated for a two-week period during the month of June.

Our travelers descended from their vantage point and passed the Church of Saint-Laurent on their right. They crossed a little, low bridge of stone, the Passellus Sancti Martini, over a stagnant gully which was the ancient bed of the Seine.[46] A few more miles and the Church of Saint-Martin stood far back at the left on a low hill, surrounded by its own *munitio*, or stockade. It had a dry moat. This abbey church owned most of the vineyards through which the travelers were passing.[47] Saint-Nicholas was next on the left, and now houses rather than vines were bordering the highway, bringing with them the inevitable "stench of mediaeval civilization." The pavement was in still greater disrepair, being covered with a light layer of mud which caused those using it to wonder whether it were paved after all. Alexander and his friends reached the gate of Saint-Merri. The wooden drawbridge was down, and the *serjant* on duty gave little more than a casual glance at them as they paid their toll and entered the suburb.

This right-bank enclosure was the new business district for the city, which lay on the island just beyond. There was a winding cross-thoroughfare which led to the Chastelet gate and then on to the Church of Saint-Germain l'Auxerois, paralleling the road to Clichy, but nearer the river. This main artery, often referred to officially in documents as the Ruga Sancti Germani, left the stockade on the east at the Porte Baudoyer. So great was the need for space that the suburb was expanding considerably outside the stockade at Porte Baudoyer.[48] Many a fine house was being erected outside the Porte on the road to Charenton, and before the Barres, which was the name given to that part of the stockade stretching from Baudoyer to the river. These people felt secure because the Templars had their stronghold at the Barres, facing on the river.[49]

The Temple was a group of strong houses, with their own landing in the river, which the order preferred, rather than a donjon or tower. The accommodation afforded by this group of houses was sufficient to care handsomely for a large number, so that guests of royal distinction who came with huge equipage and train were usually lodged there. Such a visitor was the English royal chancellor, Thomas Becket, who came to Paris in 1157 to carry away the little French princess. Giraldus has described Becket's procession.[50] First there came two hundred and fifty male servitors, on foot, who were singing English songs. Following them were huntsmen with fine dogs on double leashes. Then came eight carts, each drawn by five horses, with a driver (probably walking) leading a dog. Leather coverings were fastened over the loads in these carts. Two of them carried beer or ale in iron-bound casks; one cart held the furniture of a chapel; another, all the necessary fittings for a bedchamber; still another bore the *expensa;* and a sixth carried kitchen utensils. The remaining two were loaded with room hangings, sacks of clothing, and so on. At a proper distance behind these walked twelve pack animals, each with a rider on its back—and a monkey. These sumpters were loaded with boxes of linen, silver, golden utensils, cups, plates, bowls, roundels, clothing, and books. One of the animals carried sacred vessels and ornaments for an altar. Following all this baggage were knights leading their "destriers," or war horses, as they rode along on palfreys. Youths came after them with birds on their wrists. These were squires. The officers of the household followed; next came more knights and clergy, riding two and two. Last of all appeared Chancellor Thomas and his associates. This costly procession was headed for the Temple, but I doubt that even that fine group of buildings could have housed so many. Probably adjacent householders were persuaded to vacate for a time.

In the very heart of the enclosed area, extending to the river, was a gravelly depression called the Grève, on which no houses were built.[51] Until very recently this had been the site of the weekly Paris Market, but the King had transferred the Market to the Campelli, close by the cemetery of the Holy Innocents.[52] It had become too difficult for peasants to drive their carts into the stockade through the crowded streets. The Grève had since become the wine market and chief point of unloading for boats bringing wine to Paris.[53] These came down the river. The location was attractive because it was open, and many of the wealthy now had houses facing it. The Church of Saint-Gervais stood just inside the Porte Baudoyer. It is not unlikely that this church and that of Saint-Merri were responsible in the first place for the enclosing of this suburb and for the growth of its business district. The Grant Pont, as the big bridge was called, was a considerable barrier to boats coming up or down the river. Those coming from Rouen could unload better below the bridge, just as the wine boats coming down from the region of the Saône preferred the Grève. Salt, cattle, and fish were the principal cargoes from Rouen, and these were unloaded and sold at the Chastelet; wood, grain, and hay, in addition to wine, were handled at the upper quays.[54] There was a great deal of food in evidence here at Paris—enough to arouse comment from strangers.[55]

The Grant Pont was a beehive of activity.[56] It was a stone bridge, about eighteen feet wide, set on a span of five or six arches. Its surface was probably a conglomerate, pebbles set in concrete. The roadway down the center was lined on both sides by small houses, little more than booths or stalls, set against a high parapet, which could be defended militarily. Presumably there was a catwalk along the top of each parapet, and perhaps there were low crenels. The houses or stalls were roofed with the usual steep, peaked roofs of tile or slate. No section of Paris was more secure from robbery or attack than this fortified bridge. It is easy to understand why it was occupied chiefly by money-changers, and presumably by a few goldsmiths and leather-goods merchants also at this date. Each little house had a counter open to the roadway, and inevitably a steep ladder or stair mounting to a *soler*, or upstairs room. This upper floor might well have had a fancy window facing on the roadway, as was common at the time. I do not believe that merchants as wealthy as those operating on the Grant Pont would have established living quarters in such a restricted area. In a document of 1163 a man buys a *fenestram nummulariam supra Magnum Pontem*, which is evidence enough that these structures were only booths and not houses. Perhaps when the counters were closed at night, goods and fixtures were stored above. There was a constant passing on foot over this bridge, and some traffic on horse. It was the principal entrance to the Cité, as well as the money center. We can be certain that Alexander stopped with one of those changers and had his ready money converted into *deniers parisis*. The changer sat before a deep tray full of money.

He held a balance or scale.[57] A typical balance consisted of a grip held in the hand, continued by a vertical bar to which the weighing arm was bolted at the center so that the arm swung freely up and down. At each end of the weighing arm dangled a heavy cord, supporting a cauldron-shaped metal basket. The changer gave a certain ratio of *parisis* for the foreign silver, according to predetermined purity. I have a fond idea that if we had brought him a United States silver dollar he would have allowed us twenty-five *parisis* before deducting the proper amount for his commission. Sterling deniers were superior in ratio to the *parisis*, but there were many counterfeits of sterling and Alexander's money would have been subjected to much biting, and ringing on the table.[58]

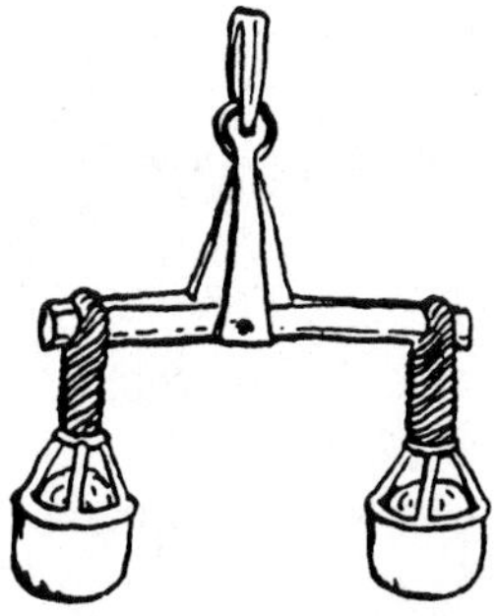

The Chastelet, which guarded the land end of this bridge, was a tower gate such as might then be found in any large town. It had guardrooms and underground cells, like those we imagined at Newgate in London. In addition, this was the Porte de Paris.[59] The Ruga Sancti Germani crossed the Chaussée de Saint-Lazare at this point, and there was some sort of entrance to the suburban stockade (on which we are not precisely informed). Was there a gate admitting into the stockade, or was there just an open stretch in the palisade at this place? If there had been a stone archway, this should have left some trace, in name at least, as at Saint-Merri and Baudoyer. These were cited as landmarks in later documents, long after the stockade had been removed. (Philip Augustus began his wall on the right bank in 1190.) As we have already indicated, meat, fish, and salt were heavily traded at this point. The Church of Saint-Jacques de la Boucherie stood on a small rise near where the stockade ended. The butchers were congregated in that vicinity by royal order, although many continued to trade on the left bank, and a few privileged ones were permitted to sell in the Cité.[60] Bakers and fish sellers had their stalls close by. This was the noisiest corner, as well as the busiest, in all Paris. It was difficult to make much speed across the Seine over the Grant Pont. Anyone in a hurry—and there were not many—would be advised to take a ferry across, farther up the river.

We will suppose that Alexander Neckam spent his first night at the hospice associated with Saint-Gervais, at the Porte Baudoyer.[61] There was perhaps a sign of some sort over this lodging. A student was far from being a novelty in this thriving city of some 250,000 souls. The difficulty lay in how to house the population in an area which should have contained no more than one-third that number. Hospices for transients were gradually becoming more frequent. Travelers coming in from the west might stop at the new hospice at the Church of St. Thomas the Martyr, on a road that ran between the Clichy highway and the extension of the Ruga Sancti Germani, which continued on to the village of Chaillot. This hospice on the Rue Saint-Thomas was in an area commonly called the Louvre. Sainte-Opportune, in the Campelli at the market place, would soon begin to provide lodgings.

On the following day, Alexander's immediate task was to report to his master and, through him, select his permanent residence. We will imagine him setting out on foot, shortly after daylight, toward the quarter occupied by the schools.[62] He crossed the Grant Pont, elbowing and shoving his way through the throng. The street which continued straight before him was known as the Street before the King's Palace. The royal residence was on the right hand, separated by a wall from the rest of the island. There was a gate in this wall opening onto a shallow *place* where some fishmongers were selling their wares. Alexander turned up the second street to the left, just before reaching the fish sellers. This cross street was the Rue de la Draperie. As the name implied, it was occupied mostly by drapers, who stood behind their counters with open shop fronts. This was a rich trade, and the street was agreeable and well kept. It was quite long and brought the traveler into the main street of the student section, which was Rue de la Lanterne to his left and Rue de la Juiverie to his right. There were some remains of Roman paving on this street. In ancient times it had been a continuation of the Roman road which brought Alexander to Paris. Perhaps still visible in 1178 were some of the ruins of the old bridge which had connected this road directly with the mainland. The entire island still had its Roman wall around it. This was in a bad state of repair, despite the praise of the turreted city quoted from Nigel Wireker. The wall did not come to the water's edge; it stood back some ten or twelve feet, leaving a narrow no man's land around the edge of the island, which was punctuated by an occasional quay or landing platform. One such quay was the Porte Saint-Landry, which served as a landing for those who had business within the Cloister Notre Dame.

The Rue de la Juiverie extended for a single block, in the modern sense. There was a large synagogue (to be converted later into the Madeleine Church) on the northeastern corner; apparently there were twenty-four houses occupied by Jews.[63] Some of these residents may have been bakers, as numerous bakeshops were there.[64] The presence of the Jewish colony in the heart of the student quarter probably had significance. Moneylending was their important activity, and they must have had plenty of business with students, even with those among the clerics. Officially, there was almost no anti-Semitism at that date. The King, Louis VII, was very just in his dealings with the Jews, and he allowed them to prosper and to mingle fully with the population. There was perhaps some intermarriage. Many Jews came to own buildings occupied by Christian clerics.[65] Unofficially, however, there was a smoldering antagonism against this display of non-Christian wealth in the heart of Notre Dame. (Immediately after his accession to the throne, Philip Augustus exiled the Jews for a short period. On their return, they did not come back to this area, but occupied a district on the right bank.) On that morning in 1178 when Alexander stepped into the Rue de la Juiverie, we can believe that the air was prosperous and that there was a bustle of activity on that single block. A turn to the left, at the end of the street, brought the stroller into the Rue Saint-Christofle, which led to the Campus Rosaeus, Saint-Pierre de Buef, and the parvis of the cathedral. A network of crooked streets which ran off to the left of the Rue Saint-Christofle was filled with small houses that provided student lodgings—Rue de Petite-Orberie, Rue des Oubloiiers (later Rue de la Licorne), the winding Rue des trois Canettes, Rue de la Pomme (later Rue de Perpignan), Rue de Saint-Pierre, and so on. These streets were vastly overcrowded, and yet the Bishop of Paris had forbidden the housing of students within the nearby cloister of the cathedral.[66] Alexander walked past the Church of Saint-Christofle, on his right, and then found himself in the presence of an immense building activity. Houses had been cleared around the then cathedral church, which nestled against the old Roman wall on the south side of the island. Behind this church the wall had already been removed for a few hundred yards, and the choir of the new Cathedral of Notre Dame, which had been begun in 1163, was now almost complete. The choir straddled the line of the Roman wall at that point, and the nave, when it should be finished, would cover part of the site of the Merovingian cathedral. Alexander walked reverently into this old roughly built structure.[67] There was a narthex, or entry vestibule. The interior was very shabby, in need of a restoration which it would never get, but there was some beauty that could still be seen. The nave was long and low, basilica shaped, with two rows of columns dividing off the side aisles. These columns were of black and white veined marble and were topped by white stone capitals carved in the shape of acanthus leaves. The floor was in mosaic tile, with intersecting circles and other geometric figures. The ceiling beams were gilded with ancient and faded gold. The chancel and altar were in the apse at the eastern end. Some marble paneling was visible there on the walls. The great organ of the choirmaster Leoninus stood perhaps behind the altar in the apse. When Alexander was there, a covering had been lowered over it by a rope from the ceiling. When the young man left the building, he noted that the outer roof was of old-fashioned tiles. Opposite this cathedral there was a new street, recently cut through—the Rue neuve Notre Dame. He returned by this route, on his way to the Rue du Petit Pont, and he remarked that the Hospital of St. Mary (later to be called the Hôtel-Dieu) was built on the left hand between the crumbling Roman wall and the edge of the water. This building ran the entire block, from the Parvis to the Petit Pont. So crowded were the students in their effort to find lodgings that some eighteen of them were quartered in a single room in this hospital. In the year 1180, Josse of London received permission to organize these young men into what was to be the oldest college of the University of Paris —the Dix-huit Clercs. In exchange for lodging and a very small amount of money these clerics were to act as mourners for the pauper dead.[68]

The Petit Pont aroused great admiration in all those who saw it for the first time.[69] The entrance to the bridge had been somewhat widened in 1153–54. Houses of wood were constructed on each side of this stone bridge. These, in need of space, projected slightly over the outer edge of the bridge. They were not in a continuous line, but were divided in several places by open spaces. There could not have been more than five houses to a side, with perhaps two open spaces setting these off. We suggest that the bridge itself was supported by three or four arches. The open spaces between the houses were surprising to Alexander. They were called *exedrae*, and they made it possible for those strolling on the bridge to gaze at the river. It seems that there were stone seats, facing each other, in each of these spaces. Masters and students could sit by the river in this way and hold their discussions in the open air.[70] Students used to stand there and watch the diving into the water on a hot day. I do not doubt that they did some diving from those places, themselves, weather permitting. Swimming, however, was not a common accomplishment in the twelfth century. The houses must have been very small. Unlike the stalls on the Grant Pont, these houses were most assuredly used for living quarters, and they may have been two and three stories high with one small room on each floor. It is probable that Adam dou Petit Pont lived in one of these structures and that he taught his students on the ground-floor area usually appropriated for a shop. In winter he would sit there close to a charcoal burner, possibly a basin, while on warm days he may have moved out to an *exedra*, or open-air seat. Traffic was, of course, heavy before his door. Students paced up and down on the muddy pavement. But a teacher in the twelfth century liked auditors of all kinds; the more who stopped to hear, the better it was for his fame. We can picture such a scene. The little room is open toward the bridge. To the rear it has a pair of windows overlooking the Seine. The stone floor is covered with dry rushes in the winter, with green things in the spring and summer. Students sit on the floor, maybe on an occasional bench. The teacher has a chair with a back and armrests. He may have a reading stand before him and a low stool for a footrest.

Since a teacher had to do much writing, we will describe in Alexander's own words, at this point, the materials used by a scribe:

> Let him have a razor or knife for scraping pages of parchment or skin; let him have a "biting" pumice for cleaning the sheets, and a little scraper for making equal the surface of the skin. He should have a piece of lead and a ruler with which he may rule the margins on both sides—on the back and on the side from which the flesh has been removed.
>
> There should be a fold of four sheets (a quaternion). I do not use the word *quaternio* because that means "a squad in the army." Let these leaves be held together at top and bottom by a strip [of parchment threaded through]. The scribe should have a bookmark cord and a pointed tool about which he can say, "I have pricked [*punxi*] not pinked [*pupigi*] my quaternion." Let him sit in a chair with both arms high, reinforcing the back rest, and with a stool at the feet. Let the writer have a heating basin[71] covered with a cap; he should have a knife with which he can shape a quill pen; let this be prepared for writing with the inside fuzzy scale scraped out, and let there be a boar's or goat's tooth for polishing the parchment, so that the ink of a letter may not run (I do not say a whole alphabet); he should

have something with which letters can be canceled. Let him have an indicator [*speculum*] or line marker [*cavilla*] in order that he may not make a costly delay from error.[72] There should be hot coals in the heating container so that the ink may dry more quickly on the parchment in foggy or wet weather.[73] Let there be a small window through which light can enter; if perchance the blowing of the north wind attacks the principal window, let this be supplied with a screen of linen or of parchment, distinct in color; green and black offer more comfort to the eyes.[74] Whiteness, when too intense, disturbs the sight and throws it into disorder. There should be red lead for forming red Phoenician or Punic letters or capitals. Let there be dark powder and blue which was discovered by Solomon [that is, ultramarine].

The notary or scribe should know when he is about to write ψ, when an aspirate, when ω, when o, when ζ, when η, when δ, when small ϝ, when τ, when υ, when ι, when σ, when antisigma (ɔ), in order that he may not make a barbarism in writing or a slip in speaking; a wrong letter is frequent among barbarians. He should know where to put *bimos signi* [?], transposition, where reverse order, where a comma representing a diphthong. Furthermore, let a style of writing be acquired for seals, manuscripts, and documents, transactions, another manner for a text, another kind for glosses. But a gloss, for brevity, should be written by titles [abbreviations].[75]

This description doubtless applies to a professional scribe, or manufacturer of books and documents, rather than to a mere student or teacher, but it gives information on what was required by anyone writing.[76] The first essentials were the high-backed chair with arms, a footstool, and a sort of reading desk on which to place the parchment and the other materials. Such essentials are reproduced in illumination after illumination. At times a white cloth was draped over the writing or reading desk. The inkhorn, a genuine cow horn, was placed in a round hole; it had a tight cover so that it could be carried about at one's belt. The vellum or parchment was marked off and ruled with a lead point, or simply with a blind point. The quill pen, which had replaced the reed pen by this time, had to be kept stored long enough for the oil of the goose to dry out; then it was cut and trimmed. The erasing process was much like that used with a mimeograph stencil today. Once the offending letter was erased with a knife, the surface had to be rubbed with a tooth. Anyone copying a book needed to lay a long, narrow strip of parchment into place to mark the column and the line where he stopped, in order to avoid a costly skip of the text. Apparently a sort of screen of linen or of parchment (perhaps even paper, which was being manufactured at the time) could be set or hung at a window. The information on Greek letters need not be taken too seriously. These characters were copied from some ancient grammarian. It should be noted that different styles of writing are prescribed. Information is given also on the preparation of fresh parchment, a task which was probably undertaken by the teacher or scholar himself. We know that parchment and vellum were bought at fairs and that the skins were at that time in a semirough state.

In those days, when books circulated in manuscript, a book was considered published when it was *anonciez*, or announced; at least, that is the way Marie de France expresses it.[77] One way of accomplishing such an announcement was to make a formal presentation to a high personage such as the king, or a prominent count or duke. The author seldom wrote a book out at length in his own hand on vellum or parchment. Such writing was more apt to be done on wax tablets, which could then be passed to a professional scribe for copying off fair. Very probably the author of a vernacular work dictated to a scribe. Professional copyists were specially employed by booksellers, and many monasteries also made a business of copying and binding books.

By way of digression at this point, we may ask how long it took a twelfth-century author to compose a work. Gaimar needed some twelve months to compose about 6,500 lines: "Gaimar devoted March and April and all twelve months before he had translated about the kings."[78] To complete his *Topographia Hibernica* (in Latin, of course) Giraldus says that he spent three years; but his *Expugnatio Hibernica* required only two years.[79] All sorts of people were writing. For this we quote Guernes de Sainte-Maxence: "All these other romances which clerks, laymen, monks, or ladies have made about the Martyr, much have I heard them lie."[80] This includes just about anybody who could read or write.

We can assume that Adam dou Petit Pont was at his desk, or discoursing with students, when Alexander came to see him. Possibly he had made previous arrangements by letter with Alexander on the subject of a room. If the experience of John of Salisbury was typical, it is likely that Alexander had to pay a year's rent in advance, before moving in.[81] If Alexander had a considerable sum of money with him, he would leave it with the teacher for safekeeping.

Adam dou Petit Pont was an old man at this time, about seventy-three. (His death was to come in 1183.) Like many other teachers at Paris, he was an Englishman by birth and early education. He encouraged many subtleties of dialectic; indeed, he and his pupils were famous for that. He was most independent in spirit. At the same time, he believed very heartily in grammar and rhetoric. Otherwise, Alexander would hardly have studied with him, for this student shows throughout his writings a passion for etymology and language per se. In addition to the Greek alphabet, Alexander made shift to know some Hebrew.[82] This last must have come from an acquaintance with some Jewish scholar of the Rue de la Juiverie. We may wonder why Adam dou Petit Pont would have persisted in maintaining his quarters on the Petit Pont, surrounded by unquestionable discomforts. The rooms were excessively small, and it must have been impossible to provide kitchen facilities. Perhaps Alexander, and most of his neighbors, had their food brought in, hot, from a nearby cookshop. There was such a cookshop, according to evidence, on one of the little streets leading down to the river from the Rue de la Huchette. Adam probably remained on the bridge because his fame was associated with that address. Then again many visitors strolled by there in the course of a day and must have stopped for a while in his doorway, through which the teacher's brilliant words were plainly audible.

Some students came to Paris with letters of recommendation addressed to the King, to Abbot Richard of Saint-Victor, and to other important personages.[83] We are assuming that Alexander Neckam did not possess one of these. The King could not do much to carry out such a trust, except to interfere when a student got into trouble; but Abbot Richard had taken the task quite seriously. He was frequently disappointed in his charges, for he complained of the lack of seriousness and the dearth of religion in the schools.[84] There could have been a slight feeling of rivalry here, as Saint-Victor (and Sainte-Geneviève) had theological schools which rivaled those of Notre Dame and Petit Pont. The Abbey of Saint-Victor was approached by a road which led out of the market place of the Rue de Garlande. It was just a few hundred yards from there to the abbey buildings.

Chapter IV

Lodgings in the City

AT THE south end of the Petit Pont, crowded with students, was the Petit Chastelet, a stone tower gate which was less imposing than the one protecting the Grant Pont. One had to pass through the Petit Chastelet in going to the left bank of the Seine. The view offered there was not apparent to anyone standing on the Petit Pont, as the houses and the Chastelet itself lay between. It was only after Alexander had passed through the deep, narrow archway of the gate that he got his first view of the road to Orléans. The road continued directly ahead, up a sharp rise, and disappeared in the distance over the hill. We would have appreciated the view more than Alexander did; for a moment we would have imagined ourselves in Pompeii or ancient Rome.[1] The road was Roman made, about twenty-seven feet wide, cobbled with stones set in concrete. There was a similar road, the Rue de Garlande, which ran off at an angle to the left; this was less wide, although at one time it had been the main highway between Paris and Lugdunum, leading eventually to Rome. On the hillside, to the right of the Orléans road, were obvious Roman buildings, the Thermes and the so-called Palais de Hautefeuille. There were also some traces of a Roman aqueduct.

Alexander followed the Rue de Garlande as far as the

Monastery of Sainte-Geneviève which was prominent on the hill, to the left. Until it had climbed nearly to the monastery this Rue de Garlande had no houses; it was bordered by the usual vineyards. It led first to a broad market place (soon to be called Place Maubert) and then turned sharply up the slope. Before reaching this place, near the Orléans road, Alexander saw a new little church, dedicated to Saint-Julien-le-pauvre. This was a favorite with students, who loved to hold their disputations there. Beyond Saint-Julien, still short of the future Place Maubert, a track turned off toward the river where hay and straw were piled for sale. Alexander Neckam followed along the Rue de Garlande and continued up the hill toward the monastery. There was a bourg, or small village, attached to Sainte-Geneviève. The center of this was a street called the Rue des Sept Voies, which owed its name to the fact that no fewer than seven roads led into it, and five of these were *culs-de-sac*. Alexander crossed this street and circled back toward the Orléans road, along the ridge. Soon he spied once more the Palais de Hautefeuille[2] and the little Church of Saint-Estienne (-des-Grés), straight ahead.

The Palais de Hautefeuille was a massive Roman building, in fair condition at that time. It inspired considerable curiosity, even in a twelfth-century community. Some thought it had been built by the Saracens (pagan Roman and Saracen were often confused); others believed it to be the family home of Ganelon the traitor. It was a rectangular structure, about three hundred by four hundred feet. The outer wall was double and in 1178 the roof may still have been present, resting on a few short columns supported by the double wall. Inside were two more walls and pagan altars and columns. This may have been the capitol of Lutetia; but that is only a supposition. It could have been a temple. When Alexander saw it, this Palais de Hautefeuille was used by the "Water Merchants of Paris" as their court and meeting house. It was referred to as the "Parleoir des borjois." The Merchants held their assemblies in the center court, which may not have been roofed over. The wall of Philip Augustus was unkind to this building when it passed through it after 1211. Still later the Dominicans erected part of their new convent on its heavy understructure.

Looking toward the city from the Parleoir des borjois, Alexander surely wondered at the Thermes, a trapezoidal building with very few windows, unadorned, which stood in a field to the left, farther down the hill. It was surrounded by a few barns and outhouses.[3] Even its pastoral setting did not make it inviting. It was entered by a small door on the side which faced the Orléans road. At this time it was being used as a manor house—and later acquired the title of palace—but no one guessed what its original use may have been. We are no cleverer today. It had been serviced by an aqueduct of which some sections were still visible to Alexander, standing not high off the ground. The Church of Saint-Séverin was new and flourishing, but private dwellings were still few in number on this hillside. The various fields were partitioned off by hedgerows, and perhaps by a few hedges. The area surrounding the Petit Chastelet, at the very door of Paris, was the Clos Mauvoisin, which was now broken up for building. The Rue de Garlande got its name because it passed through the Clos de Garlande; farther along, toward Saint-Victor, was the Clos de Chardonneret. Nearer the summit of the hill and Sainte-Geneviève was the Clos Bruneau.[4] The Thermes and its adjacent buildings were in the large Clos de Laas, which was the property of the Abbey of Saint-Germain-des-Prés. The Abbot was contemplating the partitioning of this Clos de Laas for building, but when Alexander first stood there only the Bourg du Petit Pont, the old Clos Mauvoisin, was showing building activity. The street which paralleled the river here, going toward Saint-Victor, was already filled with the houses of butchers and other tradesmen, who rented their upper rooms to students. It had received the designation of Rue de la Boucherie. Where this street swung across the Orléans road, its name changed to Rue de la Huchette. Little alleys, scarcely more than paths, led down to the river's edge. Continuing along the Rue de la Huchette toward the fortified monastery of Saint-Germain-des-Prés, Alexander had a view of the well-trodden Pré-aux-clercs, the recreation field, which lay between Saint-Germain-des-Prés and the river. This field was a constant source of bickering between the monastery and the students. The young folk did not always behave themselves. Like Smithfield in London, this site was used for games, perhaps dancing, and undoubtedly for tourneys; but it had never been a market place.[5] Privileged audiences could remain in the King's garden, seated on the Roman wall, and watch games and other exercises in the Pré-aux-clercs, a hundred yards away.[6]

We are imagining that Alexander's new quarters were in a house on the river side of the Rue de la Boucherie. From the upstairs window one could crane his neck and see the pleasant fields of Saint-Victor off to the left. There was a new ditch or canal at the end of the street, which had been dug at the request of the abbey to carry the waters of the Bièvre across their lands. This emptied into the Seine. So much of the canal ran through unpolluted fields that it was clear and pleasant. A little bridge called the Poncel carried strollers over this canal. The rumble of the mill wheels was so common at that point that it usually went unnoticed. It was a question, which did not bother Alexander, when the

Bourg du Petit Pont would eventually reach the villages clustering around Saint-Victor, Sainte-Geneviève, and Saint-Germain-des-Prés. That date was not far distant—the early thirteenth century.[7]

A visitor to a new place soon becomes aware of its inconveniences, especially when the visitor speaks the same language, more or less, and can soon feel at home. A perpetual source of irritation to the students was the civil authority. The provost of Paris, who ruled the city and the district for twenty miles around, in the king's name, lived in the Petit Chastelet. Most of the king's *serjanz*, and others responsible to the provost for the maintenance of order, were located at the Grant Chastelet on the other bank of the river.[8] There was another provost, the provost of the merchants, whose only duty was to head that "Water Merchants of Paris" association which we have located in the Parleoir des borjois. This association, or hansa, was a thorn in the side of free trade. It had ancient royal privileges, which King Louis VII had recently ratified. It had a monopoly on all water traffic coming up the river from Normandy. No boat laden with beef, salt, etc. could approach nearer than Mantes unless the owner belonged to the Paris hansa, or unless he chose a "companion" from that association who would share fifty-fifty in the profits. At the date of Alexander's first coming to Paris these privileges had not been extended to include ships bringing cargoes downstream. This extension was made in 1192. Violations of the monopoly were tried at the Parleoir des borjois and confiscation resulted. Fortunately, the association had no jurisdiction over goods carried by land. For the king collected the *droiture du roi* at the city gates.[9]

There were other restrictions on trade. No merchant was permitted to sell in his own shop on Saturdays. On that day sales had to be made at the Campelli, outside the Porte de Paris. This had its advantages. Merchants came on that day from nearby towns and brought new and interesting wares. Also many local goods which might have lain hidden in the regular shops, unnoticed, were given better display. The bakers were not allowed to use the public ovens on Saturdays and certain saints' days. This meant no fresh bread for at least sixty days in the year. Every Sunday bakers were permitted to sell their leftover bread in the square before the cathedral church.

We have referred to civil jurisdiction in the city of Paris. The full picture was somewhat complicated. Civil courts were maintained by the royal provost and by the *avouez* (lay representatives) of the bishop of Paris, the abbot of Sainte-Geneviève, and the abbot of Saint-Germain-des-Prés. The last mentioned was the authority for the little islands off the tip of the Cité, and for his own village and the Clos de Laas. The abbot of Sainte-Geneviève controlled most of the area between the Petit Chastelet and his abbey. The bishop of Paris was overlord of the Grant Pont, the Cloister Notre Dame, the little islands upstream from the Cité—the Isle de Notre Dame, the Isle des Vaches, and the Isle des Javiaus—and certain other places. Infringement on the bishop's civil rights by the royal provost was bitterly opposed. It must be remembered also that the bishop had canon law authority over all the students and others in clerical status. When the herald read *bans*, or official decrees, in the Cité, it was customary to read them in the name of the king and the bishop of Paris. The bishop maintained the oldest and most popular public oven, a hundred yards below the Grant Pont on the riverbank. It was called the Four l'Evesque.[10] The abbots also had ovens which served their villages and immediate neighbors. These ovens, as well as mills and wine presses, were *banalités*, or feudal monopolies of the abbots in their role as overlords.

The citizens of Paris were very fond of bread and pastry. They loved *gaufres* (waffles), *nieules* (light pastry), *canestel* (little cakes), and *oublies* (wafers).[11] Everywhere on the streets were sold meat and fruit pasties, carried about by the *talemeliers* in little baskets covered with white cloth. These pasties were turnovers in shape.[12] The favorite varieties were chopped ham, chicken, and eel, all of them well seasoned with pepper. Others were of soft cheese and egg.[13] As in London, there was a constant clatter of street cries. There were menders of furs, menders of *henaps*, *regrattiers*, and so on.[14] The *regrattiers* were vegetable and fruit merchants who could sell some other things, such as candles.[15] There was an organized group of *crieurs* for wine who were employed by the royal provost. These people visited the taverns each morning and learned what wine was available (*vin a broche*), and where. As they walked through the streets, they carried a bowl of wine that could be sampled, and they would beat against this with a small stick to attract attention. The taverns were obliged to contribute well for the service.[16] It was becoming quite a "racket." The Moslem Usamah remarked upon this custom of "crying the wine" as it was carried to the Holy Land by the Franks. Usamah used to stay at a certain lodginghouse in Nablus. "The house had windows which opened on the road, and there stood opposite to it on the other side of the road a house belonging to a Frank who sold wine for the merchants. He would take some wine in a bottle and go around announcing it by shouting: 'So-and-so, the merchant, has just opened a cask full of this wine. He who wants to buy some of it will find it in such and such a place.' "[17]

For several pages we have been ignoring Alexander

Neckam and his new lodging. Jehan de Hauteville describes such student quarters in his *Architrenius*, which has been summarized as follows:

They dwell in a poor house with an old woman who cooks only vegetables and never prepares a sheep save on feast-days. A dirty fellow waits on the table and just such a person buys the wine in the city. After the meal the student sits on a rickety chair [see description on p. 69] and uses a light, doubtless a candle which goes out continually and disturbs the ideas. So he sits all night long and learns the seven liberal arts. Often he falls asleep at his work and is troubled by bad dreams until Aurora announces the day and he must hasten to the college and stand before the teacher. And he wins in no way the mighty with his knowledge. But through the grace of Nature and Fortune he wins a bride at the end of the poem.[18]

In the following century, the thirteenth, John of Garland wrote in much the same way:

I eat sparingly in my little room, not high up in a castle. I have no silver money, nor do the Fates give me estates. Beets, beans, and peas are here looked upon as fine dishes and we joke about meat, which is not in our menu for a very good reason. The size of the wine skin on the table depends on the purse, which is never large.[19]

We know from Nigel Wireker's remark in his *Speculum stultorum* (before 1180) that the ass Burnellus associated himself at the University of Paris with the English because they were subtle, courteous, and generous.[20] From this we assume that the English students tended to congregate together. Burnellus found two vices in the English community: the fondness for food, and the habit of "Wassail! Drink-hail!"

From passages such as these it is possible to form a picture of how the twelfth-century student must have lodged. Someone, perhaps an old woman, would rent her two or three upstairs rooms to students. One of these rooms would be the main front room, or *salle*, which contained a fireplace. Beds would be set up there at night, and during the day it would serve as dining room and lounging room for all the students in the house.[21] Surely a scribe's chair was to be found there, by the fire, which they all took turns in using. Twice a day the old woman, or other proprietor, cooked the food which they could pay for, and a manservant ran errands and bought the wine. The proprietress doubtless slept in the kitchen, or, if she had a husband, it is possible that they reserved for themselves a bed somewhere on an upper floor. We suspect that each student had to provide his own bed, which, with sheets, pillow, and coverlet, was worth some twenty sous, or about ten of our dollars. This price is furnished us in a document of the Hôtel-Dieu, from the year 1168, which required each canon of the cathedral to bequeath his bed or the equivalent to the Hôtel-Dieu.[22]

Alexander Neckam was not without means, so we are assuming that he was more comfortably installed than some of his fellows. We will imagine that he was able to rent for himself the inner room on the second floor, which gave him more space for his belongings. His meals and much of his free time would be passed with his companions who occupied the *salle* or outer room. Alexander describes the fittings of an average bedchamber:

> In the bedchamber let a curtain go around the walls decently, or a scenic canopy, for the avoiding of flies and spiders. From the style or epistyle of a column a tapestry should hang appropriately. [There was no such fancy column in his student room!] Near the bed let there be placed a chair to which a stool may be added, and a bench nearby the bed. On the bed itself should be placed a feather mattress to which a bolster is attached. A quilted pad of striped cloth should cover this on

St. Mark with scribe's chair and desk
Courtesy Louvre Museum

Chapter house from Pontaut, France, reassembled at
The Cloisters, New York
Courtesy The Metropolitan Museum of Art, The Cloisters

which a cushion for the head can be placed. Then sheets of muslin, ordinary cotton, or at least pure linen, should be laid. Next a coverlet of green cloth or of coarse wool, of which the fur lining is badger, cat, beaver, or sable, should be put—all this if there is lacking purple and down. A perch should be nearby on which can rest a hawk. . . . From another pole let there hang clothing . . . and let there be also a chambermaid whose face may charm and render tranquil the chamber, who, when she finds time to do so may knit or unknit silk thread, or make knots of orphreys [gold lace], or may sew linen garments and woolen clothes, or may mend.[23] Let her have gloves with the finger tips removed; she should have a leather case protecting the finger from needle pricks, which is vulgarly called a "thimble." She must have scissors[24] and a spool of thread and various sizes of needles—small and thin for embroidery, others not so thin for feather stitching, moderately fine ones for ordinary sewing, bigger ones for the knitting of a cloak, still larger ones for threading laces.[25]

There is frequent mention in twelfth-century literature of draping the walls of a chamber with hangings.[26] This was the commonest and easiest way to shut out drafts, and it also gave a rich appearance. As the art of tapestry weaving (in the Gobelin sense) was not developed until the fourteenth century, we infer that such curtains were just heavy linen, dyed a solid color.[27] Probably they hung free from the top of the wall.[28] More elaborate houses had their walls sealed with plaster or a wood paneling, or both: "Then they came into the room which was painted and paneled with enamels and precious stones";[29] "in his rich and lofty palace, built of squared stones covered with lime, vaulted, paneled [*lambruschiez*] with colors painted on, and chiseling."[30] The plastered walls could also be decorated with painted designs or murals.[31] This was more often the case in religious edifices and in palaces of regal size.[32] And yet the little apartment occupied by the lady in Marie de France's

Guigemar is painted in this way with a design showing Venus casting into a fire the *Remedia amoris* of Ovid. A calendar could be painted on the wall: a list of days intervening before some important event, as in the *Yvain* of Chrétien de Troyes: "My lady has painted in her bedchamber all the days and all the seasons."[33]

Early in the twelfth century Baudri de Bourgueil described the elaborate bedchamber of the Countess Adele.[34] There the walls were covered with hangings and not with plaster or paneling—but what hangings! The designs must have been embroidered in colored worsted, as we find in the Bayeux Tapestry. On one wall Creation, earthly Paradise, and the Deluge were pictured; on the second wall there were scenes from Noah, continuing on to the Kings of Judah. A third wall bore designs from Greek mythology, the siege of Troy, and Roman history. The bed of the lady was in a small alcove which opened from the fourth wall. There a single hanging draped around the bed showed the Battle of Hastings (like the Bayeux Tapestry). The wooden beams of a room were usually painted. In this case, the ceiling showed the constellations—the signs of the zodiac—and the names and courses of the planets. The floor of this same rich chamber was laid with tiles representing a map of the world: seas, rivers, mountains, and towns in Asia, Europe, and Africa. The bed, too, was carved and painted: the Quadrivium was shown at the headpiece, the Trivium at the foot, and Medicine on the side. In all probability this description of the room and bed is exaggerated, but if it were half true, the chamber must have been so cluttered with design that it could produce only insomnia. Our protagonist, Alexander Neckam, would have been lucky to have a hanging around his walls of a single solid color. His ceiling was of wood, coated with a lacquer or varnish finish, perhaps over an undercoat of color. Behind the wall hanging dismounted tables and other furnishings were stored when not in use.

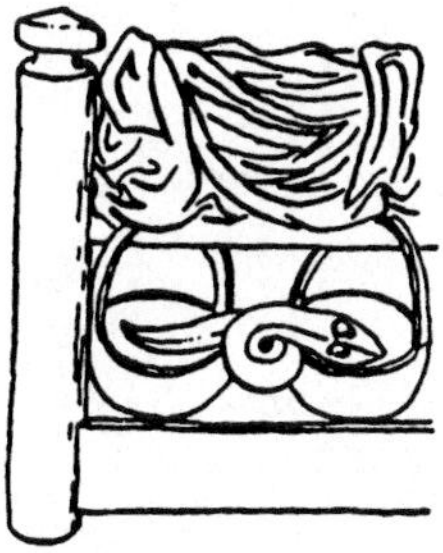

The picture of a typical bed, which we quoted from Alexander, needs some further comment.[35] The main part of such a bed was a rectangular frame of wood which had a bedcord of silk, probably red, or perhaps of leather thongs. This frame (*espondes*) was fastened by loops (*crepons*) to head and foot pieces (*peçuels*). This was the simplest kind of bed and could be put together very easily at nightfall and dismounted in the morning. The feet were apt to have an outward curve, often resembling an animal or bird claw. There was usually a knob at the top of each post. We see from contemporary pictures that this simple type of bedframe could be reinforced. There could be a third frame for one of the sides. Apparently also a side rail could be fitted on each of the two sides to help brace the ends and to prevent the covers and mattresses from slipping off. Although such beds were easily portable, one or two would be left standing, if a room was not crowded, to serve as benches or seats.[36] A number of *coutes*, thin padded mattresses, could be laid on top of the first mattress, which was stuffed with feathers. Some of the details of fancy beds must be taken with a grain of salt. Take this for instance:

In a bed of which the hooks are of silver, the knobs are of red gold, and the frame pieces are all of ivory. All the cords are of red silk. There are two or four padded mattresses, and bolsters and sheets of velvet, and pillows, and a coverlet of marten's fur embroidered with birds, beasts, and flowers.[37]

The name for the sidepieces of the bedframe was *limons*.[38]

Here is an over-all picture of the furnishings of a bedchamber, in a few words: "The duke searched the room, which was all paved. There was not a wall hanging that he did not move . . . nor a small box, nor a big locked chest that the duke did not unlock and open that night."[39] Clothing, books, etc. were kept in chests ranged around the wall. Clothing for immediate use, however, was hung on a pole, high on the wall. This pole took the place of our modern closet. Add to these details a scattering of rushes on the tile or stone floor, an occasional bench or stool, and a colored mattress or a small rug which could be unrolled for sitting on the floor, and our picture is complete. If the room were the *salle* on the second floor, it would certainly have a fireplace; otherwise it might be heated only by a charcoal brazier, probably in the form of a large metal dish. Candles were the source of light.[40] One type of candlestick, or candelabra, stood high from the floor, with small spikes or "pricks" where the candles were impaled. Table-size candlesticks also were used. All these were apt to be made of wrought iron, occasionally ornamented with enamels at the base. Small lanterns, perhaps of horn, were used for moving about.

If Alexander preferred to eat in his own room, this was effected by the setting up of two or more trestles on which boards were placed. We are assuming that this table was set up in the *salle* of his lodginghouse and that he ate there with the other students. A table board of gold is recorded as having belonged to Joan, the daughter of Henry II of England, who married in Sicily.[41] A gold board must have meant a wooden board with plates of thin gold attached to it. A fair white cloth, reaching to the ground, or nearly so, was draped over the table, and benches were set at the sides. The *Chanson de Guillaume* mentions that for the Count's great hall there were benches and forms, with an upper table and a lower table.[42] These were probably set in a T. The host, or principal diner at the meal, used a high-backed chair at the head of the table, with his back to the fireplace. In an affluent household there was a raised floor, or dais, at the fireplace end, where those who were of higher rank sat and ate.[43] The table was set with salt containers of various shapes—sometimes in the form of a boat—with round, flat loaves of bread, a wooden bowl for every two people, a few trenchers or roundels on which food could be placed and cut, and knives that resembled our hunting knives.[44] If the host were wealthy, a small side table was set up where one or more varlets did the cutting for those who dined or supped.

In this *salle*, or perhaps in the pantry, there might stand a small buffet, with a flat top and with a small cupboard below where *henaps* could be kept.[45] People were called to the table by an act known as *corner l'iaue*, "blow for the water." In the average household this meant to go to several wooden or metal basins which were chained to a shelf or stand and wash, perhaps making use of soft soap which had the consistency of mutton fat.[46] A long towel was used. On a more formal occasion the guests seated themselves first on benches running the length of each side of the table, and then the servitors circulated a basin, ewer, and towel. We imagine that the hands were held over the basin and water was simply poured over them. The towel got most of the dirt and became wet and clammy.[47]

Food was carried up from the kitchen without much respect for distance. Meat was brought in on the spit, while vegetables of different kinds, having been boiled together, were piled on a platter, or perhaps a large flat trencher. The service dishes were placed on the right hand and the sauce dish on the left. It was customary to serve two pieces of bread at a time.[48] Juicy foods were sopped pretty liberally with the help of the bread, two people eating from the same bowl. Special attention was paid to sauces, wherein the true secret of the culinary art was supposed to lie. Neckam leaves us some recipes:

> A roast of pork is prepared diligently on a grid, frequently basted, and laid on the grid just as the hot coals cease to smoke. Let condiment be avoided other than pure salt or a simple garlic sauce. It does not hurt to sprinkle a cut-up capon with pepper. A domestic fowl may be quite tender, having been turned on a long spit, but it needs a strong garlic sauce, diluted with wine or vinegar [that is, green juice of grapes or apples]. Flavor a hen which has been cleaned and cut up into pieces, with cumin, if it is well boiled; but if it has been roasted, let it be treated with frequent drippings of fat, nor does it refuse garlic sauce; it will be most tasty with simple sauce.[49] Let fish that have been cleaned be cooked in a mixture of wine and water; afterwards they should be taken with green "savory" which is made from sage, parsley, dittany, thyme, costus, garlic, and pepper; do not omit salt. One who takes this is especially exhilarated and restored by a raisin wine which is clear to the bottom of the cup, in its clarity similar to the tears of a penitent, and the color is that of an oxhorn. It descends like lightning upon one who takes it—most tasty as an almond nut, quick as a squirrel, frisky as a kid, strong in the manner of a house of Cistercians or gray monks, emitting a kind of spark; it is supplied with the subtlety of a syllogism of Petit Pont; delicate as a fine cotton, it exceeds crystal in its coolness.[50]

This demonstrates that Alexander loved raisin wine and that he had a considerable enthusiasm for things of the table. The *chansons de geste* frequently list on the menu "cranes and geese and peppered peacocks."[51] Since neither the crane nor the peacock would be considered edible today, this surprises us. Such meat is tough and stringy and was not at all adapted to the "scorbutic teeth and gums" of a twelfth-century man. We have evidence, however, that peacocks were actually served in Elizabethan times, so there is little reason to doubt the evidence of the *chansons de geste*. Probably the cranes were served because they were captured with great sport by the hunting falcons and the mediaeval man liked to eat whatever he brought home from the hunt. The peacock had some associations of nobility, and it was surely boiled until its flesh was tender.

A meal began with a blessing, after the hand washing had been accomplished. No one should think that eating at this time was a sort of "catch as catch can." Even the dogs were expected to behave: "When greedy dogs stand before the board is there not need for a rod? As oft as any of them shall snatch toward thee, and taketh from thee thy food, wilt thou not as often smite? Else it would snatch from thee all that thou hadst. . . ."[52] There are various treatises on personal etiquette at the table. One is just twenty-three lines long, which we call the *Quisque es in mensa* from its opening words.[53] This prohibits belching, touching the nose or ears while at table, the use of a toothpick, and elbows on table, and insists that the hands and nails be clean and that the mouth be emptied and lips wiped before drinking out of the *henap*. Bones were to be placed in the bowl or *escuele*, or thrown on the floor for the dogs. John of Garland, in his *Morale scholarium*, infers that the *henap* should be held by the base when drinking, and that wine should be poured with both hands on the jug. An expensive *henap* often was a *coupe couverclee*, provided with a cover.[54] The *henap* was passed from hand to hand. When two people ate from the same *escuele*, and one was a lady or a person of high rank, it was considered correct for the man or the lesser person to wait upon the other.[55] He handled the napkin, broke the bread, cut the cake, and passed the *henap* and the platters of food. When Henry II and his son the Young King ate from the same *escuele*, we presume that the Young King thus attended his father.[56] The carver at the side table was expected to exercise normal cleanliness. There is an amusing passage in the *Roman de Renart* where poor, simple Ysengrim—who is carving in mittens—is accused of wiping his nose and his mouth while doing the carving, and he is suspected of doing even less sanitary things.[57]

In his student lodging, at the table which was set up in the *salle* for Alexander and his companions, it is hardly likely that any special etiquette was followed.

The linen was removed at the close of a meal, and those who had been at table were required to wash their hands once more. If minstrels were present, the members of the household made themselves as comfortable as they could and listened for a while; the *henap* was passed around freely. This procedure was not limited to special occasions only. It was quite common to have someone sing or tell a story after a meal, even in a small manor house. It will be noted that we made no mention above of table forks or spoons. Forks, of course, were not even made. Spoons existed, but they were passed around only as a particular favor when the need was felt. Wace tells a story which begins in this way: "I do not know what they had to eat but they needed spoons. A chamberlain had the spoons. . . ."[58] The spoons were counted before and after use. In Wace's story a certain knight concealed one of them. We have already mentioned that soups and sauces were taken with the aid of bread. Very few adults at that time had an adequate set of teeth. Solid pieces of food were handled with the fingers. The bill of fare could include pork, mutton, venison, wild ducks, hens, capons, and fish, well washed down.[59] The wild boar was a special kind of pork with stronger flavor. The flesh of the boar is no treat to the taste of a *gourmet*. It was because the boar, like the crane, represented difficult game in the field that his flesh was served with occasional enthusiasm. Beans, beets, and peas were served, but the first two were considered poor fare. Peas were rather popular at the best of tables. Bread (three kinds, at least) was indispensable, and mention is frequently made of a *gastel*, or cake. Apparently such a cake was a mixture of brown flour, sweetening, and shortening. The sweetening was honey, which is only a third as strong as our modern sugar, and the shortening was a vegetable oil, probably olive oil. The resulting cake must have been very similar to what we now call Scotch shortbread. I believe that the Scots got their recipe in the first place from the French. After it was baked, the French *gastel* could be compared in shape to a round, flat stone.[60] The baking of bread is described in the *Chevalerie Ogier le Danois*.[61]

The above picture represents a well-to-do household rather than a student lodging. Some of the very poor could not even afford to set a table: "For a poor man who has no money does not sit by a fire, nor sit at a table, rather he eats on his lap. The dogs flock around him and take the bread from his hands."[62] Apparently a prosperous fisherman lived quite well. In the *Vie de Saint Gregoire* the fisherman's wife served him white wheat bread, fish, and a mazer of wine. He would take only coarse bread and water. More prosperous peasants were fond of boiled milk and hot clabber.

Sometimes they boiled bits of cake or bread with the milk, and the result was called a *morterel* and was eaten in an *escuele* with a spoon. This might be accompanied by cheese and a *composte*. The *composte* consisted of fruit and herbs preserved in wine or in a salt pickling fluid.[63]

It is time for us to accompany Alexander on a trip to the kitchen, from which dishes were carried up the narrow stairway, one or two flights, to serve his table. The kitchen was at the rear of the house on the ground floor, or it could be another flight down in a sort of half-basement. The chief essential in a kitchen was the large fireplace. Not far from this, perhaps in a projection of the foundation wall, a few feet off the ground, was the opening of the *garde-robe* pit.[64] Into this the kitchen waste was thrown, accompanied probably by some human waste. We might guess that a fastidious cook would place over this a wooden cover that could be lifted off at will. This pit was emptied at intervals by a "Maistre Fifi," who removed the waste in buckets, through the superior opening, and carried it out through the kitchen, and perhaps the upper floor of the house.[65] Water was kept in a large open vat, or *tine*. This was kept filled during the day by a servant or by a professional water porter who might have contracted to do the job. This man carried a yoke, called a *grouge*, across his shoulders, with a pail dangling at each end. The source of the water was problematical. We know from a doctor writing in the seventeenth century that the wells of the Paris area were brackish, that the water of the Seine was more tasty, but that it gave dysentery to all except those who were natives of the region. While reflecting on the possibilities of the Seine as a source of water, the reader should remember that it had a swifter flow than it has now. Since the nineteenth century the course of the Seine has been slowed by canal locks and weirs so that it now gives a different appearance. Today it is a sluggish stream.

Here is Alexander's own list of required utensils in a kitchen:

In a kitchen there should be a small table on which cabbage may be minced, and also lentils, peas, shelled beans, beans in the pod, millet, onions, and other vegetables of the kind that can be cut up. There should be also pots, tripods, a mortar, a hatchet, a pestle, a stirring stick, a hook, a cauldron, a bronze vessel, a small pan, a baking pan, a meathook, a griddle, small pitchers, a trencher, a bowl, a platter, a pickling vat, and knives for cleaning fish. In a *vivarium* let fish be kept, in which they can be caught by net, fork, spear, or light hook, or with a basket.[66] The chief cook should have a cupboard [*capanna*] in the kitchen where he may store away aromatic spices, and bread flour sifted through a sieve—and used also for feeding small fish—may be hidden away there.[67] Let there be also a cleaning place where the entrails and feathers of ducks and other domestic fowl can be removed and the birds cleaned. Likewise there should be a large spoon for removing foam and skimming. Also there should be hot water for scalding fowl.[68]

Have a pepper mill, and a hand [flour ?] mill. Small fish for cooking should be put into a pickling mixture, that is, water mixed with salt. . . .[69] To be sure, pickling is not for all fish, for these are of different kinds: mullets, soles, sea eels, lampreys, mackerel, turbot, sperlings, gudgeons, sea bream, young tunnies, cod, plaice, stargazers [?], anglers, herring, lobsters fried in half an egg, *bougues*, sea mullets, and oysters. There should be also a *garde-robe* pit through which the filth of the kitchen may be evacuated. In the pantry let there be shaggy towels [*gausapes*], tablecloth, and an ordinary hand towel which shall hang from a pole to avoid mice.[70] Knives should be kept in the pantry, an engraved saucedish, a saltcellar, a cheese container, a candelabra, a lantern,[71] a candlestick, and baskets.[72] In the cellar or storeroom should be casks, tuns, wineskins,[73] cups, cup cases [*henapiers*],[74] spoons, ewers, basins, baskets, pure wine, cider, beer, unfermented wine, mixed wine, claret, nectar, mead . . . *piument,* pear wine, red wine, wine from Auvergne, clove-spiced wine for gluttons whose thirst is unquenchable. . . .[75]

We have no description of a hand mill, but there is a mill worked by a foot treadle, for grinding grain, on a capital at Vézelay.[76] The treadle works a heavy flanged wheel which enmeshes so as to turn a vertical screw, likely of stone, which grinds in a perforated millstone at the bottom of a hopper. The operator who works the treadle is pouring grain from a sack into the funnel-shaped hopper while another man is receiving the flour in a sack as it is carried down through the hole.

Pots were placed on the tripods over the open fire, and spits were turned before the flame, doubtless by the hand of a kitchen knave. The fire was not supposed to go out. When it did die out, the cook or the housewife sent to a neighbor for a hot coal. The average house, however, had a *fuisil,* or fire-striking iron. This was a piece of iron, two or three inches long, which had a bronze handle. From a side view this instrument had the appearance of a very small flatiron.[77] It was struck against a piece of flint so that sparks fell onto some charred tow.[78]

The reader is doubtless interested in the pantry, or *dispense,* and the storeroom, which are described by Alexander. We assume that the cellar or storeroom was downstairs adjacent to the kitchen. I cannot locate the pantry. It was perhaps there that the bowls for washing hands stood on a ledge, or on a stand. We know that pantry work was considered very honorable, but that kitchen service was low. That being so, we can rest assured that the pantry would be abovestairs, somewhere adjacent to the *salle.*

We stated in an earlier chapter that more detail would be given about the construction of twelfth-century houses. In Exeter there is a stone house well preserved (and restored) which has only one room, on the ground floor. The entry is by a door in the middle of the front wall. Such a single room must have been combined kitchen, *salle*, and bedchamber, and yet the builder could not have been too indigent since he erected a house of stone. At Southampton the so-called King John House was unquestionably a wharf storage building with a single room for the wharfinger's family on the upper floor, reached by a long stairway which skirted the back wall of the storage court, which was open to the air. The house of a well-to-do person who did not manufacture or trade on his premises would have been somewhat as follows. Inside the entrance door was a vestibule with a stair leading straight up. A door opening on the side of the top landing led into a *salle*, which was the principal room, with its ornamental windows fronting on the street. There was a fireplace at one end. The floor was tiled or of stone. Opening off from this was an inner room, a private apartment which could be reached only by going through the *salle*. It was used as a sleeping room, or conceivably it could have been given over to women's work or to storage. In a town house there was frequently a floor above. This would be reached by a stairway in a tower situated at one side of the main *salle*. The room upstairs would be occupied by some members of the family, or perhaps it was rented out. It was called a *soler*. On the ground floor a door would open to the side of the vestibule and lead into a pantry, which, in turn, opened into the kitchen. Such a simple plan could, of course, be varied considerably. Occasionally the ground floor of a wealthy house was divided into small chambers which were rented on a permanent basis to poorer people.[79] Some houses were large enough for the stair to go up the center rather than at one side. In that case a door would open from each side of the entrance vestibule and from both sides of the upper landing. This doubled the number of rooms. To match the main *salle* on one side would be a women's workroom on the other. A single small room could be given over to the storing of clothing. As we have said a few pages earlier, in some cases the kitchen was placed in a half-basement. The so-called Jew's House in Lincoln had rooms opening off from both sides of the central stairway.

The problem of locating the latrine was a serious one. Such a convenience was called a *longaigne*, which is to be translated "far-off place." Obviously the householders wished to isolate such a chamber, even though their limited space made it difficult. In the *Life of St. Gregory* the latrine is spoken of as a retiring place where tablets could be read without interruption.[80] I am inclined to think that where the space permitted a *garde-robe* pit was dug apart from the house and a shed and wooden platform were placed over it. The Assise of 1189 in London demanded that such a pit should not be less than two and one-half feet from the property line.[81] Boccaccio's *Decamerone* tells of an outdoor platform that collapsed under the occupant. This platform, however, was built in very unsanitary fashion over an open court.[82] In some town houses the latrine must have been placed in the inner sleeping apartment, off from the main *salle*, with a chute provided to a pit in the floor of the cellar. This shaft would have an opening into the cellar through which it could be emptied. Words spoken above in the sleeping apartment would have an uncanny habit of being heard in the cellar as they drifted down the shaft.[83] The ideal arrangement, practiced in a royal palace or a wealthy household, as in the halls attached to the royal castle at Salisbury, was to have a special latrine tower to which a door opened off from the *salle* or from an anteroom. Any small house so provided was indeed lucky. I am afraid that more often the waste pit near the kitchen fire took care of sewage as well as kitchen refuse. The *Life of St. Gregory* informs us that in a larger household the user of a latrine was escorted there, and assisted, by a chamberlain.[84]

Windows were small and high, except those of the main *salle*. A window on the ground floor could have an iron grating before it, to discourage thieves. The windows of the *salle* were given much attention. Frequently they were double with a thin dividing column through the center. The houses that have survived to the present day were mostly expensive houses so that we are obliged to describe windows in houses of that class. These had sculptured tympana.[85] In larger houses there would be a whole row of such windows, side by side, giving the effect of a gallery. In small houses, such as those found at Chartres, there would be one lone double window. No glass panes were in use as yet. A window was screened with black or green cloth to protect against the cold of winter.[86] Lower-floor windows had removable wooden shutters or coverings.[87] It was customary to hang bird cages, usually square and made of wicker, in the window during the warmer months.[88]

We have been describing houses built of stone, because they are the only kind that have been preserved. But most of the dwellings of the twelfth century were made of wood. For these we must have recourse to representations in the Bayeux Tapestry and in a few other sources. In a manuscript of the mid-thirteenth century there is a fairly good representation of a wooden house which cannot have differed much from the type used in the previous century.[89]

The wooden siding is made of vertical boards, like boards and batten without the battens. There is a little "lift" or roof projecting over the entrance door, or before the entire lower floor of the house. The door is a double door. The upstairs in the illustration looks more like a loge or balcony, but this was drawn with excessively large windows in order to show the figure of a lady taking a bath for which a maid carries the water in a small cauldron. One of the downstairs windows of this house has a shutter which fits the opening without any overlap. (In a peasant house mentioned in an earlier chapter we described the shutter as hinged at the top and falling against the side of the house.) The Bayeux Tapestry depicts wooden houses with the same little "lift" or portico as we have just mentioned.[90] Apparently this roof could be supported at the outer corners by fancy wooden posts. In one of the houses of the tapestry there is an actual balcony on top of such a projecting roof. Balconies could not have been uncommon, for Fitzstephen, in his description of the water tourney on the Thames, mentioned that people crowded onto the balconies of houses facing the river.[91] It is evident also from the tapestry that where a house did not have a common wall with its neighbor its outer walls were reinforced by tall posts which served as buttresses. These too could have fancy capitals. Unquestionably it was such fancy posts and ornately carved beams, as well as tile facings and elaborate wooden moldings, that gave some houses the "gingerbready" look which Alexander Neckam deplored. He was disturbed also over the outer thrust of the house walls. He insisted

that no walls, even those from wooden beams, should make equidistant lines. See that wooden walls be built in proper proportions, that they have no greater thickness at the bottom than at the top; the surfaces should not be equidistant. It is obligatory that the more the walls rise from the ground the more distance there should be between them. For, since all stress naturally inclines to the center of the earth, the walls should be associated in angularity.[92]

This is a strange engineering theory. He means that a house which is not a perfect square or rectangle in its floor plan is more secure than one that is. Elsewhere Alexander describes in brief the construction of a country house:

Let the main hall be furnished with a vestibule near which the portico may be properly set up. There should be also an outer court which is named from *ater* because kitchens used to be constructed near open spaces in order that the passers-by might smell the odor and vapor of the kitchen. In the hall let there be posts set apart with proper distances. There is need for nails, poles, siding, beams, and crosspieces extending to the roof. Rafters are required, reaching across the house. Walls should not be strictly parallel; the higher they rise, the farther apart they should be, otherwise all the structure will be threatened by ruin and there will be a hazard. Let windows be suitably placed in the house, looking toward the east, in which gourds or "twisted pots" should be placed, on the outside, in which may be kept storax from Aleppo, but not Trojan storax, . . . Serapian balsam, balm of Mecca, euphorbia, Persian gum, mastic, black poplar ointment, laurel oil, juice of green grapes, elder oil, and castoreum. [These are to bring the proper odors in through the window.] Let some basket weave be added to the roof and let the whole be covered or thatched with marsh reed, or, if planking is laid up there, this can be covered with tiles or slates. Have a ceiling to expel the treacherous air from the house. Let the projection or base of the outer wall be supplied with posts. The door should have a lock and a latch, bars, pegs, and bolt. Swinging or double doors may lead in from the portico and should be supplied with hinges in the proper manner.[93]

And he says elsewhere:

A roof is added, subject to ceilings and beams. What shall I say about carvings and paintings except that wealth supports stupidity? Roofs that keep out the winter should be sufficient. But the destructive luxury of wealth and the deadly vanity of a city have subjected men to the yoke of miserable slavery and have thought up so many illegal inventions that no one can enumerate them. However, it is necessary that the carvings of crossbeams should hold up spider webs. Expect superfluous and vain inventions in buildings, clothing, foods, harness, cloaks, and various other furnishings, and you can say with reason: "O Vanity, O Superfluity."

Alexander does not mention the possibility of a balcony.[94] He records, as he did in describing the structure of a boat, that wicker weave was used to reinforce joints, but he says nothing of stucco construction over a series of uprights erected for the outer wall. On these uprights a wicker lath would be interwoven before the application of some sort of cement.[95]

A block of stone (*perron*) might serve as a door stoop, or such a stone, similar to the old carriage mounting blocks in modern cities, could be placed a short distance away from the building. It was used to aid a knight or lady in mounting a horse. People sometimes sat on the stoop: "Outside at the *perron* where she goes to sit."[96] The pleasure of such sitting was questionable as the street was never inviting. Except on main roads there was almost no paving. The black Paris mud, which caused a wit to trace the name Lutetia from *lutum*, "mud," was sticky and unpleasant.[97] Streets were leveled down so that they sloped toward the center, from each side. This meant that a stream flowed down the middle of the road during rainy days, serving as a cleansing agent. There was without a doubt some paving carried out in the twelfth century, in imitation of the surface of an old Roman road. The lower layers of a Roman pavement would not be copied. Blocks were laid and cemented with a mortar of sand, lime, and river mud to make a road called a *chemin ferré*. (The ancient Roman cement was very hard, consisting of lime, rubble, and volcanic ash.) Where a road went through a bog, a foundation was made of logs of oak.[98]

Although streams of water were encouraged to flow down the middle of the streets, there was a shortage of drainage ditches for these to empty into. Fortunately many of the Paris streets sloped toward the river, or toward the Bièvre. Drainage must have been remarkably bad on the Cité itself—in the royal palace and in the Cloister of Notre Dame.[99] A ditch that was dug remained open to the air. Filth found its way constantly into the muddy streets. Chamber pots and washbasins could be emptied too by pitching the contents from the window. To avoid such foulness on a dry day, and the rushing gutter on a wet day, many rode through the streets on horseback, and the others used heavy shoes with very high, thick soles. The *chape* was a protection from water thrown from above. (It is easy to recognize the origins of our modern polite rule that a gentleman should walk on the outside while the lady takes the wall.) Streets were never lighted, of course. Those who were obliged to venture abroad after *couvre-feu*—seven or eight o'clock in the evening, by modern time, according to the season of the year—were apt to be accompanied by a boy with a torch or lantern. To be sure, the houses were usually lit up at an earlier hour and, as the streets were not wide, the illumination may have been sufficient at five or six o'clock, modern time, on a winter evening. Policing of the streets late at night was ineffective. There was a watchman on the principal tower of the city's defenses, presumably the Grant Chastelet at Paris, who blew a horn at the first break of day. A knight of the watch was on duty each night, and he had under him certain *serjanz,* and a *corvée* of tradesmen who were obliged to stand watch through the city. The tradesmen were selected by a rotation system among the guilds. Despite these precautions, the best protection was afforded by good stout wooden shutters on the lower windows, and a heavy door or strong lock. I doubt that the open shop fronts were boarded over. It seems more likely that the merchants removed their portable wares into a section of the house that could be bolted up. At a much later date Villon mentions vagrants who spent the night under merchants' counters. But the stairway tower which led to the upper floor would be locked with extreme care.[100]

The heavy outer door, which was usually double, was locked by a bar or beam fitted across it on the inside and held in place in two metal slots. A smaller, single door must have been fitted with a common latch, consisting of a small bar which pivoted at one end. This could be lifted from the outside by a latchstring, a thong or cord which hung out through a hole. Thus we have the traditional saying: "The latchstring is out." On the inside, a metal ring was attached to the bar or bolt and served to lift it.[101] In more expensive buildings the doors were fitted with locks and keys. Many keys have been preserved from the twelfth and thirteenth centuries in our museums. They were heavier than we should expect, because locks turned rather clumsily, but not all were as heavy as this one: "He held a key and struck him in the face with it, so rudely that down he fell."[102] A ring with several of these large keys could be worn at the belt by a housewife, or by the seneschal of a wealthy household. Apparently padlocks of a kind were also in use. Guernes remarks about a door which lay in the path of St. Thomas Becket, on the day of his murder: "But that one was closed with a great lock [*loc*]. . . . When he wished to twist the lock it fell in his hands."[103]

We will now take leave of individual houses and accompany Alexander in another journey over the city of Paris. A traveler who approached the city in 1210 would have noted the following, according to the author of a *chanson de geste:*

That day they rode and traveled until they saw Paris, the admirable city, with many a church, many a high church tower, and abbeys of great nobility. They saw the Seine with its deep fords, and the mills of which there were many; they saw the ships which bring wheat, wine, salt, and great wealth. . . .[104]

Just where men on horseback could have been fording the river is not immediately apparent to us today; but there has been a rise in the level of the water due to the weirs and canal locks of the nineteenth century. The Seine in 1180 was shallower and swifter. Presumably these fords existed where one or more of the smaller islands could serve as midpoints. Water mills were the common device for grinding grain. Windmills were a recent invention in Normandy and had not spread very far before the close of the century. There were a number of water mills under the arches of the two Paris bridges. No contemporary of Alexander has described these for us in detail. We are obliged to turn to a fourteenth-century illustration and hope that there was little change in the two-hundred-year interval.[105] This later picture shows each mill constructed on a floating hull, or boat. The wheel is over the side; the millstones and the operator are on a cupola-shaped platform with peaked roof which is built amidships on each hull. A ladder leads up to this. Sacks of grain are being brought in small boats and passed up to the millers. Each miller pours the grain into a funnel which is over the stone. The milled flour is pouring into sacks held beneath the platform. We assume that the action of a screw turning in the millstone is similar to what we observe in the smaller mill pictured at Vézelay. A mill erected on a floating hull could be shifted to allow traffic to pass under the bridge.

This same fourteenth-century manuscript pictures the small boats which operated on the Seine. They were low in the water, and the lines of the gunwale show that they were slightly arched with bow and stern a little high. Some are being paddled from the stern; others are being rowed. The oarsman sits in the prow and not amidships as is done today.

Fishing rights above the bridges, as far as the Marne, belonged to the king, but his bailiff gave licenses very freely.[106] The Seine had many more fish than it does under modern conditions, and there was a profitable trade. *Vivaria*, or fish enclosures, were constructed in various places, close to the banks. There was a path along the left bank of the river which was used by horses maneuvering and drawing boats.[107] Usually two horses worked to a boat, and a rope was led from them to the peak of the mast. Such a tow had to be released as the boat approached the Petit Pont, but it was reattached easily when the boat had gone through the arches. We will assume that short willow trees were planted effectively along the edges of the banks to prevent soil slip.[108]

If Neckam had taken a ferry across the Seine, farther down the river, he would have been impressed by various things other than the water mills, the horse towpath, and the bridges hidden by their houses. At the tip of the great island on which the main city lay was the king's *cour*, or palace. Our earliest picture of this dates from 1412, and is an illumination for the month of June in the famous *Tresriches heures* of the Duc de Berry.[109] This represents a later group of buildings which was begun for Philip the Fair, early in the fourteenth century. These aid us somewhat in attempting a reconstruction of the palace in the time of Louis VII. The principal thing was the garden with its trellis of pliable wood and its trees. We know from Abelard that the royal authorities opened this to the student public at certain times.[110] We can imagine the plants that grew there by reading Alexander's description of a proper kind of garden:

It should be ornamented with roses and lilies, the heliotrope, violets, and mandrakes. One should have also parsley, costus, fennel, southernwood, coriander, sage, savory, hyssop, mint, rue, dittany, celery, pyrethrum, lettuce, cress, and peonies. There should be made beds for onions, leeks, garlic, pumpkins, and shallots. A garden is distinguished when it has growing there cucumbers, the soporific poppy, daffodils, and acanthus. There should not be lacking pot vegetables such as beets, dog's mercury, orach, sorrel, and mallows. Anise, mustard, white pepper, and absinthe give usefulness to any garden. A noble garden will show you also medlars [very similar to persimmons], quinces, bon chrétien pears, peaches, pears of St. Regulus, pomegranates, lemons, oranges, almonds, dates which are the fruit of palm trees, and figs.[111]

Alexander then remarks that unfortunately certain useful herbs do not grow in European gardens: ginger, clove, cinnamon, licorice, zedoary, incense, myrrh, aloes, oil of myrrh, rosin, storax, balsam, galbanum, cypress, nard, Arabian oil of myrrh (*gutta*), and cassia fistula. The following medicinal herbs, however, can be cultivated there: saffron, sandyx, thyme, pennyroyal, borage, purslane, and

wild spikenard which gently brings forth through the upper orifice the disturbed content of the "father of the family," by which I mean stomach. Colewort and ragwort excite love, but the marvelous frigidity of psyllium seed offers a remedy for that affliction. Myrtle too is a friend of temperance. . . . Those who are experienced in such matters distinguish between the heliotrope and our "heliotrope" which is called calendula, and between mugwort and our native "mugwort" which is feverfew. It happens that the wool-blade is one shrub and the silver-leaved wool-blade is another. The iris grows a purple flower; the Florentine iris or ireos has a white one. The gladiolus bears a yellow one; but the burweed has no flower. Other noted herbs are horehound, hound's-tongue or *cynoglossa*, parsley, *macedonium* [?], bryony, groundsel, wild myrrh or angelica, *regina*, coriander—three heaven-gazing species. But Macer and Dioscorides, and many others, diligently inquire into the properties and effects of herbs, wherefore we pass to other things.[112]

Probably many of the plants and herbs which Alexander says could grow in these gardens were there at the tip of the island, some of them trained against the remains of the Roman wall. Very little grass was grown in a mediaeval garden. The walks may have been bordered with acanthus.

The Roman wall could not have been very attractive any longer.[113] The foundation or footing stones of this rampart were miscellaneous blocks of stone brought by the builders from various ruins—old temples, houses, and so forth. Here and there, where this footing was uncovered, one could make out dedicatory inscriptions to household gods and citizens who had departed long ago. On this motley foundation the Romans had built up a typical wall of brick and cement. The bricks were thin and varied in design, as was usual with Roman work. This wall had no towers—just a battered walk along its top, with low crenels. Here and there a narrow stair was built against the side. There was certainly such a stairway in the stretch of wall that enclosed the garden. An opening in the wall at the very tip of the island had a wooden gate, allowing authorized people who came by water to make an entrance into the garden.

The two small islands off the tip of the Cité sheltered this garden entrance, but the flow of the river caused a back eddy in the intervening water which some people did not care to navigate. The little islands were empty and overgrown with weeds and grass.[114] Some wood may have been stacked there at times. There was also a marshy strip of land, a green-covered island which hugged close to the left side of the Cité. This is still visible in the *Tresriches heures*. This had no use; it was just a lush green strip. The buildings of the royal court, beyond the garden, can only be approximated by us. Doubtless there was a large hall, of Merovingian or Roman construction. It had a broad stone stair fronting on the street, with a large mounting block a short distance away at the foot of these stairs. It was possible for a knight to ride on his horse up the stairway and enter the hall, although this was not encouraged. We have evidence that the garden extended to directly behind this hall.[115] In addition there must have been a fortified tower or donjon, surrounded by a small dry moat. There was a small church, the Chapel of St. Nicholas. It is possible to picture the relative location of these buildings by studying the relative positions in the later establishment of Philip the Fair; but this can never be determined with absolute accuracy.

Chapter V

Gown

In order to illustrate the intellectual climate of Paris at this time, and to comment upon some of its social complexities, we will add another dash of fiction to our discussion. It has already been assumed that Alexander Neckam, possessing a little more money than the average, has rented from an elderly proprietress the inner room on the second floor, which he occupies by himself. We will add to this an assumption that three other students, less affluent, are occupying the *salle* or principal room, outside his door. They set up their beds there every night, sometimes forgetting to take them down in the morning, and Alexander joins them there twice a day for the two meals that are served by their hostess. Like that student group mentioned by Jehan de Hauteville, they have a single manservant who fetches water and wine and does other errands.[1] We are pretending that the address is Rue de la Boucherie, close by the Church of Saint-Julien-le-pauvre. The single window in Alexander's room was high, but it looked out over the river and gave a perfect view of that area on the Cité where the new cathedral church of Notre Dame was being erected, slowly, in all its glory. This was not a bad vantage point for a newcomer who was enthusiastic for the sights of Paris. Looking down toward the left, Alexander could even see into the back window of Adam's house on the Petit Pont, very dimly, but sufficiently to tell whether the teacher was engaged with students.

The companions who shared the *salle* as living quarters were each typical of a class of student. One was a monk, who, after two or three years in a cloister, had grown restless and taken sudden leave. He still wore his habit, but he was in Paris without the knowledge or consent of his superiors. Despite many fulminations by the Church authorities against such wanderers, faulty communications and poor keeping of records made it almost impossible to check up on them. If this young "monk" wished the protection and advantages that could come to him from the house of his order that was in or near Paris, too often he received them on the strength of his own statements.

Another of the companions was a young secular canon—too young, and undoubtedly too secular in his viewpoint, for the benefice he was enjoying. The benefice was not a rich one, so he was short of funds.[2] He owed it to lay patronage back home. He, too, was studying in Paris without bothering to secure permission beforehand or afterwards. He was expecting to take up medicine at Montpellier, after studies in the quadrivium at Paris, and then he hoped to go on to Bologna for a stiff course in the civil law. Nigel Wireker had a biting pen, but he was certainly truthful in describing students of this class.[3] They come home from Montpellier bringing pots and jars, and they attach themselves to a rich patron who is responsible for their receiving a benefice. They wear fancy clothes. Eventually they grow disgusted with feeling pulses and examining urine. They rush off to Bologna. When they return they are unusually controversial and are fond of big words. They are ready to dash off to Rome to have the slightest little dispute settled at the Lateran Court. This youth, at the time he lived near Alexander, was not very serious about his studies. He was interested above all in people and their reactions; he could find very little of that in a discussion of Boethius' treatises. Wireker mentions the student who gazes at the passers-by when he should be paying careful attention to the master. He dreams almost constantly of hunting. Although this canon must remain a shadowy figure to us, I will apply to him the physical characterization which Alexander Neckam gives to a certain type which he calls the *arrogans*.[4] Modern youth would perhaps prefer the term "phony." Alexander says of such a youth that he tended to move all the parts of his body as he stood. His eyebrows would be arched, he kept glancing out of the corner of his eyes, he blushed easily, he would clap and stretch out his hands with no provocation. He often crossed his legs while sitting and would talk with his hands, mouth wide open. Such an exquisite youth would shake his hair, lisping now in a weak voice and now roaring like a hog caller (this simile is mine). Since Alexander pictures the type so well, I feel no compunction in assuming that he could have had such a young gentleman in the room adjacent. John of Salisbury said of this kind: "They consider that riches only are the fruit of wisdom."[5]

The third student was more irregular. He had the simple tonsure, but his mind was concentrated upon the tavern and on dicing and the women. He was clever, though, at poetry (both Latin and vernacular), and he had a pleasant singing voice. This young man was frankly not interested in getting ahead in the Church or in professional circles. What he desired was to make acquaintances who would be profitable to him later in his career as a minstrel and wandering scholar.[6] He had been at the schools in Orléans and had come to Paris only because of the larger circle of people which he expected to find in the shadow of Notre Dame. The "monk" had visions of returning eventually to his cloister, or to a better one, after he had had his fill of the good life; the canon wanted to rise high in medicine or the law, or both; Alexander was a serious student, bent upon becoming himself a scholar and teacher of note; but the "singing cleric" was a worldly man, and he loved verses more than he did the sacred offices. While remaining at the schools, he was one of those "faint-hearted" described by a preacher who said that some clerks with benefices could hardly rise for the morning offices; others when the offices were said betook themselves to the *spectacula*.[7]

But guiding Providence often makes us change our minds and our aspirations. Perhaps a dream would come, and this worldly man might change into another Serlo of Wilton, another Folquet of Marseilles. Serlo, after his conversion and his becoming a Cistercian abbot, would eat only bread and water for a day if he chanced to hear a performance of one of his secular lyrics. The renegade monk might also have a decided change of heart. He could be like that historic figure who attached himself to a cloister, expecting to make off with the sacred vessels, but who saw the light in time and eventually was named prior. The *arrogans*, in turn, could become a serious physician or a worthy lawyer. The wheel of Fortune changed so easily in the twelfth century.

These three, sometimes joined by Alexander, were not averse to a good time: "Everyone blames and reproves a young fellow . . . whom one does not see to be gay and cheery; that is the way you should be. School is not everything for you."[8] In December and January, as well as at Eastertide, there were the *ludi theatrales*, the plays which were put on at the monasteries, and occasionally in the cloister of the Cathedral. Some of these *ludi*, like the *Jeu de Saint-Nicholas* and the *Jeu d'Adam*, had very entertaining comedy. It will be remembered that the Christmas season lasted from Christmas to the Feast of the Purification on February 2, but the hearty entertainment was on Christmas Day, St. Stephen's (December 26), St. John the Evangelist's (December 27), and Holy Innocents' (December 28). On the three days after Christmas it had long been the custom of the Church authorities to allow the youngest clerks and novices to take over and celebrate in a "childish" way. This was particularly true for Holy Innocents', which began, of course, at sundown on December 27.[9] The irreverent behavior which invariably resulted was not taken too seriously. The boys recited a parody of the Martyrology, at Prime. In some places, at a date not precisely determined, there arose a *messe des fous*. In the spring and warmer months caroles were danced on the hillsides just outside Paris. Giraldus remarks that the Black Monks, the Cluniacs, permitted the use of their land for this sort of entertainment. In a carole those not participating in the round dance would sit side by side, perhaps on a sloping hillside, a natural amphitheater.[10] The dancers, and some of the audience, provided the music by clapping and chanting a ballad or other dance song. Sometimes the words may have been acted out. I am inclined to believe that this was so with a *pastourelle;* the girl stood in the middle of a circle and someone, girl or boy, mimicked the accosting knight. The circle of dancers served as a chorus. On occasion a cleric would lead such a dance.[11] We know also that the dances were held in churchyards.[12]

An amusement of a different kind was afforded by a wealthy man who gave a banquet or dinner. This was not always on some special occasion. Thomas Becket, when he was chancellor of England, used to throw open his great hall to all those who wished to come and eat and drink. A wealthy man of this kind might stop with the Templars, outside the Porte Baudoyer. The Templars themselves were not hostile to excessively good cheer.[13] But a visitor to such a party did not have an "awfully good time," unless he were a person of some prominence or a clever minstrel. The tables were long and the meat and drink got very scarce toward the lower end. The young *scholasticus vagans* of Alexander's household could get some enjoyment from it. He was furnished an opportunity to present his wares, in Latin or French, and he occasionally received a warm welcome. Peter Pictor, who spent his days ornamenting ceilings and painting the walls of wealthy patrons' houses, remarked earlier in the century that some of the high ecclesiasts would rather listen to the fatuous verses of a jongleur than to the well-composed stanzas of a serious Latin poet, meaning himself.[14] Of course, ordinary households also were in the habit of listening to entertainers, after a meal, when these were available, and there was always the minstrel who gathered a group of listeners before a church or in an open place on the street. These men recited everything from saint's life to *chanson de geste*. Some of them were acrobats, and others led around a hapless bear or a trained monkey. They were good for a laugh, and the cost was very little. Each person might contribute a maille (half-denier).

There was other amusement, less innocent, furnished by the taverns and the houses of prostitution. The taverns were buildings open to the street, like the usual shop. The room was filled with benches and stools, and there was an occasional table board laid on two trestles. In taverns it was customary to drink and roll the dice.[15] Little food was sold there, but it could be brought in from a street vendor or from a nearby cookshop. The two more worldly members of the group at the house on the Rue de la Boucherie were probably frequent attenders; we hope that Alexander and the canon dropped in only occasionally, for a cup of wine. As it was against the law to strike a cleric or to arrest him except on authority from the bishop, it was very difficult to keep order in these places. On the wall behind the counter there were poles, and maybe hooks, from which dangled the wearing apparel left by drinkers who could not pay their scot.[16] The tavern keeper was in the pawnbroking business, although he was seldom a Jew. Casks of wine, rather long, with diameter greater in the middle than at the ends, reposed on low wooden racks. They had a small air hole at the top, and wine was drawn from a plugged hole on one end. A large *henap* filled may have cost a denier, depending upon the value of the wine. As for the women, it was not necessary to seek out the quarters where they practiced the oldest profession. There was much competition also from the serving maids and the tradeswomen who had daily contact with the normal life of the city. It was the girl's family rather than the civil law which watched over her virtue. Rape was sometimes very severely punished; but this severity depended upon factors that were not constant.[17] Boys and girls entered very young into the life of the community, often at the age of twelve or thirteen. Child labor was of everyday occurrence. They were not always sheltered at that age, and their decisions were made with immature minds.

I do not wish to give the impression that Alexander as the serious student of our group belonged to a class that was greatly in the minority. Serious clerks may have made up a half of the university community; another fourth could

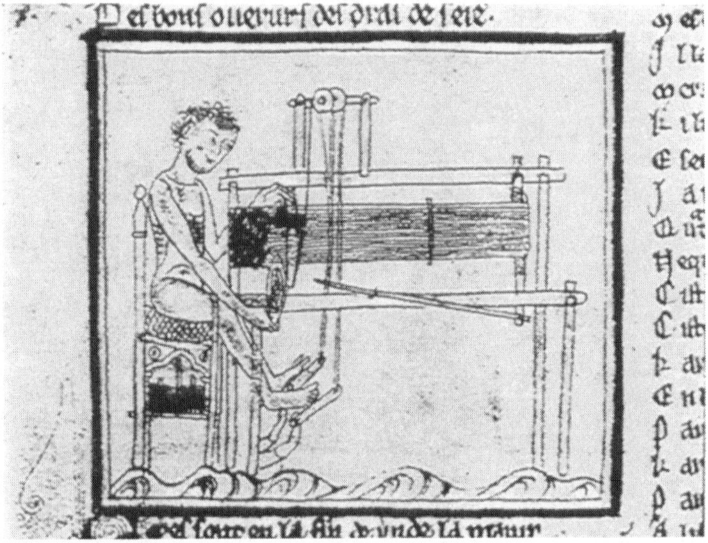

Treadle loom, from MS O.9.4
Courtesy Trinity College, Cambridge

Loge with loom, from MS R.17.1
Courtesy Trinity College, Cambridge

Illumination showing "companions of the bath"
Courtesy British Museum

have been constituted by the worldly but reputable group of which the canon was representative. The stray monks and wandering minstrels were there, however, and should not be forgotten. Some great literature was composed by such delinquents, for respectability and distinguished art do not go hand in hand.

When asked to define knowledge, Alexander doubtless gave the traditional answer.[18] There were the trivium, which consisted of grammar, rhetoric, and dialectic; the quadrivium, made up of arithmetic, geometry, music, and astronomy; and, in addition, theology, civil and canon law, and medicine. The last three were taught separately and with some concentration, but the other subjects were often not studied in any sequence, and the *lector* (or teacher) might combine dialectic with any of the others. Normally a student such as Alexander followed the trivium and the quadrivium for several years before beginning theology, and then, if curiosity and money were not lacking, the two laws and medicine might follow. Hugues of Saint-Victor had even proposed a different system of classification: he divided philosophy or learning into theoretical, practical, mechanical, and logical. The trivium fitted under logical, and the quadrivium, with theology, came under theoretical. The lectures given by Adam dou Petit Pont combined grammar and dialectic, although rhetoric was not completely absent. Following a hint given by John of Salisbury on the methodology used by Bernard de Chartres, we will assume that young Neckam attended two sessions a day with Adam, his *lector*. The principal one was in the afternoon, perhaps from two to four o'clock modern time. This began with an exposition of a text and then could be followed by a short question, or disputation, period. Perhaps Adam ended with a brief sermon and then all said the Pater

Noster. Exercises were assigned for the next day. The morning session could have been spent, as it was in Bernard's classes, with reading and correcting of the students' tasks.

In the exposition period the *lector* or master studied the construction of certain phrases and then commented on the author's ideas and discussed subtly the precise meanings of the words. The teacher certainly used a prepared commentary or gloss on the text that was being studied. As books were hard to get, the students were encouraged to copy out, or copy down, paragraphs of the texts that were being analyzed. For their exercises they would change prose into verse, and vice versa, or they would write something similar in the style of their model author. When studying a theological text, or one on rhetoric, the teacher indicated three stages of meaning. There was *historia*, or literal sense; then there was allegory, or doctrine; and finally there was the moral implication, or *sententia*. The chief text in theology at this time was the *Liber sententiarum* of Peter Lombard, which was meant to be a collection of moral questions for use in discussion. Peter Comestor's *Historia scholastica* (1173) was an arrangement of the history of Christianity made in a way that brought out the allegorical and moral possibilities of interpretation. Very frequently the teacher did not discuss a complete text of an author. He made use of *flores*, or chrestomathies, in which a series of selections from different writers were read and discussed. These passages might be arranged in order of occurrence in the full texts, or they might be placed in some scriptural sequence or in a sequence that presented a logical order of doctrine. Adam dou Petit Pont was particularly famous for his sharp syllogisms. His course in grammar must have taken the form of a study of the philosophy of language. He, and most of his fellows, believed firmly that the names of things had a natural appropriateness. Therefore these *lectores* encouraged etymological explanations whenever possible, and often when they were totally "impossible." Alexander Neckam continued this practice in most of his own writings. Both the *Old* and the *New Logic* of Aristotle were now in use. These were, of course, constant reference books for Adam, and we may imagine that he had his Aristotle text placed on a stand close by his professorial chair and reading desk. The old man was no mean theologian. In 1179 he was to be one of the English representatives who attended an important council in Rome.

It will be noted that grammar and rhetoric were receiving a strong dialectic tinge in the schools of Paris. This fact was much decried by contemporaries, but the tendency grew constantly stronger. Aristotle's *Logica nova* (*Analytica priora et posteriora*, *Topici*, *Sophistici elenchi*) even more than the *Logica vetus* (Boethius' translation of the *Categories* and *Periermenias*, with the *Isagoge* of Porphyry) had captured the imagination of most of the *lectores* and students in Paris since the year 1160. Before setting up as a *lector* on the Petit Pont or in the Cité, a scholar was obliged to receive a *licentia docendi* from the *scholasticus* or chancellor of the cathedral chapter of Notre Dame. A similar official of the Abbey of Sainte-Geneviève gave permission to teach on the left bank of the Seine. The new master would have to give evidence that he had pursued his subject diligently with acknowledged teachers and that they approved of his setting up on his own. We will quote (p. 157) from Gerald the Welshman on this subject. A new *lector* would begin with an opening lecture to which students and other teachers were invited. There would be a dinner, and the old teacher would indicate his approval.

Other masters would recommend that their pupils frequent the new classroom.

Nigel Wireker has his character Burnellus frequent the English students in Paris. Doubtless there was some congregating of student clerics according to origin and interests; but there were no organized "Nations" as yet, in the twelfth century.

Alexander was wakened at dawn by the blowing of the watchman's horn from the tower of the Grant Chastelet. This was sounded as the upper rim of the sun appeared on the horizon. It was already growing light before the sun showed itself. We will assume that Alexander hurried through his dressing, possibly making use of a washbasin which dangled from a chain in the *salle* or in the dispensary, or perhaps even in the kitchen court below. At this time he may have scooped up a handful of French soap from a wooden bowl nearby.[19] This soft soap was made by boiling mutton fat in a *leissive* of wood ash and caustic soda. Two other kinds of soap were the Saracen and the *savon esparterois* used by Jews. We are not suggesting that the use of toilet soap was common as yet, but it was certainly employed as an enema and for the removal of surplus, visible dirt. It is reasonable to assume that Alexander stopped for Mass on most mornings at the Church of Saint-Julien-le-pauvre, before rushing to the house of Adam on the Petit Pont. During the class the students sat on straw, or stools, or an occasional bench, while the teacher occupied his high-backed chair. We have said that much of this morning period was devoted to correcting of themes. After several hours of it the students walked in groups, or talked with the teacher, until the time to return to quarters for their first meal at about ten o'clock (our time). We suspect that fast was often broken before that with a cup of wine, and perhaps with a famous Parisian pasty. With dinner over, in an hour or two, most people rested in some way. By another hour they were up (*relevée*) and then came the two hours of class in the afternoon. This was the principal exposition, as John of Salisbury has hinted.[20] It was followed by more private discussion and amusement before supper at Vespers. After this meal, we can assume, the students took to their books by candlelight; and some worked far into the night. A few must have made their way to the tavern. On holy days, which were frequent, there were no classes and more real sport. Students strolled or rode into the country; they participated in games on the Pré-aux-clercs. There were always groups of them who were looking for mischief.

Since Alexander had a room to himself, we picture him as following the advice given by a certain priest to Giraldus. The priest was an old man who had seen many successive groups of students at Paris. "When a man of letters sits in his chimney corner with a book, he is his own best company."[21] Alexander has left us a copious treatment of what he thought of the seven arts in Chapter 173 of his *De naturis rerum*.[22] He was conservative in some ways, and he showed preference for the trivium, which, before the twelfth century, was the sum total of learning. But he thought that the trivium could be improperly used. Grammar is supposed to teach us to speak well and correctly—but do we do it? Rhetoric was designed to give us eloquence, but those who use it are bent upon the wrong purposes. Dialectic is to enable us to distinguish right from wrong, and yet we employ it to make the wrong appear right. Alexander was bitter on this point. He took sides in the squabble of his day which divided the advocates of grammar and rhetoric from the dialecticians. He gives many examples of the ridiculous state into which dialectic had fallen in the mouths of its practitioners. "Sortes," the "Mr. X" of the twelfth-century logicians, could be proved to be anything at all.[23] Alexander did not care much for the quadrivium: arithmetic, geometry (Euclid), astronomy, and music. That is, he registered on parchment his disapproval, but he displayed keen curiosity just the same. Zoology and gemmology were not school subjects in his century, but he was much interested in them, and by the time he wrote the *De naturis rerum* he had studied these fields with the aid of Solinus, Pliny, Aristotle, Cassiodorus, and Boethius. Herbs also fascinated him. We infer that his practice of arithmetic was limited to the use of the calculating board, which we can picture in his room in Paris. This board consisted of a low table top to be set on legs of a kind. On it was a center line, through which crosslines were spaced, alternating long and short. The longer crosslines marked single units and the shorter lines indicated "fives." Calculations were made with metal or bone counters which were placed on the proper lines in making additions, and taken therefrom when subtraction was in order. I doubt that Alexander had an astrolabe. He could not have resisted describing one if he had owned it. This instrument was useful in astronomy and geometry (or that part of it which now belongs to trigonometry). Alexander has one first observation to his credit in popular astronomy. He is the first to tell us of the legend of the man in the moon. He repeats a popular Latin distich on this: "The peasant in the moon, whom a pack on the back weighs down, shows that to steal thorns helps no one."[24]

As Alexander settled into his lodging, we will assume that he took stock of the availability of books.[25] He could not have brought many with him, traveling light as he did. He must have contacted the booksellers, buying some titles and renting copies of certain others. Books at the time were not always bound separately. A volume might contain within its plain wooden boards (often covered with skin) a number of works, usually related in subject matter. Possibly Alexander brought from Dunstable, in his saddlebags, the chief grammatical texts: the *Institutiones* of Priscian, the *Ars minor* of Donatus, the famous *Eclogue* of Theodulus, and the commentary on Martianus Capella by Remigius of Auxerre. He may have brought, also, some of the books needed for the study of rhetoric: the *Rhetorica ad Herennium*, Cicero's *De Oratore*, and the works of Quintilian. He might have purchased in Paris the *Old* and *New Logic* of Aristotle; the *Historia scholastica* of Peter Comestor, the *scholasticus* or chancellor of the Paris schools who had just died; and the *De universitate* of Bernard Sylvester. This book by Bernard was a favorite with the poets. It gave a picture of *Natura* as the *mater generationis*. As a prospective theologian Alexander assumedly purchased also the *Liber sententiarum* of Peter Lombard. The young canon, whom we shall designate hereafter as Bernard, was following courses in the quadrivium. He required the works of Boethius, Pliny, Euclid, Ptolemy, and Solinus. As this canon had a hankering for the law he may have started already to dicker for the *Code* and the *Digest*, as well as for the *Decretum* of Gratian and the decretals of Pope Alexander III. If medical books could be purchased by either Alexander or Canon Bernard, their choice would have fallen on the *Prognostica* of Hippocrates, the *Pantegni*, something by Galen, and various treatises by Isaac. The books of Dioscorides and Macer on herbs also were desirable. Alexander showed at a later date the results of some medical study. It is possible that he got his first acquaintance with medicine at this time. We will give the canon the benefit of a doubt and assign to his personal library a missal, a Psalter, and a breviary. He might have owned a hymnal. Probably the "monk" and the minstrel possessed very little in the way of books. As Giraldus had occasion to say once: "Today there are in the Church clerks without the science of letters just as there are many knights without skill and practice in arms, who are called by others 'Knights of Saint Mary.' "[26]

Books were valuable property.[27] They could be sold, pawned, and rented.[28] Those who wanted to hold on to them were obliged to take some care. An important book, frequently used, might be chained to its reading desk or shelf. We can conclude that Alexander and young Bernard kept theirs in chests for which they had keys.[29] I am going to hazard a guess that either Bernard or Alexander soon rented an *Ars dictandi* by Bernard de Meun. This was a condensation of the larger *Summa dictaminis* of Bernard Sylvester. These were home courses in secretarial science. They explained how to write letters and gave many specimens for all occasions which could be adapted to anyone's use.[30] Commonest among these letter forms were those asking for money from relatives.[31] Letter writing as an art was encouraged by the schools at Orléans, which were distinguished for their more frivolous varieties of learning. A serious student at Paris must have glanced up the hill toward Orléans in much the same way that the modern student in a large, distinguished university looks with scorn toward a more practical institution in the same locality.

A learned kind of entertainment which attracted Alexander and Bernard, possibly the "monk" also, was the public disputations held by students and professors on the holy days and on other special occasions. A visiting scholar might announce a lecture, or a series of lectures, just as Giraldus did at Oxford. On three successive days Giraldus read from his *Description of Ireland*, and each day was for a different kind of auditor, including laymen.[32] In Paris, Giraldus tells us, it was customary to have public expositions of canon law on a Sunday. The opening lectures of a new teacher were apt to be attended with avidity, particularly if he stacked the audience with his friends and well-wishers. More common were those occasions when someone set up various propositions which he was prepared to defend against all comers. At times these defenses took on a very serious character when a teacher's doctrine was suspect, and he was required to defend himself against heresy. Some of these "defenses" may have been held at Saint-Julien-le-pauvre, which had the advantage of being located in the Burgum Parvi Pontis. They were usually held in churches, on an afternoon, after *relevée*, and they could continue for a while after supper. As a general rule, there was little activity by candlelight in the twelfth century. Lacking elaborate means for illumination, the people naturally preferred to live by the sun. The large wax candles, called *cierges*, which were the very ultimate in efficiency, were expensive. The people rose at daybreak (*point du jour*) and retired as it grew dark, except in the dead of winter when darkness fell not long after four o'clock (modern time). In that cold, dark season the hours from four to seven-thirty were usually passed beside a bright fire in the chimney place. But at the other seasons of the year activity by natural light could continue until seven or eight, and in mid-summer it was still twilight when they went to bed.

As in London, and in every large city, certain churches were designated to ring their bells to mark the canonical hours, from which the townspeople took their time. Apparently three churches—Sainte-Opportune, Saint-Merri, and the Cathedral—were doing this at the date Alexander was in Paris. The mediaeval man was very conscious of *midi*, when the sun was directly overhead, and he reckoned by it when he was traveling about. The hour of Sext coincided with *midi* only a few times during the year. Most folk who were at home were taking their rest as the sun reached its zenith.

We might speak at this point about the types of recluses: the monks and the hermits. Nigel Wireker lists the monastic orders when he has his protagonist, Burnellus, consider them all.[33] They were the Hospitalers (wearing the white cross), the Black Monks or Cluniacs, the Cistercians, the Order of Grammont, the Carthusians, the Augustinians or black canons, the Order of Prémontré, those of Semplingham, the Benedictines, and the Templars. Most of these were represented in some way in the vicinity of Paris. They were the same in England, too. Perhaps the "Friar" Tuck of Robin Hood's band was a Black Monk; he was certainly not the Franciscan who is so anachronistically portrayed in all our modern versions of the legend. In an age such as the twelfth century, which was inefficient in its approach to social and statistical matters, it is a wonder that the Church was able to keep as good a centralized control as it often did. But some of the individual monastic houses got out of hand, and critics, both lay and clerical, did not allow it to be passed over.[34] In the *Anseÿs de Mes:*

The monks drink in violence and strife of the best wines which God has established. They eat bread as white as hail; of all flesh do they eat also, so that their bellies are full and stuffed and they almost burst through the middle. But real [holy men] the hermits do not act so. They have bread of barley, kneaded with water, and wild fruit which they have gathered in the woods, and various herbs and roots also. When Bauclus had been in the abbey to the point that he had his fill of ease and bread and wine he realized that he would not be saved in this way. In a wood that was some seven hundred yards away he became a hermit, for fourteen or fifteen years. He did not eat of bread or flour, or anything which was not a root. His back became so thin from fasting that he could hardly stand upon his feet. . . .[35]

Chrétien de Troyes presents a picture, similar to this, of a hermit whose bread is filled with barley straw, and who has no meat and no wine.[36] He eats meat only when it is brought to him by the knight Yvain. Hermits were not uncommon in the twelfth century. There were two dominant psychological reasons which influenced such individuals to abandon their fellow men. Some were literal-minded and believed that luxury and petty vices could not be avoided in any society as life was then constituted. Others must have been oppressed by crowding and developed a kind of agoraphobia. A person was seldom alone in town or country, or in most monastic communities. There were surely a few high-strung people who had a desire to escape from this.

A typical large Benedictine abbey had the following monastic officials: abbot, prior, subprior, third prior, sacristan, subsacristan, cellarer, subcellarer, guestmaster, *camerarius*, *subcamerarius*, *refectorarius*, *subrefectorarius*, precentor, succentor, librarian, shrine custodian, pittancer, and physician.[37] The sacristan was treasurer and chief bailiff; his assistant was directly in charge of workmen who labored on buildings, etc. The cellarer may be called the seneschal of the establishment. The guestmaster served directly under the cellarer. The duties of cellarer and sacristan were sufficiently similar, so that they were occasionally at odds over their respective responsibilities. We might have included another office in our list, that of almoner to the abbot. Some of the farm lands of an abbey could be managed by a monk who was permitted to live out of the abbey in a manor house. The behavior of such a member of the community was observed strictly, and he was subject to replacement at any time.

The dress of the monks varied with the order. The reader should bear in mind, however, that the habits worn were basically similar to the plainest dress of lay peasants. The villein who worked in the fields had his long hooded frock of undyed wool or linen, girded with a tie belt or perhaps with a clasp. On his feet were heavy shoes with very thick soles. The various orders of monks stylized their particular peasant dress and kept it uniform. Furthermore, the monk wore no headgear at all, whereas the peasant had a broad-brimmed hat, or, at times, a snood. Despite such similarity I find it difficult to identify some of the items in a monk's dress as given in the following passage: "He took the cowl, the frock, and the *estamine* [woolen cloak?], also the big boots, the *tribous* [?], and the fur garment [*pellice*]."[38]

There were certain essential rooms, or buildings, in a monastery: chapter house, refectory, calefactory, dormitory, infirmary, cloister and library, church, and hospice or guest house. Marie de France says: "The abbot comes to speak to them, he begs them to stop, and he will show them his dormitory, his chapter house, his refectory. . . ."[39] The chapter house was the assembly hall of the community. There is a splendid specimen of such a hall, taken from Pontaut (France), which has been set up again in The Cloisters in New York City.[40] The members of the community, in this particular example, sat along a stone ledge on three sides of the hall. The abbot's seat is not determined. This chapter house of which we are speaking formed an alcove off from the cloister, separated from it by three magnificent arches, one of them over the doorway. The refectory, or dining room, could have a platform at one end, where the abbot had his table. Sometimes it had a reading pulpit high on the wall where a reader was placed. The calefactory was the social room in some of the orders. This was not essential. The dormitories were seldom built with any idea of permanence, and usually they have not survived. The guest house had no special charm. The cloister, usually with a garden in the center, was of great importance. Here the religious would stroll, pray, and meditate, and in many communities they sat along the inner wall, copying and studying. Care was frequently lavished on the capitals which supported the roof of such a cloister. In The Cloisters of New York City there are some excellent examples of smaller cloisters which have been brought over from France and set up exactly as they were.

Close to Alexander's lodging were the Augustinian canons who maintained both Saint-Victor and Sainte-Geneviève, up on the hill. Neckam was always welcome in both of these houses, particularly because of his associations with this order back in England. The Augustinians were extremely extroverted. They provided hospitals for the sick and lodgings for travelers, and above all they were concerned with education. As we have had occasion to comment, those of Saint-Victor and Sainte-Geneviève provided theological training. If Alexander had come to Paris in quest of theology instead of grammar and dialectic, he would have gone to one of these two schools.

Benedictines of various kinds were close at hand. The Cluniac community was represented by Saint-Martin-des-Champs, that huge agricultural foundation which had so impressed our travelers as they drew near the suburb of the right bank on the day of their arrival. With the aid of hired labor (*hôtes*) these monks were clearing the marshy districts to the northeast of the city. The Abbot of Cluny kept a firm hand on all his subordinate houses, and this very centralization made them agents of transmission for new prevailing ideas. The monks of Cluny were tremendously concerned with the recovery of Spain, and with the promotion of the pilgrimage to Compostela. Since the time of the great abbot Peter the Venerable, who died in 1156, they had made enlightened efforts to convert the Saracens and the Jews. It was at their Abbey of Saint-Martin-des-Champs that Alexander and his companions saw and heard many jongleurs of the better type. The monks themselves permitted performances of dramas, and even lighter entertainment, such as caroles.

Not far from the king's palace, on the island of the Cité, were the Benedictines of Saint-Barthélemy and Saint-Magloire, who were subject to the Abbey of Saint-Marmoutier at Tours. There were other, smaller groups of Benedictines, autonomous except for obligations to their General Chapter. First in size and importance was the Abbey of Saint-Germain-des-Prés. This large community with its stone rampart and drawbridge stood close to the Seine adjacent to the Pré-aux-clercs. Ordinary students were not always welcome within its portals because of the many disputes and contentions which had arisen over cases of jurisdiction. Since Pope Alexander III had dedicated the abbey church in 1163, this community was exempt from the authority of Bishop Maurice de Sully and owed obedience directly to the Holy See. The Abbot was feudal overlord of the land which lay close by the Petit Pont. His own village of Saint-Germain was a thriving town which since 1170 had enjoyed the privileges of being a commune.

Because of his intimacy with the Abbot of St. Albans,

in England, Alexander Neckam was given some special privileges by the Abbot of Saint-Germain and was, on occasion, allowed to see the intricate machinery of administration which held together so active an enterprise.

The actual administration of a large Benedictine abbey in the twelfth century is depicted most graphically in the account given by Jocelin of the Abbey of Bury-St. Edmund's. We shall draw on this. The abbot was in every sense of the word a feudal overlord, with the additional authority pertaining to his religious office. He could discipline a monk by sending him into exile. Control over the abbot's own acts belonged only to a papal legate sent for an occasional inspection. The sacristan provided the income for the upkeep of the abbot's house from the feudal rents which belonged to the abbot. These were distinct from the rents of the monastery proper. When the abbot's post was vacant, the royal authority stepped in and administered his revenues until a new incumbent was elected and approved. In 1181 the King gave permission to the Archbishop of Norway to live in the abbot's house at St. Edmund's and to receive ten shillings a day.[41] This was during the interim following the death of Abbot Hugh.

Once an abbot had been elected, and consecrated with his miter and ring, he was brought in great ceremony to the abbey church and took his seat on the west side of the choir. He was greeted by his knight vassals as well as by his monks. He was supposed to maintain hospitality for these vassals, and others, on a scale somewhat similar to that of a baron or count. He named a steward and kept account of the manors and the servile holdings and of the services required. Abbot Samson, when elected at St. Edmund's, constructed new hunting parks, stocked them with beasts, and kept a kennel and a huntsman. He himself did not follow the chase. He was required, however, to keep apart the revenues of the monastery and the revenues belonging to his own office. St. Edmund's had a special custom: the monastery entertained all monks and secular priests who were received as guests; the abbot paid for the entertainment of other guests when he was in residence. When he was absent, the monastery did all entertaining on its own responsibility. Abbot Samson bought several stone houses outside the abbey enclosure in which the monastery schools were conducted. Previous to this purchase each student was obliged to pay a denier or a maille twice a year for rent, as well as another small fee for instruction.[42]

The abbot received gifts on the Feast of the Circumcision from all his vassals, like any feudal lord. He collected knight's service from his vassals, which included scutage, reliefs, and aids. The burghers of Saint-Germain doubtless paid to their abbot an annual sum (perhaps sixty marks) for the liberties of their commune. The buyers of the abbot, or of the cellarer, had the right to make first purchase of all supplies that were brought to the abbey towns for sale. There were many diverse customs and tolls which were collected by the monastery.[43]

Benedictine monks were required to spend four hours and more a day in the choir of their church, and a certain number of hours in manual labor. At the time when Alexander Neckam visited Saint-Germain, the Benedictine order was no longer playing a leading part in intellectual activity.[44] But the Abbey of Saint-Germain-des-Prés certainly had a fine library, and the monks were expected to devote from three to five hours a day to reading. At the beginning of Lent each monk received from the library a book, which was usually kept a year. Probably some copying of manuscripts was done during the hours allotted to manual labor.

Jocelin refers to a certain council as being held at "the season of bloodletting when the cloistered monks were wont to reveal the secrets of their hearts in turn, and to discuss matters one with another."[45] Jocelin is literal when he refers to the season of bloodletting. It was a practice five times a year for the monks to be bled, and we know that this was used as a period of bathing and relaxation.

In the dormitory buildings at Saint-Germain the professed monks were each housed in a small partitioned compartment which was called a cell. There was a whole series of these along each long wall. The novices, on the other hand, had a *domus* of their own, which was a large single room filled with beds.[46] The infirmary also was a separate *domus*. In the center of this infirmary hall was a narrow pallet where the members of the community were placed in their last hour, clothed in a hair shirt and sprinkled with ashes.[47] There was a physician as well as an *infirmarius*. Jocelin says that Master Walter, the physician at St. Edmund's Abbey, received fees from the practice of medicine, from which we assume that he was allowed to have a practice outside the cloister.[48]

The outer gate of the monastery was kept by an old monk, the *portarius*, who had a cell arranged close by. As a guest entered or left the enclosure, the *portarius* saluted him with bowed head, except special guests before whom the porter prostrated himself on the ground.[49]

Usually when Alexander finished his visits to the Abbey of Saint-Germain it was Vespers and he hurried through the busy commune which surrounded the abbey, intent upon getting back for supper on the Rue de la Boucherie. The road which led toward Petit Pont passed through a few vineyards and fields before houses increased in number, and the road became the Rue de la Huchette. It was a familiar path for all students, as it was the route which they took to the Pré-aux-clercs. Surely Alexander sometimes looked back as he passed along the more open stretch of this road. The great abbey with its high fortified enclosure must have stood impressive against the setting sun on a winter's afternoon. Perhaps it was then that he decided his future would lie with the busy Augustinian order rather than with the Benedictines who were housed here so strictly within their moat and drawbridge.

> saddles, and another shields. One man manufactures bridles, another spurs. Some polish sword blades, others full cloth, and some are dyers. Some prick the fabrics and others clip them, and these here are melting gold and silver. They make rich and lovely pieces: cups, drinking vessels, and eating bowls [*escueles*], and jewels worked in with enamels; also rings, belts, and pins. One could certainly believe that in that town there was a fair every day, it was so full of wealth. It was filled with wax, pepper, cochineal dye, and with vair and gris [fine furs], and with every kind of merchandise.[3]

Still other trades are pictured in another description: "A hundred burghers are tavern keepers, a hundred are bakers, a hundred are butchers, and a hundred are fishermen. Another hundred are merchants who sail to the Indies [*Inde major*], and three hundred there are who do other things."[4]

For a nearly complete list of the trades it is necessary to consult the *Livre des mestiers* of Estienne Boileau, which was prepared in Paris in the thirteenth century. We will limit ourselves to comment on a selected group. For the privilege of practicing a trade in the city it was necessary to pay a fee to the royal provost. Many of the trades were organized into corporate guilds with rules and regulations. This began during the course of the twelfth century. Most of the groups owed service to the *guet*, or "watch," which they thoroughly detested. Men over sixty, men whose wives were in childbirth, sick people, those in trades which served directly the armed knights and the Church, and those in trades which were considered foul—these were exempted from the *guet*. A list of the exempted tradesmen that came under these categories is interesting: arrow and bow manufacturers, armorers, shieldmakers, stationers and book dealers, painters or illuminators, sculptors, embroiderers, goldsmiths, and apothecaries; and among the "foul," skinners, bath keepers, and tavern keepers. Most trades were not allowed to work by candlelight, or after Vespers, unless the peculiar nature of their calling required it, such as heating of furnaces, etc. On Friday night many had to close up their regular shops and prepare to carry their goods to the Campelli, outside the Porte de Paris.[5] Needless to say, certain holy days, like the Feast of the Purification (February 2), the Feast of the Annunciation (March 25), the Feast of the Assumption (August 15), the Feast of the Nativity of the Blessed Virgin (September 8), and various others, were required to be kept by all. Some trades had their own special holy days.

It was forbidden to call a patron away from the stall of a nearby competitor; he must stroll over of his own accord. Provision merchants were forbidden to go out into the country to get supplies. They were required to wait for the produce or fish to be brought to the proper place in Paris, where it could be purchased wholesale. Charcoal was not to be bought up for storing (for purposes of resale) between Easter and All Saints'. Restrictions were so many that we wonder how it was possible to make a profit. We may infer that many merchants disobeyed the regulations. Boileau lists a hundred trades. Some of these are a surprise to us: makers of small objects of lead and tin and makers of nails for fastening onto belts. Wax sellers, pepper merchants, and apothecaries were associated together. The oil merchant sold olive oil, almond oil, walnut oil, linseed oil, and poppy oil. He is of interest to us because we are concerned over the type of shortening used in cooking and the oil bases used in paints.[6]

The apothecaries sold aromatic spices, which were required in every kitchen except the humblest. People who were troubled with nervous stomachs, which needed warming, would carry around with them various spices which they ate like our modern candy. Thus, Thomas Becket "ate both ginger and clove by the handful; his wine he always diluted with water." The apothecary sold also herbs and other substances that had medicinal value. We cannot begin to name all of these, but here are some of them: antimony, acacia, agaric, asphodel, garlic, sal ammoniac, anise, wormwood, anacardium, almonds, aristolochia, amber, henna, yellow arsenic or orpiment, balsam, borage, betony, acanthus, bugloss, camphor, cassia fistula, cardamom, castorea, cubebs, cinnamon, caraway, hemlock, calamine, costus, endives, euphorbia, hellebore of several kinds, henbane, and gum arabic.[7] No prescription from a physician was required. There were expensive cures and cheap cures. Perhaps the most expensive was *mumie*, which was imported from Egypt and could be purchased by only the well-to-do. It had formerly been used as an embalming fluid and was efficacious against bleeding. Pictures that we have of apothecary shops show shelves around the wall containing boxes and jars. The apothecaries are seated on the floor, or on low stools, mixing drugs with very large pestles and mortars on their laps.

Many clerical doctors, who had studied in the schools, were attached to patrons. Such protectors used their services personally, or sent them to friends and vassals. As to whether there was any considerable number of orthodox physicians practicing on their own, I cannot say. These remarks are, of course, applicable to the late twelfth century. Conditions changed within the next few centuries.[8] The average person, when ill, called upon an empiric, a *mire* or *miresse* who practiced without the aid of Galen or Hippocrates.[9] By modern standards these empirics were safer than the others. Whether the physician was a secular cleric, a monk, or a lay empiric, it was possible to spend a fortune on his services. A knight serving in the guard of Edward the Confessor "had lost all his wealth on doctors trying to find health." He was finally healed by the saintly king.[10] There were many maimed people, and the halt and the blind were always moving about the streets in a mediaeval city. Those who were mentally afflicted were not confined, unless their ailment was dangerous to those around them. A considerable number of cripples must have been spastics who suffered cerebral palsy as a result of birth injury. These are the *contraiz.* The *Life of Saint Edward the Confessor* describes such a man in detail: the leg was pulled up against the thigh, and the heels were twisted around; all the body below the waist was uncontrollable. Apparently this man dragged along the ground with two "little hand crutches."[11] A similar cripple placed himself inside a basin and dragged himself over the ground. The first of these unfortunates claimed that he had been to Rome six times looking for a cure. Wooden legs were in use, sometimes richly ornamented.[12]

Practitioners in the twelfth century were continually hoping to simplify the practice of medicine. They had "wonder salves"—a green salve, a red salve, and so on—which they claimed could be applied with sure results. Many formulas for such salves are found in the *materiae medicae.* They had many regimes for improving one's general health.[13] They advised resting after meals to aid the digestion.[14] Bathing in mineral springs, such as those at Bath, was thought to be efficacious against cold humors. This bathing was most helpful, therefore, in old age.[15] Jewish physicians taught that it was better to drink water at mealtimes because water is heavier than wine and therefore better for the digestion.[16] Wine should be taken an hour after eating to augment the natural heat. Hard foods were not good for the kidneys.[17] People were advised to let blood on general principles four times a year.[18] Special strengthening drinks were prescribed.[19] Some sickly folk, like the fictitious Uther, father of King Arthur, drank only cold water.[20] Foods such as cheese, garlic, and pepper were forbidden.[21] Women were brought out of a faint by sprinkling with water.[22]

The art of surgery was still not separated from medicine. Those who had studied their art out of books had three problems with which they were constantly engaged. The first was to keep the humors in balance. The humors—phlegm, blood, bile, and black bile—were cold and moist, hot and moist, hot and dry, and cold and dry, respectively. These qualities were the complexions of the humors. All drugs of the pharmacopoeia were classified according to their degrees of moisture, dryness, heat, and cold, and they were prescribed so as to maintain the proper balance of the humors within the body. The physician "discovered" how these were out of balance by examining visually the urine, sometimes the stool, and by feeling the pulse of the right wrist. He would count up to a hundred beats.[23] This routine did not take long, so a physician could make a phenomenal number of calls in a morning.

The second problem was that of treating fevers. These were classified roughly into tertian, quartan, daily, and hectic. Sometimes pestilential fever was given separately. Among these the modern observer will recognize malaria, tuberculosis, nervous tension, influenza, and, under the heading hectic, the terrible diseases such as typhoid, scarlet fever, and typhus. These classifications were according to the intervals at which the fever recurred—every third day, every fourth—or according to the severity of the onset.

A third problem, which the twelfth-century *mire* could cope with more satisfactorily, was that of healing wounds, visible sores, and skin diseases. These were very common indeed. The physician, and the victim himself, knew the need for bandaging with strips of linen, often torn from a shirt.[24] No idea of asepsis was held, but empirically some use was made of alcohol (in wine) and of white of egg (which is sterile when broken immediately before use). Counterirritants and plasters were popular. Bad tissue was cut away and the exposed area was doused in white of egg and drains were inserted to draw off the bad humors.[25] Pus was usually encouraged to provide healing by second intention. A deep wound, such as that made by an arrow, was kept open with a paraffin tent—a finger of paraffin set into the hollow—and a drain was added. In gynecology a tent of cloth was inserted with some medication at the tip. There was very little cutting on the part of orthodox physicians, except for cataract, abscesses, and trepanning. It was considered sinful to cut into a living body so that lithotomists were not in good repute. Some of them were remarkable surgeons for their time. Certain Italian families, like the Preciani, wandered about practicing this art. When they arrived in a community, various physicians contrived to notify sufferers who were willing to take the risk. The operation was a daring one. The "staff," a rod invented later to prevent the operator from cutting too far, was not yet devised.[26] The ulcers and skin diseases were very many. Usamah gives us a "Frankish remedy" for scrofula: "Take uncrushed leaves of glasswort, burn them, then soak the ashes in olive oil and sharp vinegar. Treat the scrofula with them until the spot on which it is growing is eaten up. Then take burnt lead, soak it in ghee butter and treat him with it. That will cure him."[27] One Bernard, treasurer of Fulk of Anjou, King of Jerusalem, had a compound fracture of the leg, in fourteen places. The Frankish physician washed the wounded limb frequently in strong vinegar alcohol. By this treatment all cuts were healed. Bad wounds were always sewed up with thread (probably silk when it was available). A wound in the *vuit buc*, probably the side at the waistline, was not greatly dreaded.[28] Cendal, a silk material, was preferred for bandages.[29]

All births were attended by midwives; men were forbidden to be present on pain of death.[30] However, as Marie demonstrates in her *Milon*, infant care was rather good, once the child had been brought safely into the world.[31] If such care had not been sensible, few of us would be here today. The baby was kept wrapped in swaddling bands, which are loose linen or wool wrappings with broad cloth bands, wrapped in crisscross fashion, holding the material firm around him. The child was lifted, bathed, and changed every three hours. It was nursed on those occasions by wet nurses, as nothing but human milk could be given a suckling. Two babes who were nursed by the same woman, although they were not related by blood, often felt a bond in after years. Richard I was nursed by Alexander's mother. This type of nursing was kept up longer than we breast feed our children in the modern world—well into the second year, probably. When the child became a runabout, a maid was designated to watch him.[32]

The burial of the dead was a matter for the Church. After death the body was turned over to the men or women of a religious order, who washed the body and, usually, sewed it up in deerskin.[33] The body was then carried on a bier, consisting of two poles with wooden crosspieces, attended by the clergy and mourners. It was draped with a black pall.[34] The corpse of a prominent person, lay or clerical, might be laid to rest in a stone sarcophagus which was sealed up with lead.[35] For a considerable time it was customary to treat such a tomb with marked reverence: "covered with a silken cloth, surrounded by burning lamps and wax candles."[36] These lamps would have been like a modern votive light—an enclosed bowl with a wick inserted into oil. The sarcophagus could stand in a chapel or in a crypt. It was sometimes placed under the floor stones, or tiles, of a church building. People of lesser rank were taken to church burial grounds, such as that of the Holy Innocents, and interred. We assume that a simple wooden coffin was used. A flat tombstone could be laid on the grave, with name cut or painted thereon. It was considered praiseworthy, says John of Garland in his *Morale scholarium*, to say a prayer for the dead when passing a cemetery. A description of a funeral procession, as given by Chrétien, is interesting:

> The candles and the crosses went first, with the nuns from a convent; then followed the clerics with sacred books and thuribles. . . . [The widow and the vassals followed the bier making very loud and visible grief.] When the nuns and the priests had held the service, they returned from the church and came to the grave.[37]

The horse of the dead knight was often led before the bier.[38]

Because preservative embalming was not practiced, bodies were soon destroyed by decay. After a few years the bones could be lifted out of a grave in a burial ground and stacked with others, making possible further use of the space. The process of preparing the dead is summed up quite well in the *Mort Aymeri:* "They prepared it rather well and richly; they embalmed with balsam and ointment and sewed the body tight in deerskin."[39] The ointment and the balsam had no preservative qualities, of course.

Now turning to the trades proper established in the city

of Paris, we find high in esteem the goldsmith. Theophilus Rugerus gives ample details on goldsmithery, and we will use his treatise to illustrate further the brief discussion offered by Alexander. Alexander says:

> The goldsmith should have a furnace with a hole at the top so that the smoke can get out by all exits. One hand should operate the bellows with a light pressure and the greatest diligence, so that the air inside the bellows, being pressed through the tubes, may blow up the coals and that the constant spread of it may feed the fire. Let there be an anvil of extreme hardness on which iron and gold may be softened and may take the required form.[40] They can be stretched and pulled with the tongs and the hammer. There should be a hammer also for making gold leaf, as well as sheets of silver, tin, brass, iron, or copper. The goldsmith must have a very sharp chisel by which he can engrave in amber, diamond, or *ophelta* [?], or marble, or jacinth, emerald, sapphire, or pearl, and form many figures. He should have a hardness stone for testing metals, and one for comparing steel with iron. He must also have a rabbit's-foot for smoothing, polishing, and wiping the surface of gold and silver, and the small particles of metal should be collected in a leather apron. He must have small boxes, flasks, and containers, of pottery, and a toothed saw and a gold file, as well as gold and silver wire, by which broken objects can be mended or properly constructed. The goldsmith should be skilled in feathery work as well as in bas-relief, in fusing as well as in hammering. His apprentice must have a waxed or painted table, or one covered with clay, for portraying little flowers and drawing in various ways.[41] That he may do this conveniently let him have litharge and chalk. He must know how to distinguish solid gold from brass and copper, that he may not purchase brass for gold. . . .[42]

Despite the list of gems given here and in the lapidaries, the stones in common use in the period were the sapphire and various kinds of quartz: jasper, moss agate, colored chalcedonies, sardonyx, amethyst, citrine, and plain crystal.

Emeralds and rubies were very few, and the diamond, of course, could not be polished in any way. Garnets were used, but often a luminous foil was painted on the culet or underside, and the stone was called a carbuncle. The jacinth and jargon were supposedly varieties of what we call the zircon; but many of them may actually have been brownish citrines. Because glass was so easy to handle, it was frequently employed, with a colored foil on the underside.[43] The only method of polishing was "bruting," a process of rubbing stones together. This meant that the finished product had an irregular cabochon shape. The stone was set onto a metal surface by soldering gold or silver wire around it.[44] Very few gems were engraved at this period; most of those used had survived from the ancient world. Engraving of a kind was done on softer minerals. The apprentice working at the table was probably chalking out designs to be soldered to or cut on the metal surfaces. He used a kind of chalk or litharge which could easily be erased. Alexander expatiates again, elsewhere, on those who cheat by selling brass for gold. Perhaps he himself had been cheated in this way.[45]

There is an intimate picture of a petty merchant and his wares which is sketched in a few lines by John of Garland, writing forty years after the date that concerns us. The variety of objects which the merchant offers for sale tickles our fancy: "William, our neighbor, has in the market these things before him to be sold: needles and needlecases, cleansing material or soap, mirrors, razors, whetstones, *fuisils* or fire-striking irons, and spindles."[46] This is no great assembly of goods for sale, but William must have been surrounded by eager housewives.

Although the average merchant was expected to close shop and transport his wares to the Campelli every Saturday, the real thrill at the fair, for the Parisian shoppers, was offered by itinerant merchants who carried scarce products from town to town, and from fair to fair.[47] These people were particularly in evidence at the annual fairs of Saint-Lazare and Saint-Germain, not to mention the Lendit. In the *Charroi de Nimes*, William Shortnose is only posing as a merchant in order to gain entrance to the town, but the picture which he presents is a good one: "Barons, be patient, the most expensive things are coming last . . . among the first are inks, sulphur, incense, quicksilver, alum, *graine* [cochineal dye], peppers, saffron, furs, tanned leather, shoe leather, and marten skins. . . ."[48] A merchant like this was a combination of chemical importer and tanner.[49]

Alexander is the first to describe mirrors of glass with a lead backing: "Take away the lead which is behind the glass and there will be no image of the one looking in."[50] Probably metal mirrors also were still in use. There does not seem to have been much glass manufacture at Paris, as neither Alexander nor Estienne Boileau refers to it. Theophilus, however, gives a full description of the processes involved.[51] The chief use for glass at the time was in stained windows. The mixture was two parts beechwood ash to one of clean sharp sand. The mixture was put in pots into the furnace. When it was removed therefrom, the glass blower, using a long tube, formed a cylinder by blowing a bladder and cutting off the top and bottom. A white-hot cutting iron was employed. This cylinder was stored and then reheated, cut, and rolled out flat into a sheet. This was drawn upon, to secure the required designs, and then glazed with the coloring matter, once more in a furnace. The leading was handled much as it is today. Glass was used for *henaps*, or drinking cups, also.[52]

As our protagonist gazed out of his back window, he could distinguish quite clearly the building operations which were in progress on the new cathedral church of Notre Dame. The choir had recently been completed (in 1177). Nowhere does Alexander Neckam enumerate for us the techniques employed in such a huge building enterprise. We must supply such details from elsewhere. First, the land was measured by a *geometricus*.[53] We presume that a quadrant was used for laying off the angles, and a pole for marking the distances. There was a master to whom the direction of the construction was entrusted. He had under him a *magister lathomus*, or head stonecutter, who saw to it that the stones were properly dressed before being raised into position. This dressing was accomplished right there on the building site. The workmen were stonecutters, masons, cement and mortar mixers (*mortarii*),[54] carpenters (*lignorum artifices*), and unskilled laborers. Much of the pay of these workingmen was received in beer, wine, loaves of bread, and articles of clothing, so that it is most difficult to estimate their wage. I have record that the unskilled workers received two or three deniers a day in cash, and the skilled workers some nine deniers.[55] Hoisting of stones and beams was done with a windlass that resembled the capstan on a boat. The spokes were turned, and the hoisting rope was reaved through pulleys. Perhaps the ropes were wetted down before being pulled. The masons stood on scaffolding made from heavy branches and rough logs tied in position.[56] Hand-hewn boards were too precious for such rough purposes. The master doubtless planned in his mind approximately the design which he intended to follow and the method which would enable him to overcome architectural difficulties. There is no reason to deny that he could have sketched some detailed operations on parchment, or on wax tablets, as Villard de Honnecourt did in the following century. Thick walls were seldom solid, except in military construction. The two sides of the wall would be erected with dressed stones facing outward, and then the space in between would be filled with rubble.[57] Today, in repairing such walls, a liquid cement is pumped into this space and allowed to harden. Where the ground was boggy, wooden piles were driven. The stone for such an enterprise as the construction of the new cathedral was brought by barge from Normandy. These barges, heavy with stone, were surely being towed quite regularly up the Seine, by horse power, and were passing under one of the arches of the Petit Pont before depositing their loads at a quay constructed for this very purpose, just a hundred feet or so from where the building was in progress. The stones were being shoved up the slope on wooden rollers. The shouts of the bargemen could not have failed to attract the attention of the scholars on the Petit Pont, who must have leaned over the parapet in the little exedras and made themselves a nuisance to the barges that passed beneath. These workmen in the warmer months wore only their *braies*, or linen underdrawers, a snood or felt cap tied under the chin, and heavy shoes. In colder weather they put on coarse frocks, and *chapes* with hoods.

A weaver at work is described by Alexander:

> A weaver is a horseman on terra firma who leans upon two stirrups and who gives rein constantly to the horse, content with a short journey; but the stirrups representing the condition of his fortune enjoy mutual vicissitudes, since when the one goes up the other is depressed without any indication of rancor.

These two figures of speech describing the weaver will require explanation before we proceed further. The weaver sat on a chair before his loom, with his feet resting on two treadles, compared by Alexander to the stirrups of a horseman. As the operator pushes down on one treadle, the "mounting" heddle raises the threads of one "shed"; when the other treadle is depressed, the first "shed" descends and the other goes up.

The weaver has a [breast] roller to which the cloth to be rolled up is fastened. Let there be beamlike strips marked with holes and facing each other from opposing sides, with wires shaped like a shepherd's crook and the strips going the same way as the warp threads, also [let there be] linen threads as slender as those that are properly associated with fringes [tied to] rods in the heddles, these threads at set intervals; let the weaver draw the warp threads [with such a heddle], the upper series of threads and then the lower. When the weft has been passed through by means of a shuttle, let him beat down the work accomplished, and let the shuttle have an iron or wooden bobbin between open spaces. The bobbin should be filled from a spool, and this spool should be covered in the manner of a clew of yarn with a weight. Let the material of the weft thread be pulled from this weighted spool, so that the one hand of the weaver tosses the shuttle to the other, to be returned vice versa.

But in vain does one weave a cloth unless previously iron combs, working upon the wool, to be softened by flame, have carded the strands in long and reciprocal endeavor. Thus the better and finer parts of the combed wool may be reserved for the thread, with the woolly dregs like coarse tow being left over. Afterwards let the wool thread be aided by the application of madder or woad such as is done in Beauvais, or let the material to be dyed be saturated with frequent dipping in *graine*. Then let the weaver reclaim it; but before it makes its appearance in the form of clothing, it should be subjected to the care of the fuller, demanding frequent washing.[58]

Weaving is so complicated to the uninitiate that we were obliged to make our translation of Alexander's text with the sketch of a twelfth-century loom before us. The weaver sits in a high-backed chair with his feet on the treadles or pedals. The loom has a rectangular frame, and the warp threads run horizontal: they are stretched from the "cane roller" to the "breast roller." On the top of the loom is a frame resembling goal posts. This frame has a pulley over which there passes the thong from the two treadles. As the thong moves down on one side, it lifts the opposite heddle; when it reverses motion, it lifts the other heddle. A spool which feeds the shuttle is not visible in our illustration. The weaver is making a diaper weave, as is shown by a bale which is being rolled up.

The principle of weaving is this. A number of strands of thread, wool or linen, are looped together on a warping board (or the equivalent) and the result is then set up on the loom, with the "cane roller" at the far end and the "breast roller" at the end where the weaver sits. The proper distance between these warp threads is maintained by the wire teeth of the raddles. A heddle consists of two short strips of wood with threads stretched between—one for every two warp threads. These heddle threads, or "leashes," are then looped over alternate warp threads. This means that when one heddle is lifted, it pulls up alternate warps; when the other heddle is lifted, it draws up the remaining warp threads. Each heddle is controlled by a treadle. Diaper weaving was very common at this time. There the weaver does not make plain weave such as we have been describing. The background of the cloth is woven with just one heddle; the second heddle is used to draw out the warp threads that control the design. As it is impossible to get a complicated design with just two heddles, obviously some of the design must have been set into the warp threads by using threads of a different texture at the proper intervals. The background on a diaper weave is not so tight as that of plain weave, because the weft has not been passed alternately through different warp threads. This means that diaper cloth is more absorbent of moisture, and such cloth was therefore suitable for tablecloths and other usages where absorbent material is desirable. Different weft threads could be used, of course, by merely selecting a different bobbin and shuttle at regulated intervals. In a design that was complicated the weaver was obliged to use artistic judgment like any creative artist.[59]

In samite a skein of six silk threads was employed for the warp; this made a strong silk material, a kind of satin. Cendal, or taffeta, was silk woven plain without design; it was glossy on both sides. There is some question about the true nature of *ciclaton*. Apparently the word goes back to Arabic *siglatûn*, and it seems to indicate a silk cloth into which are woven circular seals, or coin dots, of a different color from the background. This would be the same as *paile roé*. We do not know the exact weave of scarlet silk which is often mentioned.[60]

These silks all came from Sicily or Byzantium, or from further east through Alexandria. Since most of them reached France by way of Montpellier, that city was a kind of style center for the best-dressed man and woman of the twelfth century. Often some threads of spun gold or silver were included in the weft.[61] If the gold threads were numerous, the stuff was called *orfrois* or orphreys. Weaving in France, the Low Countries, and England was done with linen and wool threads, sometimes supplemented by cotton. Cotton was the rarest of these three materials, having to be imported from Africa or Mediterranean islands. Cloth could be made heavier by using more skeins in the warp threads, and also by twisting them. "Burel" was a quite loose, plain weave of wool cloth; serge was a tighter weave with twisted warps and possibly even in the twelfth century with the weft crossing over one warp and then under two or more warps, and so on in alternation. Canvas was a loosely woven, heavy linen. Tighter, finer linen was *chainsil*, "shirt cloth." If a cotton weft was used with linen warps, the result was fustian.

Two kinds of rugs were made in Paris: native and Saracen weave. We recognize the Oriental variety, with tied worsted knots, but we are not certain of the native French weave.[62]

The fuller was the "cleaner" of the Middle Ages. He preshrank all fabrics before they were made into clothing. His treatment with fuller's earth (hydrous silicate of alumina) gave body to the wool and helped it take the dye. This also was a cleaning mixture when diluted in hot water, or perhaps in the ammonia of urine. The fuller put the cloth into a trough with his mixture and then walked it with his bare feet; hence Walker and Fuller denote the same trade in England.[63] There were laundresses in the twelfth century. The clothing was soaked in a *leissive*, in a wooden trough, and then was pounded in water to get rid of the loosened dirt. We have observed that wood ashes and caustic soda were mixed to form the *leissive*. Sometimes the first soaking must have been in pure water. Theobald of Cologne drank the water in which he washed the clothes of his monastery.[64]

There were professional embroiderers and needleworkers who were women. Here is a typical example:

> Mahalt she was called and she was a worker; marvelously did she know how to work, to embroider fine gold upon purple silk, to ornament with regal jewels, she knew how to place gems and good stones better than anyone before her. Her fame in this was such that she was sought after by the highest nobles, honored and demanded for her art.[65]

A powerful countess asks her to finish a task as quickly as possible. Unfortunately the Feast of St. Edward the Martyr is due to fall and the woman is annoyed because she must shut up her shop for a day. Her assistant does not understand the identity of St. Edward the Martyr and unwittingly blasphemes against King Edward the Confessor, claiming that she would not take a holiday for him. She is afflicted with a painful ailment in consequence.

Distinction was very clear at this time between the cobbler (*savetier*) and the shoemaker (*cordouanier*). John of Garland refers to the cobblers as being "low" and "vile"; they repaired old shoes. The shoemakers manufactured new footwear, with their "sharp knife, and leather blackened with dye. They sew together their shoes with an awl, a turned-up tool, and pigs' bristles [for thread]."[66]

The dyer had tubs or vats which he heated over a fire. His common dyes were woad, madder, and *graine*. This last was quite expensive. John of Garland notes that a dyer was a marked man out among company because of the coloring which remained under his nails.[67] In the *Roman de Renart* the vat has been placed under a window. Apparently the color was tempered with wood ashes and the combining of the ingredients required experience and skill.[68] Cloth was not the only substance that was colored in this way. In the fabliau *Dou prestre teint* mention is made of dyeing a wooden crucifix.

We have given Alexander's description of a goldsmith at work. He says nothing of a more essential tradesman of this kind—the blacksmith. In order to comprehend the smith's work with iron, we must first say a few words about mining.[69] The twelfth-century man had access to the alluvial deposits of tin in Cornwall and Britain, as well as certain alluvial deposits of coal, silver, and gold. A little digging may have been indulged in, but very little indeed. The shafts that were sunk were shallow, and they followed a visible lode into the earth for a short distance. Britain furnished tin, lead, and silver. Much of the gold used came from the Iberian Peninsula. Presumably the iron deposits in France, Britain, and Spain were worked on the spot. Poitou and Verdun produced fine steel. We know from the lapidaries that hematite, magnetite, and limonite were the common iron ores that were appreciated. A pit was dug on a windy hilltop. A few drains were inserted to allow the molten iron to be drawn off down the hill. A layer of burning charcoal was placed in the pit, followed by a layer of ore, and so on, in alternation. The whole was then sealed with earth at the top. Such a smelter was most inefficient, but the iron that was drawn off did have some carbon in it.

Next came the job of the blacksmith. We have some illustrations showing him at work. He had a furnace burning charcoal, and occasionally mineral coal.[70] This furnace was table high, with a back and a hood. A pair of bellows kept the fire going. After the crude bloom obtained from the smelter was reheated, the smith took a chunk as desired and put it on his anvil, using a long pair of pincers. The anvil might be set on a wooden stump. Then he pounded this heated mass, hour after hour, beating it into shape. He would reheat, observe the proper temper, and once more continue the pounding. This labor gave the smith tremendous muscles and, at the same time, converted the mild steel of the original bloom into a wrought product with the molecules in the right direction. Of course, if the required amount of carbon did not, by chance, unite with the iron in the smelting pit, then the smith was working with wrought iron. He probably did not recognize any difference other than the variations in temper and malleability. These are harder in steel than in iron.[71] Chunks of the original bloom could be drawn through a hole, with strong pincers, and made into thick wire.[72] After a few such drawings, each time through a smaller hole in a plate, the steel (or wrought iron) would have to be retempered. Finally the correct thickness was reached and lengths were cut which could be pounded around a bar of the required size, forming the links of mild steel to be used in manufacturing chain mail. These last few processes were done, of course, by an armorer. If a bloom from the smelting pit appeared too soft, it was called *fer*, not *acier*, and it was employed for commoner uses. As to whether a twelfth-century smith knew how to produce iron as distinct from steel, we cannot say. Perhaps a few did realize that the difference lay in the character of the smelting. Copper and calamine were mingled together, producing bronze.

Theophilus describes an ideal workshop for metal forging and design.[73] It should be a long hall with many windows on the south side. These windows should be five feet apart, a foot above the ground, and should measure three by two feet. A wall, reaching to the ceiling, should divide the hall into two parts: one side for work with copper, tin, and lead; the other, further subdivided into two compartments, for silver and for gold. Theophilus says that to temper iron or steel it should be heated to a glow, sprinkled with powdered ox horn and salt, and plunged into water.[74]

There were various kinds of carpenters: housebuilders, shipbuilders, coopers, wheelwrights, cartwrights, and so on. The twelfth century lumped them together.[75] We quote from Wace:

> The carpenters who came there had great axes dangling from their necks, plainers and adzes draped at their sides; . . . they brought timber from the ships and dragged it to the spot . . . already bored and smoothed off. They brought, in large casks, the joining pegs completely dressed. Before it was evening, they

had constructed a wooden castle; they made a ditch around it.[76]

This is the first evidence I have seen of a prefabricated building!

Wace has enumerated the common tools: axe, adze, plainer, wooden pegs, to which we add iron nails, hammers, and a heavy, clumsy saw, similar to that we use on the woodpile today. The plainers were two-handled and resembled the modern drawknife. Theophilus gives many details on nails. They were about the length of a finger, in three shapes: square, triangular, or round, according to need.[77] There was a special "iron" for putting the heads on nails.[78] The common glue for inside work, cabinetmaking, was a casein glue. To make this, soft cheese was pounded in warm water in a mortar. This was squeezed and allowed to harden. It was then ground to a powder and mixed with quicklime. Much interior woodwork was covered with leather. This was usually untanned horse or ass hide which was made to adhere to the wood by means of this glue.[79] Where our modern cabinetmakers would use veneer, the twelfth-century workman covered the surfaces with leather. For things exposed to weather the artisan had a hide glue. Wood and metal files existed. We have no definite information on the chisel, but since stone and wood carvers used such a tool, we can be sure the carpenter had it also. Here is another passage from Wace: "He had lumber brought and trees carried from all parts of Normandy—pegs made and boards planed, to construct ships and skiffs."[80] John of Garland remarks: "Carpenters make various things with different tools, which we observe in tubmakers who build tubs, containers shod with iron, large measures, wine casks

uable cups by turning quartz on a crude lathe. This was a slow process with the means at their command and could not have been practiced very frequently. Pottery, when made, was turned on a table having at its base a large wheel which was kicked into motion by the potter's feet.[87]

All this time we have been thinking of Alexander Neckam as newly arrived in Paris. But it must have taken him a long time to make the observations which we have recorded. We will therefore carry forward our story and imagine that several years have passed. Louis VII of France has made his journey to Canterbury in August, 1179, which resulted in an illness that proved fatal to him on September 19, 1180. The king was now Philip Augustus, a boy of fifteen, who was busy planning to recover Normandy from old Henry II of England. International complications were now in evidence again. Philip was entertaining the young King Henry in Paris, while the latter was plotting against his father. (Young Henry died in 1183, and then Geoffrey of Brittany became King Philip's guest, until he fell off his horse in 1186 and died in Paris.) The presence of the renegade prince in Paris was embarrassing to Alexander Neckam. Perhaps it was during Henry's stay that Alexander began to see more of the court, and of castles, which we shall describe in the next chapter. Adam dou Petit Pont died in 1183. It may be that Alexander took over his actual classroom on the bridge. Certainly this Alexander was a clever teacher, capable of attracting a flock of students. He remained fond of grammar always, but he had gone on to study medicine, the two laws, and theology. He was insatiably curious about natural phenomena, although he took much of his information on those subjects, without questioning, from the ancient textbooks: Horace, Vergil, Ovid, Juvenal, Lucan, Claudian, Martial, Cassiodorus, Solinus,

Aristotle, and, above all, Pliny. We have no account of Alexander's first experience as a teacher in Paris, but we can borrow from that of Giraldus, who narrates in the third person his own "baptism of fire":

The students hastened with great eagerness to write down all his cases, word for word, as they came from his mouth. . . . A certain noble canon of Notre Dame, son of the Baron of Mont Maurice, who had just been chosen dean of a certain church because of his docility and his love of erudition, on leaving the lecture spoke with Gerald in private and asked him how many years he had studied at Bologna. When Gerald replied that he had never been there, the canon asked where he had studied law. When he learned that Gerald had studied only three years, there in Paris, he went away filled with admiration. Gerald's teacher, whom Gerald visited after dinner, applauded and congratulated his pupil and added: "I would not have taken a hundred sous that you should have been prevented from speaking today before so fine an assemblage of scholars." Matthew of Anjou, who was promoted to cardinal, on taking leave of his students, advised them to go study with young Gerald. They did so and Gerald lectured daily at his lodging: in the morning on the Distinctions of Gratian, in the afternoon on his Cases.[88]

Giraldus (or Gerald) was in Paris when Alexander went there, so that they may have known each other, but Giraldus was older. We can imagine Alexander giving his first lecture before an invited audience and receiving the admiring plaudits at the close.[89] Perhaps his master, Adam, expressed an enthusiasm that was as keen as that shown by the teacher of Giraldus. Doubtless Alexander ceased to live now in his lodging in the Rue de la Boucherie. That was no sort of place to receive students. The "companions" would be separated for good. We can make no guess about the activity of the wayward "monk." Bernard the canon returned, perhaps, to his native heath, for the practice of medicine, or of law. The Goliard might have begun to sing such a song as this:

> My intent is to die in a tavern
> Where wine is closest to the mouth of the dying;
> Then the choir of angels will sing more gladly:
> "May God be propitious to this man of drink."[90]

The date for our next chapter will be 1183–85. Alexander returned to Dunstable in 1186, abandoning his Paris fame. The reason for his departure may have been the strained conditions which now existed between English and French during the final years of the reign of Henry II of England.

Chapter VII

The Baron and His Castle

WHEN Giraldus was leaving France, in 1178 or thereabout, he stopped for a while at Arras. In the morning he looked from the window of his lodging, gazing toward the market place, and saw the men of Philip of Flanders setting up their tilting targets. Soon he saw many youths, *tyrones et robusti juvenes*, breaking lances on some of the targets and piercing others. When he beheld the Count himself, he saw him accompanied by his barons, all clothed in silk. The exercise lasted an hour. The Count left, followed by the others, and all was silent. Giraldus was provoked to reflection on the ways of life.[1] I am citing this passage because it is a good starting point for us to begin describing the dress and the customs of the noble class of the time.

The baron when clothed in nonmilitary dress was much like the burgher except for a greater display of wealth in silks and embroidery. No night clothing of any kind was worn in the twelfth century, by man or woman, so we start from scratch when we clothe our subject early in the morning. Alexander mentions the articles of dress:

Let a man at rest [not traveling] have a *pellice* [fur-lined garment], and a *cote* or *bliaut* provided with sleeves and openings, slit at the crotch. *Braies* are needed to cover the lower limbs, and stockings or *chauces* should be worn around the legs, while covering the feet with laced boots or leather shoes. An undershirt of muslin, silk, or cotton, or linen—the fur of the outer mantle should be gris or vair [gray squirrel], or rabbit, or *lérot* [dormouse ?], and the mantle's edging can be of sable or marten, or beaver, or of otter, or fox fur. . . .[2]

The first garment which the man put on was his *braies*, or loose linen underdrawers, fastened at the waist by the *braiel*, a belt of cloth usually studded with metal buttons and nails.[3] Next the *chauces* were drawn on. These stockings were of wool or silk, with a wide band placed above or below the knee as a garter. They were thicker than hose we would wear today, but the mediaeval wearer wanted them as *dougees* or "fine" as he could get them. The *chainse* was now added; this had long tight sleeves, as a rule, and these had to be sewed on the wearer every time the shirt was put on. Such a shirt could be *risdee*, or "pleated," and it could be embroidered in various ways.[4] Over the shirt went the *cote*, or *bliaut*, which was the principal outer garment. This could be of rich silk, sometimes brocaded, sometimes embroidered. This garment might be called also a *sorcot*. Its sleeves were full, but fairly short, allowing the tight-fitting sleeves of the *chainse* to be visible to the wrist. After 1180 the sleeves of the *bliaut* tended to become longer and tighter: *Bien ert seant, al puin estreit*. The neck opening was closed in front with a brooch, or *fermail*, and the side opening was laced. A well-dressed man would have a handsome embroidered neck to his *chainse*, and the *cote* was cut sufficiently low to

make this embroidery show. A poorly dressed man either dispensed with the *chainse* altogether or wore it under a *sorcot* that was higher in the neck and longer in the sleeves. Fine linen was the distinguishing mark of a "gentleman."[5] In cold weather the man wore a *pellice* or fur-lined garment, with loose sleeves or none at all. This usually went over the *cote* or *sorcot*. With the addition of shoes or boots, and an outer belt tied at the waist, the gentleman was now ready for a formal appearance. The belt might have a knot in it as a mnemonic device, made in one of the long ties. If a man had a cap, he wore it indoors as well as outdoors, without distinction.

In the absence of pockets, which did not come into use until the sixteenth century, one was obliged to use various makeshifts. A story is told of Thomas Becket sitting at table with the ends of his sleeves tied as though containing something. This was not unusual, but he was asked what was in them. He answered, "Daisies," and lo and behold, when he opened his sleeves, daisies fell out as by a miraculous act.[6] A coin, or anything else, could be carried knotted in the skirt of the *chainse*. A purse, or *ausmoniere*, hung on the belt.[7]

Ordinary shoes had thin soles, like our moccasins, and their cut showed variation. The toes were never unusually long at this date. The tops came above the anklebone and were occasionally beaded or otherwise ornamented along the edge. There was a slight slash at the front edge, making it easier to pull the shoe off and on. Sometimes there was a slightly projecting tongue in front and behind. A boot was similar to the shoe, except that the sole was considerably thicker, and there was a soft top extending halfway up the calf.[8]

The mantle was worn over the *cote*, and *pellice*, in cold

enough weather. This could fasten on the right shoulder with a brooch, or it might be pinned at the neck opening.[9] The material, as we have been informed by Alexander, could be of wool or silk with a fur edging. This was for the outside. The inside had a softer fur lining. The appearance of vair is quite apparent in some illuminations. The white fur of the squirrel formed the background, and pieces of gray were sewed onto this in ten or twelve rows of "tongues."[10] The idea is similar to what we find in ermine where the white fur has the black tufts from the stoat's tail sewed on according to design.

The average man wore his hair fairly shaggy, long at the nape of the neck, but never bobbed as all our theatrical costumers like to picture it. There was invariably a part in the middle, although the hair could be combed forward to give an appearance of bangs.[11] Both baron and burgher often wore a cap. A soft brimless one, with a forward tilt, was very stylish; on the other hand, the man might wear a very low crown with a narrow rolled brim.[12] Alexander tells the story of a monkey who, when he had spotted a bald man in a crowd, always rushed to snatch the poor fellow's hat.[13]

Color was quite brilliant in all these garments. The fashion had not yet come that considered it sensible for a layman to deck himself in somber fawn or gray. To be sure, the clergy were dressed in black or dark tones. Reds, greens, blues, and yellows were in evidence everywhere, and the designs of the materials were elaborate. From the viewpoint of our twentieth-century tastes there must have been many clashing colors. Sometimes a contrasting note of black was introduced. Yvain, for instance, was given a pair of black stockings by the ladies of the Fairy Morgue. Black *chauces* with a red *cote* would have made a striking combination.

Shoes, as we observed in our paragraph on the *cordouannier*, were most often cut from black leather. We know from the *Roman de la Rose* (first half of the thirteenth century) that there was such a thing as having a good tailor: "And so you should give your garment to someone who knows how to cut [*taillier*], who can place the stitches properly and make the sleeves fit. Shoes and boots you should have fresh and new, and see that they fit so close that the low-class fellows will argue how you got into them and how you will get out."[14] Although this testimony comes thirty or forty years after the period we are considering, the advice would surely have been the same. Let us not get into the habit of thinking that a mediaeval man just ran around in a "sack" without any standard of elegance. Good fit and rich cloth were things that he desired. We would find his dress lacking in one respect, however. Pressing clothing with a hot iron to remove wrinkles was not much in vogue. The mediaevals did make frequent use, however, of a gauffering iron, to put pleats into their linen.[15]

The dress of a woman is next to be considered.[16] Basically she matched the man, garment for garment, except that she never wore *braies*. The Middle Ages were filled with jokes about the one who wears the *braies* in the family—the boss. The cut of a lady's clothes was, of course, entirely different. Her long linen *chainse* trailed to the ground, while the *bliaut* or *cote* was nearly the same length. A little of the *chainse* might show at the bottom, as well as at the neck. Her sleeves on her *bliaut* were full and open, but they had long points which dropped from the cuff or underside of the sleeve to the ground. Preachers had many nasty things to say about these exaggerated sleeve points. Some of the points were, in fact, so long that they had to be kept knotted to avoid trailing on the floor. As was the case with the men, the wealthier women had fine tight sleeves on their shirts and these were prominent, extending to the wrist. Women of lesser style carried the sleeves of their *bliaut* to the wrist. Women habitually wore a double belt of cloth, with long ties instead of a buckle. In order to make their *bliaut* fit more snugly above the waistline, it became the fashion to slash the *chainse* and the *bliaut* from the armpit to the waist; these openings were laced, permitting a little of the bare flesh to show.[17] When in a state of undress, a woman might move about in her fur *pellice*, with or without a *chainse* underneath. It was even possible to move about in the *chainse* alone, but this was considered insufficient.[18] In cold weather women followed the prevailing custom of wearing a mantle over their other garments.[19] An attractive woman liked to wear jewelry. Giraldus speaks of this. A lovely girl whom he saw on an occasion had a belt, a purple mantle fastened with a gold pin at the breast, earrings, a necklace or "torque," rings on her fingers, which were set with stones, and a golden band around her hair. Bracelets or "armillae" were frequently worn.[20]

Women kept their hair parted in the middle, with two long plaits dropping as far toward the ground as possible. This style was so usual that it made women look somewhat alike.[21] The braids were plaited, or the strands could be intertwined with ribbon. A band around the forehead held the hair in place. A wimple could cover the hair and be held by the headband. Some older women dyed their hair when it turned gray.[22] Ladies used also white powder and vermilion coloring on their faces. Guillaume de Lorris does not complain so much about this, but he warns men not to do so: "Do not paint yourself or use cosmetics; that is for women only, or for men of bad renown."[23] Cercamon remarked about his lady: "Yes, and she is not painted up."[24]

A foppish young man might wear a band of flowers around his hair, like a woman.[25]

We have made a few comments on the dress of the less well-to-do. The dress of a peasant working in the fields will be considered in the next chapter. Here are a few descriptions of ordinary citizens. The first is of a young girl: "She had a little shirt of linen, a white *pellice* of ermine, and a *bliaut* of silk; her stockings were embroidered with gladioli designs, and her shoes, by which she was tightly shod, had May flowers."[26] Marcabrun pictures a well-to-do peasant girl (her father was a knight): "She wears *chape*, frock, and *pellice*, and a knitted shirt [*treslissa*], shoes, and woolen stockings."[27]

The dress of a male burgher, or merchant, is next: "Count William wore a frock [*gonnele*] of such burel as there was in the land, and on his legs a pair of blue stockings, shoes of ox leather, which are tight on the stockings. He girds on a belt. . . . There hangs a knife in its scabbard, very fair. . . ."[28] The fisherman who changed clothes with Tristan wore a frock which was not slit at the crotch (*sanz gerun*) since he did no riding; it was of hairy wool (*esclavine*) and had a hood attached.[29]

The men found shaving very difficult. The razor used was somewhat like a carving knife in appearance. A thirteenth-century description of the barber's equipment is this: "Barber without a razor, without scissors, who do not know how to cut or shave, you have neither basin nor towel nor the wherewithal to heat clear water."[30] Such a barber was an itinerant. As he used no shaving soap, he must have softened the beard by soaking it long in hot water. The result could only have been painful. Men in the latter half of the twelfth century were doubtless only half trimmed most of the time. They tried to keep shaven, but they did not undergo the operation more often than once a week. Consequently they were usually seen with a slight stubble, except on their shaving days.[31] Older men continued to affect the beard and mustache, which were sometimes flowing and curly.[32] Baths were taken, but not very frequently.[33] In Paris there were public bathhouses, near Saint-Jacques de la Boucherie, where it was possible to go early in the morning, shortly after rising. Private bathtubs in the home resembled wide-mouthed barrels of wood. They could be turned bottom up and used as a table stand, placed against the wall. When the tub was in use for bathing, a short pole might be added which provided a tentlike awning for the occupant. A stool was often placed inside, permitting the bather to soak for a longer time. It was pleasant to bathe in the company of a friend. Those who could afford it kept two tubs which were used side by side.[34] Water was brought from the kitchen fire. The plot of Marie's lai *Equitan* illustrates these points. When Yvain is being cared for by Lunete, "she has him bathed every day and washed and rubbed down [*aplanoiier*]."[35] The Fairy Morgue and her attendants give similar treatment: "They bathe him and wash his head; they have him shaved and rubbed down with ointment [*reoignier*]."[36] It will be evident from these passages that a knight could be handled like a modern athlete. Such treatment, of course, was special favor, and not meted out to everyone. A tired guest might have only his hands, face, and neck washed. Rescued prisoners were apt to be very unkempt, so we are not surprised that Charlemagne had certain ones "trimmed and very well barbered; their hair was cut and their nails were clipped."[37]

So far we have made little mention of gloves. These were made from lamb, rabbit, or fox skin. All classes used them, especially hunters, travelers, and knights. In seasons of extreme cold the clergy, except the celebrant and those taking Communion, wore something of the kind, and workmen also used them. The mitten was the commonest form. It could be used for carrying small sums of money.[38] You will recall that the chambermaid described by Alexander (p. 83) has the fingertips cut from her gloves, and this may have been a widespread practice among tradespeople who were constantly using their fingers.

We are now brought to the important question of the knight and his armor.

> He caused a Limoges rug to be spread before him on the ground. The other ran to get the arms. . . . And he brought them on the rug. Erec sat opposite on a leopard design which was portrayed on the rug. He prepares to arm himself. First he caused to be laced on his *chauces* of white steel. Afterwards he dons a *hauberc* so valuable that one could not cut a single link. . . . For it was made completely of silver of fine woven links. . . . When they had armed him with the *hauberc* a boy laced upon his head a helmet reinforced with a gold band more shiny than a mirror.[39]

If we omit the silver and the gold, we have a fairly good picture of the arming of a knight.

The *hauberc* was woven from a series of round metal links, usually of steel, each link locking with the six or more surrounding ones. The result was a springy mesh, weighing sixty pounds or so, which broke the force of a blow by its resilience.[40] It retarded also the blow from a sharp edge. It was not so satisfactory against an arrow well shot. There were various ways of adding to this protection. The links themselves could be doubled in number, though woven into a single coat, or a second coat of mail, perhaps only extending over the torso, could be added. A lining made of felted animal hair was sewed into the *hauberc*.[41] In addition, it was customary to wear an *auqueton* or *gambois* of quilted cotton under the mail. Some of the old-style *haubercs*, which consisted of heavy canvas or leather coats with metal rings or hard leather plates sewed over the surface, were still in use as late as the year 1200, chiefly among the *serjanz*. The *hauberc* had a short sleeve, like that of civil dress. This meant that the forearm was not protected. When the knight was going into battle, long mailed gloves or mittens could be laced to the sleeves of the *hauberc*. As is evident from the passage just quoted, many knights used *chauces* of mail. These were occasionally referred to as *genouillieres*. On the other hand, some knights preferred to wrap their legs in heavy puttees.[42] A *sorcot* of handsome cloth was often worn over the *hauberc*, giving a natty appearance.[43]

The *hauberc* had a hood, called a *coiffe*, which slipped over the head. This was, naturally, of the same material as the *hauberc* itself. A more prudent knight would place a close-fitting steel cap over this. Others set the helmet directly over the *coiffe*. The helm or helmet was pot shaped with a protecting bar, called a "nasal," extending down over the nose. The helm was laced to the *hauberc* and under the chin with leather thongs. Before entering combat, a knight laced across his mouth and over his throat a triangular piece of mail called a *ventaille*, which protected those areas. In shape the helmet could be completely pot shaped, or it might be conical; it could be rounded and have a slight tip forward similar to the style of a civilian cap.[44] Helmets were ordinarily quite heavily ornamented. Much of the goldsmith's work was expended in setting stones and filigree work on the surface of helms. This battle attire was fatiguing in warm weather. In the

Aspremont there is a comment on this.[45] In the last fifteen or twenty years of the twelfth century a great innovation was under way: the "cheesebox helm" was coming into use among those who could afford such new equipment. This was a heavy metal box which had a grating before the face and rested on the shoulders. It was some time before this style took definite hold, and even then the old nasal helm remained in use among the knights and men-at-arms who could not afford more expensive equipment.[46]

I am unable to define the "broigne" with reference to the *hauberc*. Both designate a coat of mail. It has been suggested that the broigne was a lighter variety, but I am not certain of that. These were, of course, subject to rust.[47] It was customary to keep them lacquered with a kind of varnish. The natural tinge of such a coating was yellow, so we find constant mention of a *hauberc saffré*. The varnish could contain coloring matter. Madder or sinople gave a red color which was popular. Black, white, and green were often met with. The battering of combat and weather soon removed these lacquers. The rusted garment was then rolled in a barrel of loose sand and touched up once more.[48] It was considered quite fashionable for a knight to have his arms of uniform color: that is, *hauberc*, helm, *gambois*, *chauces*, and silken *sorcot*. (Similarly, it was just as chic for a lady's costume to be matching in all details.)[49] The knight's horse could be protected by a mailed coat. We find descriptions of horse armor extending to the top of the animal's hoofs; but such an arrangement was ungainly and heavy.[50] It was all that a destrier could do to carry an armed knight nimbly into battle, and the horse's efficiency was seriously handicapped by an additional coat of mail flapping around his feet.[51]

The offensive equipment of the knight consisted of a

lance of ash wood tipped with metal, a heavy sword, and very often a mace or a battle-axe hanging at the saddle-bow.[52] The battle-axe of the period had a wooden handle and a two-headed blade. The mace was a heavy ball of iron, usually with spikes on the surface of the ball; it had an iron handle. A knight who had a following of other knights and men-at-arms nailed a "gonfanon," a square or rectangular banner, to the top of his lance shaft, just below the head. This helped to rally his followers. A knight who did not have a following could have a *penon* or streamer-like pennant. It was considered quite chic for the device on the shield, the banner, and the *cognisance* or "token" to match. Three nails are specified as holding the banner in place. During combat the gonfanon became bloodied, but the bearer was proud of this symbol of his prowess.[53] The most effective way of using the heavy lance is described by Usamah, the Moslem warrior, who fought the Franks in many a Crusade conflict: "He who is on the point of striking with his lance should hold it . . . as tightly as possible with his hand and under his arm, close to his side, and should let the horse run and effect the required thrust; for if he should move his hand while holding the lance or stretch out his arm with the lance, then his thrust would have no effect whatsoever and would result in no aim."[54] It would seem from this that no special support for the lance blow was required, other than the strength of the elbow drawn close to the side. For some years now there has been perplexity over the word *fautre* or *feutre*. Knights are frequently mentioned as holding the lance *sor le fautre*.[55] A *fautre* is usually a rug or covering. In the military sense a *fautre* is the padded cloth which is laid on the horse's saddle. A lance on the *fautre* would mean, in that sense, that the hand holding the weapon is resting on the saddlecloth, or that the butt of the lance is reposing there. When Usamah remarks that a lance should not be held out from the side, he has in mind the heavy charging lance. The *espie(u)* was a lighter variety which was hurled at arm's length. This particular weapon is common on the Bayeux Tapestry, but we have evidence that it was passing from use in the second half of the twelfth century. Of course, darts and javelins (short ones, with feathering similar to that of an arrow) remained in use and were hurled in this way, with the arm held out and back.

The sword belt also had a tie buckle, not a metal one with a tongue. The scabbard was frequently made of two pieces of wood bound together by thongs; it could be of metal. The *renges* of the belt formed a loop through which the scabbard was thrust. The crosspiece or *helz* of the sword prevented the scabbard and sword from slipping through the loop. The sword had a broad, heavy blade, usually ornamented with lettering of some kind. The grip or *poing*, and perhaps the hilt, could be wrapped with metal rings (*mangon?*), or even just wire. Then again, the hilt and grip might have lettering instead of rings or wire. At the end of the grip was the *pom*, a metal ball which served as a counterweight, balancing the weapon so that the fulcrum was at the hilt.[56]

The shield was commonly of linden wood boards, nailed side by side and cemented further with the help of casein glue. These boards were covered on the exterior with heavy hide. On the inner side was a strap through which the arm was slipped and which was called the *enarme*. To the top corners of the shield were fastened a thin strap, often a strip of cloth, which was intended to hold the shield when slung around the neck. The hide covering of the shield was painted, and perhaps varnished on top of that. It could be silver, red, blue, yellow, etc., or it might have a design painted on it: lion, leopard, fleur-de-lis, or Madonna.[57] Heraldry was only beginning to appear, and there were as yet no fixed designs owned by a family. Giraldus says that French knights preferred flowers and peaceful devices, that the English warriors wanted animals.[58] The shields were tall, and they made ideal stretchers for carrying a wounded or dead knight off the field.[59] A boss or *boucle*, probably of bronze, was fitted at the upper center. It caught the blade of the opponent's sword. A smaller, round shield was named a "targe," and it might have a series of *boucles* around the rim.[60]

When going into action against each other, two knights would take position at the required distance. They spurred forward, dropped their reins on the necks of the horses, raised their shields on the left arm, and held the lance as Usamah specified (in our quotation above). If one knight was unhorsed, the other was not obliged to get down. If he did not, he was apt to have his mount killed by the adversary who was seeking for equal advantage. If both lances were broken, or if both men were unmounted, the swords were drawn and used until the battle was over.[61] The *chansons de geste* exaggerated very much the blows given and received. Usamah is our authority as to what was considered a heavy blow. He records that one Frank cut three ribs of his Moslem adversary and with the same lance thrust severed the arm at the elbow. This was considered a great show of strength.[62]

The *serjant*, who served on foot and on horse, was a professional soldier of the bourgeois or peasant class, in the employ of baron or churchman. Sometimes it was difficult to distinguish between a *serjant* and a knight. Usamah has a story about this. He tells of a tall "knight," a Frank who wore double-linked armor and carried a spear in his hand, although he had no shield. This man was guarding the door of a tower very effectively. Later, when the Franks had been captured and the men were lined up, each to be told the amount of his ransom, this man had a high price put upon him. He laughed and admitted that he was only a *serjant*, receiving two dinars pay per month.[63] A *serjant's* armor was apt to be a generation out of date—probably consisting still of heavy canvas with rings or leather plates sewed upon it, at the date we are now considering (1184 or 1185).[64] This fighting man did not always have a helmet; he could be content with the *coiffe* over his head, and perhaps a *ventaille*.[65] When on guard duty he bore a *guisarme*. This weapon resembled a lance, but the blade had an extra point which branched downward like a hook or talon.[66] The hook could be caught in the *hauberc* of any unruly person who tried to pass without good reason. *Serjanz* carried also Danish axes, darts, javelins, and lances. Some of these men were archers, although there were many archers who were not *serjanz*. More frequently the archer was a peasant or an apprentice at a trade who could use the bow, and who was pressed into service when hostilities began.[67] The bow used was of medium length; the arrow was of wood, with either barbed or bolt type of head, feathered, of course. The arrows were carried in a quiver slung over the left shoulder. Archers were deployed behind cover.[68] The crossbow was greatly respected, and the accuracy and strength of this weapon were considered so murderous that the Second Lateran Council (in 1139) had forbidden its use. Both Richard the Lion-Hearted and King Philip Augustus were making some use of crossbowmen despite the injunction that came from Rome. By the close of the century the decision of the Council was widely disregarded; bands of crossbowmen were being hired from Italy. The operation of this weapon is quite simple. The bow itself was of steel and quite small. It had a wooden stock, forming a T with the bow. A trigger was rigged on this wooden stock with a hook that caught the bowstring. The operator would shoot with the bow in much the same way we use a modern gun, sighting down the wooden stock and pulling the trigger.[69] Most of the twelfth-century bows were not heavy enough to require a stirrup and windlass for cocking the string. An ordinary bow could shoot an arrow about 150 yards; a crossbow was good for 250 yards.[70] These distances should be borne in mind, as a mediaeval man measured distances roughly by *archies* or "bowshots" and *traiz d'arbalete* or "crossbow shots." A *serjant* was occasionally armed with a big, heavy club.

Before we turn to Alexander's description of a castle, it would be well to have a closer look at feudal society. The principal unit was the knight or "chevalier." The son of a knight could normally expect to follow in his father's footsteps and be knighted by his father's overlord, or by some other patron or relative of the family. In addition, a young man of the *serjant* class, if he became a favorite, or if he distinguished himself by bravery or devotion, could hope for the same thing. Consequently it was not rare to find knights whose parents were peasants, and even serfs. Certain of the romances, not to mention *exempla* and fabliaux, owe their plots to this circumstance.[71] Too much importance has been attached to the ceremony of making a knight. The important act was that the young man should kneel in obeisance before the other, who then gave him a slight blow with the flat of the sword, on his shoulder or the back of his neck, bidding him rise and calling him a knight. Witnesses were present if possible. It was then necessary to see that the new knight was provided with a set of arms and armor, including a horse, so that he could function. Because the twelfth-century man dearly loved a party, this simple ceremony was made the excuse for a high celebration, which was not at all necessary.[72] If it was the lord's son who was to be knighted, word might be sent to all the vassals, who were expected to contribute a "relief," or gift, and then come in person. If monetary assistance was not required, the lord might take advantage of an occasion when his court was well attended for other reasons. A number of young men of lesser fortune would be selected to stand by the young lord and receive knighthood at the same time.[73] It was largely in the thirteenth century that a mystical element was added to the procedure, emphasizing the need for purity, and demanding that the candidates should bathe, keep vigil the night before in a chapel, and so on. This was a kind of play acting. I am not saying that elements of it were not occasionally practiced in the twelfth century,[74] and I believe that in the thirteenth there were still many "spot promotions" where knighthood was conferred without the trimmings.

Once he had become a knight, the young man would hope to be given a bride and a fief. This coincidence of events was doubtless more common in the romances than it was in real life. The average young knight was expected to follow the tourneys for a while, where he could acquire reputation and a certain amount of cash. The making of money in this way was simple. At a tourney the victor of each single combat was entitled to the horse and the armor of his vanquished adversary. If enough of these were collected, even though the young man might lose his own in the course of the tourney, there were always merchants who would pay well. When the young knight more or less settled down and received a fief and usually a wife, he was still required to give service to his overlord at certain seasons of the year and in emergencies. But there were many knights who preferred to follow such service as an all-year-round profession. They allowed their fiefs to be governed *in absentia,* and they took up personal residence at the lord's castle, or nearby. They performed the duties of *chevalier dou guet* (watch officer), seneschal (major-domo), and many other services. Some of them liked fighting so much that they continued, as older men, to move about among the tourneys, looking for hostilities and private wars. These were professionals, and they were very necessary for the maintenance of society as it was then constituted. Unfortunately for the overlords, too many men found this mode of life boring and impractical. They settled down on their fiefs with their wives and children and begrudged the month, during the summer, when they were obliged to appear in person at the court, with full equipment. When possible they paid scutage, a tax which enabled the lord to hire professionals to take their place. This was when there was actual fighting. Abbot Samson hired four mercenary knights for forty days at a cost of 36 marks ($252). These men were to serve King Richard in Normandy in 1199.[75]

There were varying types of fiefs. One who had only a house and a little land was called a *chasé*—a sort of "tenant knight." Another, who was placed in charge of other knights, with a small castle and a surrounding town, was a small baron. Then there was the larger baron, who had jurisdiction over a county or shire and was therefore a count. Higher up the scale was a duke, who was the lord over a large region in a kingdom. A marquis was a count whose district was a border territory held with some insecurity. Even the small landowners might hold directly from a king or a duke. Such a landowner who owed no rents at all except service in a major emergency was called an *aloué*. In most cases, however, there was a complicated chain, a system of subinfeudation. A large landowner had under him many peoples with smaller parcels of land, some owing him knight's service (occasionally estimated in fractions, as the service of two and a half knights), and many owing *serjant's* service. The great inconsistency was that a man who was not a knight might owe the service of two and a half knights, and a knight might be obligated for a number of sergeancies. A peasant also could owe some of these services, which were above his social rank. Occasionally a knight would be unsuccessful in securing the patronage of any overlord and would be reduced to the position of a landholding peasant, or even farther down the scale. Many are the instances in the romances and *chansons de geste*, and in the *exempla* and *fabliaux*, where an impoverished knight marries his daughter to a well-to-do peasant.[76]

In this present narrative we are thinking of the small baron who holds a castle, and possibly a small town around it. In the following chapter we will be concerned with the occupant of a manor house, a *chasé*, who is not far removed from a peasant farmer, and this will bring us to consider the peasant class in some detail.

A baron followed the educational system of his class. Children born into his family were kept at home with the women until approximately seven years of age. Then they were sent elsewhere to be educated.[77] The brother of a boy's mother was an excellent choice, and this practice may have had its roots buried deep in early legal and matriarchal custom. The girls who were sent off in this way spent their time with the wife of the overlord, in the women's apartment, on the third floor of the castle. This is the explanation of the bevy of maidens who are often mentioned as being grouped around the mistress of a castle. They learned many things: sewing, embroidery, weaving, a little music, and polite conversation; often they learned to read. We know that women of this class could frequently read French, and even some Latin. This instruction would be given by the resident clerk or chaplain. The boys from the age of seven to twelve or fourteen also passed much of this time with the women. They were the *vallez*, who learned to wait on table, set up beds, and do various household duties. When their voices started to change, or perhaps even earlier as they showed manly strength, they were sent downstairs to the lord himself. There they were squires or *escuier*. The emphasis was now placed upon learning how to ride and to handle the heavy lance. The *tyrones* and *robusti juvenes* observed by Giraldus in the market place at Arras were of this kind. Just when such boys received knighthood and went their own way depended upon many factors. The boys were usually considered of age at twenty-one, but it might be earlier. Girls, of course, were ready for husbands at fourteen or fifteen years of age, and occasionally they were married off even earlier.

We will assume that a small baron near Paris, whom Alexander knows, has invited him to pay a visit. The baron is of sufficient affluence to have with him the sons and daughters of a few lesser knights. These boys relieve him of the necessity of having servant help except in the kitchen and kitchen yard. There will be also a few upstairs maids who work under the direction of the chamberlains. The land is worked by peasant tenants. One of the older squires will be designated as seneschal to oversee all the operations of the household; still others are chamberlains. A cleric, whom the baron had selected from among his serfs and sent to school specifically for this purpose, serves as household

Crenelated and buttressed wall of the Château des Comtes, Ghent

Main hall of the Château des Comtes

chancellor or secretary. He was probably not an ordained priest. A younger boy is chamberlain for the women's apartment. A professional or mercenary knight (*soudoier*) will be in charge of the stables and of the military training of the young men. He is called the constable, and it is his task to direct the practice with targets and to lead the boys on expeditions hither and yon. One or two of the squires may be designated as *mareschals* to assist in this work. If a private war breaks out, the constable will be responsible for arranging the details of combat or defense, in which case he will be obliged to use the services of some more full-fledged knights who owe service to the baron but who are seldom present at his castle. A few additional *soudoiers* also will be hired in this emergency. Minor officials were the provost and the *voiier*, or road overseer.[78] These offices would in all probability be held by *serjanz* or well-to-do peasants.

The young people slept on beds that were set up in the *grant salle* of the baron's donjon, on the second floor. The kitchen knaves lived below stairs, on shakedowns which were set out at night. The lady and her few girl attendants had their beds set up in the hall on the third floor, which was kept rather well guarded. Someone was on watch at the door which led from the spiral staircase in the thick wall of the donjon. The lord, of course, would visit his wife at night in her bed which was set apart in the women's hall. If the reader would prefer to picture the daily routine of a count, a more important baron, he has only to surround his castle with a considerable town and imagine the presence of more knights in his household. The seneschal would be a capable and trusted knight, and so on. The chancellor would be a priest and chaplain. The count's administrative duties would require the assistance of a viscount or sheriff. We do not find a great deal of information about a minor class of officers known as *hirauz*, or "heralds." These were surely men of the *serjant* class who carried messages and made announcements in the public streets and places.[79] Some of them must have had some schooling which enabled them to read and do simple ciphering. A minstrel could become a herald.[80] In a royal or ducal household the heralds would come from the noble class.

The real test of a herald's efficiency was evident when his lord announced a tourney. These affairs, which gave the same relaxation and pleasure that a modern American finds in a World Series or a championship football game, were held all year round, except during the Truces of God, but they were especially frequent just after Easter.[81] The baron holding a tourney invited many of his friends and considered it unfriendly if they did not come. Strangers were welcome if they did not provoke hostility because of personal idiosyncrasies. When the knights arrived, they were too many to lodge in the castle, even when all floor space was given over to beds. The knights were expected to rent quarters from the burghers in the town which surrounded the castle. On occasion burghers were encouraged to relinquish their houses temporarily and the knights moved in. There was a great deal of noise, and a considerable amount of minor vice, but everybody in those days took delight in the celebrations—even displaced families. The participants would be divided into groups, haphazardly or according to some prearranged plan. Sometimes one group would hold the town against another, as was the case in the *Chaitivel* of Marie de France. More often the *serjanz* and the heralds marked off a space, in an open field or between the inner and outer wall of the castle, which enabled the nonparticipants to view the exercises from good vantage points. The space between the two walls was called the *lices*, or "lists," and this term was transferred to any enclosure which was set off. The two sides lined up in double or multiple ranks, and each man proceeded to choose an adversary on the opposite side. At a given signal those who had already made mutual selection charged each other, full tilt. Then those behind them made their choices, and the fighting went merrily on. When a knight was overcome and confessed to be recreant, he made himself known to his conqueror, and then the winner remounted and looked around for another victim. In this way the field was gradually eliminated. Heralds must have kept track of the vanquished for a later squaring of accounts in horses and armor. The day's victor was highly acclaimed. From some of the romances we observe that a tourney lasting for three days was considered first-rate. A certain number of loges must have been set up to shelter the privileged ladies who sat close on the field. These must have consisted of four posts with an awning stretched across the top, and I am quite sure they never had a flooring or a railing. High-ranking ladies would be seated on low stools or cushions, and those less privileged sat on the ground strewn with rushes, or stood. I am imagining this setup because the audience at a tourney has been portrayed quite frequently in our modern illustrations and motion pictures, and the scenes portrayed resemble more the grandstand in a baseball park. The twelfth century had very little planed lumber. When the knights finally left for home, the merchants were richer, the host was poorer, and much damage had been done to hearts and reputations.

Alexander's daily contact with the baronial and fighting class had been constant during his stay in the city of Paris, but it was mostly unconscious. The royal provost lived in the fortified gate known as the Petit Chastelet, and everyone was obliged to pass through the narrow archway of this gate when he went to the suburb on the left bank. Alexander traveled back and forth a half-dozen times a day. There were knights and *serjanz* in the passageway, but they had learned through long associations to recognize a clerk intent upon his studies and practicing his usual mode of life. They simply paid no attention. Those whom they stopped for toll and questioning were driving carts or pack animals. Some of the *serjanz* were "ratty characters," who were recognized as such by the students. A Villon of the twelfth century could have found as good material in his day as François found at hand in the fifteenth century. The Grant Chastelet was even more thronged with knights and men-at-arms, but Alexander did not pass that way very often. Fortunately the presence of the king's court kept a decided hush over the military. Louis VII, followed in this by his son King Philip, had always liked Paris and was usually in residence there. Neither tolerated much disorder, and this helped to create an uneasy but peaceful atmosphere. The chief advisers of King Louis had not been of the knightly class. They were the Templar Thierri Galeran, Bouchard le Veautré, Adam Bruslard, Cadurc, and Gilbert la Fleche. They had not been popular, but money, not mayhem, had been their chief weakness. King Philip was continuing the system. His *Curia Regis* was full of professional lawyers, and he was not encouraging hereditary rights to office as claimed by certain noble families. He abolished the chancellorship in 1185. The *Curia Regis* was beginning to inquire into the conduct of affairs on the large feudal domains. Where immediate information was not presented to him, the King sent his commissaries to investigate, and judgment was suspended until they reported. At this date (1185) the Archbishop of Reims, Guillaume de Champagne, uncle to the King, had just been put in charge of the *Curia*. Already the King was experimenting with his system of bailiffs who reported directly to the King three times a year. They were to travel about and survey the collecting of revenues and the administration of royal provosts. All these details add up to the fact that Paris and the immediate surroundings were good examples of law and order during the last year that Alexander Neckam remained in France.[82] In that very year (1185) the King had called a meeting of the Parisian burghers to consider paving the main streets in Paris. To be sure, all this time, King Philip was eyeing with determination any change whereby he could limit ecclesiastical authority over the students. He was insisting that where laity and clergy were both involved the entire jurisdiction should belong to the royal courts. As yet this had been bitterly opposed by the Bishop of Paris.

Before we bring Alexander to the gate of the small castle to which he has been invited, we will give his description of a castle in general:

> If a castle is to be decently built, it should be girded by a double moat. Nature must provide the proper site as the mote or mound should be set upon native rock. Where Nature fails, the benefit of skill must take over, and a heavy massive wall, made from stone and cement, has to grow or rise as an arduous task. Outside this a fearsome stockade with squared pales and prickly briars should be well erected. Afterwards a wide ditch in the space between should be enjoyed. The foundation of the stone wall must be joined with the bowels of the earth. The wall should be supported with pilasters inside and out. The surface of it must be evened by the mason's trowel. Crenels should be separated by proper intervals. Small towers [on this wall] must flank the mainkeep, or donjon, which is set on the high place in the very center of everything.[83] [On the wall] let there not be lacking baskets containing huge boulders to be thrown down if the castle is strongly besieged. In order that

the defenders may not be obliged to surrender, there should be supplies of spelt and wheat, and haunches and bacon, and other meat put in storage: sausages and entrails, meat puddings, pork, mutton, beef, lamb, and various vegetables. One needs a spring that flows continuously, small posterns, portcullises, and underground passages by which those bringing aid may move about without being seen. One needs also lances and catapults, shields, small light targes, crossbows, clubs, slings, and sticks. Balearic slings, pegs of iron, boards, knotty cudgels, and towers hurling fire by which the assaults of the besiegers may be eluded and their purpose foiled.[84] You should have also iron beams, siege mantlets, baskets, heavy slings, and other machines. There should be there palfreys or riding horses, and pacing war horses more suitable for the use of knights. In order that the knights going out may be better cheered, there should sound together trumpets, pipes, flutes, and horns.[85] The divisions and echelons of the fighting men shall be ranged in order by the constables, even when they go forth to a tourney or lance tilting.[86] There should be poorer horses, with jolting gait, for the *serjanz* and riffraff.[87] The castle should have also prudent men, without whose advice nothing should be done in time of hostility, a power which constitutes the greatest strength and highest council of a kingdom—men by whose intercession tortures are applied more mildly, by whose sternness digressors, lawbreakers, violators of ordinances, horse thieves, and murderers may be whipped, punished, or condemned to capital punishment.[88] Their daily life should be frugal (frugality is parsimony in abundance). Their purpose is to urge to do, and to dissuade, without conjecture, for conjecture is opinion taken from circumstantial evidence. There should be also criers and heralds. Let there be present old and experienced knights; while they contend, let the balance remain undisturbed; when they achieve victory and the end of the conflict, the accounts of victory, as being the prize of victory, are not unpraiseworthily entrusted to public record. The group of knights can consist of three kinds—knights answering the feudal summons, those brought together casually,[89] and knights of the Church—whom the horn of the lord or leader urges on in a cloud of missiles, and who choose the hazards of war. They are influenced by gifts [fiefs received from the leader, the fief being a kind of payment]. There should be various dungeons or cells in the proper locations, in the depths of which prisoners are put away in hand shackles. Let there be also leg shackles and a pillory [*columbaria*], and watchmen making a noise and clamor with their horns.[90]

This is rather important, contemporary evidence of the make-up of a castle, although it is intelligible only to one who has some information already. We will assume that our reader understands it and will now accompany Alexander Neckam to the gate of the castle which he is visiting.[91] As he rode along, he noticed in the distance the donjon, or straight tower, of two or three upper floors, sitting on a *motte*, or slight rise of ground. It was circled by a stone wall, such as he himself describes. This was the *chemise* or curtain wall. Not visible to anyone just passing by was the paved court which lay between the curtain wall and the tower. This was crowded with baskets of live chickens, a few animals ready for slaughter, and all sorts of farm and kitchen gear. There was a continual squawking and baaing from that quarter to which no one paid much attention as all were used to it; they would have been more disturbed by a silence. Encircling the stone wall itself was a stockade of wooden pales. No one needed to tell Alexander as he approached that there was a deep ditch occupying the space between the two walls; this he knew. A few hundred feet away from this castle stockade was another enclosure, rectangular in shape, which obviously enclosed a pleasure garden. Some trees were visible, extending above the top of the pales. Still another enclosure, at a greater distance, was the source of whinnying noises which betrayed the fact that horses were confined there. There were a few lean-tos constructed against the horse corral. This stone tower and curtain wall would appear far more picturesque and shapely eight hundred years later, despite the ravages of time, because then there would be no trace of the wooden pales and outer wooden buildings which were absolutely necessary in the twelfth century, but which certainly detracted from the beauty of the scene. In time of hostilities the outer enclosures would have to be abandoned, and the enemy would begin by setting fire to them; but there did not seem much danger of this in 1185, the year 5 of King Philip, who kept his eye on such a donjon so near to his city of Paris.

Alexander was expected. As he came to the barred wooden gate, or wicket, in the stockade, he was sighted by the watchman on the curtain wall. Several young men, *serjanz*, were summoned by a call and they sprang to unfasten the bar. The visitor rode over the dry ditch on a drawbridge of wood which could be raised by chains. This brought him to the gatehouse in the stone curtain wall which had a sliding door of iron that could be lowered from above.[92] There was a similar door a few feet beyond at the entrance into the kitchen court, but this was almost always kept raised. Being a guest, Alexander was conducted by a little stairway in the gatehouse to the top of the crenelated wall. He walked around this, noting the baskets of rocks, sharpened sticks with points hardened in a fire, and other siege paraphernalia. He was taken around to the side away from the gatehouse, where another drawbridge led over the kitchen court into the tower. This also was provided with chains that could be pulled up at will. Alexander had left his horse with the young men at the outer gate, and he suspected that it would be led away into the corral. The porter in the gatehouse was provided with a very heavy key that he did not need to use.[93] It is just possible that there was some provision for stabling horses in the kitchen courtyard, or there might have been an entrance from there to stalls under the ground.[94] The stone curtain wall was quite thick and some rooms were probably provided in it for storage, and even living quarters.[95] A small door opening into the donjon from the court was used by the kitchen help in passing to and fro. There are numerous descriptions of the arrival of a guest at a castle in the works of Chrétien de Troyes. In one of these the owner of the tower happens to be standing on the first drawbridge.[96] For some strange reason the attendants are keeping a very poor watch; they have to be summoned by their master, who strikes with a hammer on a sheet of copper suspended from a wooden frame.

We have been picturing a donjon in the country, not surrounded by a town. Where there was a town, the outer wall, doubtless of stone, was sufficiently extensive to enclose the streets and other areas of the occupied sector. The donjon would be set in the most defensible place against the outer wall, or in the very center if that was the highest ground. The size of the courtyard, between tower and curtain wall, also varied considerably. In the castle that Alexander was visiting, this was circular in shape and the diameter was not great. It was quite possible for such a court to include a garden, with a low wall of stone, in the very heart of the fortified area. We know also of a prison stockade, an "enclosed area with large, round, sharpened stakes" inside the curtain wall.[97] Chrétien's castle gardens which he describes so charmingly may have been outside or they may have been inside. Here is one described by Marie de France: "The Queen leaned out of an ornamented window; she had three ladies with her. She beheld the King's household. . . . They had gone to amuse themselves in a garden beneath the donjon where the Queen was dwelling." This garden could have been outside the enclosure, as the Queen could have looked very easily into it from her third-floor apartment.[98] Yvain enters a large garden: "He saw reclining on his *cote* a rich man who was lying on a silken cloth, and a girl was reading to him in a romance whose name I do not know. And to hear the romance a lady had come there who was the mother."[99] A very large castle might have other buildings, in addition to the donjon, within the curtain wall. The summit of this tower, or the curtain wall itself, could be built up with a housing of wood, covered with hides to prevent setting on fire. This projection was referred to as the *hourdes*. It had a sloping roof and arrow slits for shooting through.[100]

The donjon, or keep, of a very small castle had only one room on each floor. The kitchen was at the courtyard level, from which a narrow stair, hard against the wall, led up to the principal floor where the *salle* was located. Food was carried up that narrow stair at least two times a day. The men of the household slept and ate in that one *salle*. Another stairway, in or against the wall, extended up to the women's apartment on the floor above. If there was still another floor, it would be occupied by servants or children. The roof of the castle tended to be flat with a crenelated parapet. In a larger donjon, like the one in which Alexander was visiting, there would be several small rooms on each floor in addition to the principal hall. On the main floor one of these would be a room for storing garments and other equipment; another would be a treasure room; still another would be a *longaigne* or toilet. Similar space would be provided for the women above, and might include a private chamber for the lady and her husband. In a tower of that size the stair would be placed in the thick wall. The *longaigne*, or latrine, might open directly into the ditch, wet or dry, if a donjon were built against the outer curtain wall, and not in the center of the courtyard. Such an opening was dangerous in time of siege, as it could be shot at or used as an entrance by the opposing forces. The men of Philip Augustus got into Richard's Chasteau-Gaillard by this route. A basket of *torche-culs* made of straw would always be at hand in a *longaigne*. For those who desired it, a curved stick (*gomphus*) was provided for the same purpose.[101]

Before leaving this section on the castle, we will permit ourselves a further digression and describe a royal castle, such as the one at Old Sarum in England.[102] It was in this stronghold that Eleanor of Aquitaine was confined for a considerable length of time by her husband, Henry II of England. We will consider the castle itself, inside the curtain wall, and will not speak of the town proper. The "bailey," or courtyard, was circular and very large. The donjon was placed in the northwest sector of this, hard against the curtain wall. The tower was not very high (to judge by its walls, which were relatively thin). It was divided into two good-sized rooms on each floor, a narrow room and a square one; but important here were the outer buildings which hugged the tower on three sides. On the south side, adjacent to a stairway tower, there was a low structure housing a chapel and a kitchen. Extending from this, on the east side, still close against the tower, was a two-story building containing a *salle* on its second floor. On the north side was another two-story structure, with a fine *salle* containing a fireplace made of "thin red tiles laid in herringbone fashion." This second *salle* was appropriate for female members of the family, perhaps for Queen Eleanor herself. These *salles* were entered through an antechamber at the northeast corner, which separated the two halls, and each was provided with an extensive *garde-robe* pit tower. Apparently a separate bakehouse also existed in the large courtyard, and there is a well. The cramped condition of the town may have caused the royal authorities to lavish great care on *garde-robe* pits. The two gates which provided entrance into the court were quite elaborate, and they too have such pits. Only the kitchen and the chapel could be entered directly from the donjon. To go up into the two halls which we have described, one took a stair leading from the courtyard to the northeastern antechamber. Opening into this antechamber was a strong tower room, which we assume was the treasure chamber. Queen Eleanor could have been kept quite private and incommunicado in a fastness such as this. These side structures may have been erected just previous to her imprisonment.

In a treasure chamber there would be one or more big chests, bound in iron. A specially designated treasurer had a key to these boxes. In the *Life of St. Edward the Confessor* the treasurer forgot to lock up his chest before he was called away quickly. A kitchen knave observed this and stole some of the wealth, thrusting it into his bosom.[103]

A man of the twelfth century liked the idea of a labyrinth. When he had the means of constructing a tower with exits not easily found, he did so. Take this one for instance: "Then he built with squared stones on the *motte* at Guines a round house, and he made it high in the air. . . . In this building he prepared many rooms and various things and amusements, as in a labyrinth."[104]

We return once more to Alexander. As he entered the door of the donjon to which he had been invited, he was greeted by his host. The host grasped the fingers of his guest's right or left hand and held them for a few seconds. That was the greeting of a mediaeval man.[105] Sometimes this gesture was followed by a light kiss. At times men walked hand in hand. Alexander would be told that a room had been cleared for him—one of the side rooms on the main floor, or possibly a little room in the curtain wall. He would be attended by a servitor who would help him to wash and bring him a change of clothing. Had Alexander been a knight, he might have been attended by a female. After this refreshment he took a walk with his host in the enclosed garden outside the wall.

The chief diversion of a barony was hunting. This could not be easily forgotten as dogs and hawks were visible in many places. The men rose at dawn, day after day, and pursued wild boars, or the red deer in the neighborhood. The Baron had a considerable area of land which was given over to hunting, and it was policed by his forester. Some clerics, but not Alexander, would have joined gladly in the hunt. The stag and hind (both of them red deer) were more interesting game than the roebuck and roe doe, which were also available. The fox, too, was often hunted. In pursuing the wild boar, there was great danger from the animal's tusks. Light spears were used by the huntsmen.[106] The fox was killed by the dogs, and the deer were dispatched with a hunting knife. There was an elaborate procedure in skinning a deer. Certain portions were given to the dogs. The hunting dogs were either *levrier* or *brachet.* The first of these was a short-eared hound, of which the Italian greyhound is a dwarfed breed. The *brachet* was a long-eared hound, an ancestor of the modern pointer. The *braque*, which is still bred in Portugal and elsewhere, is substantially this dog. Another breed of dog, which had no place in hunting, was the mastiff. It is still with us although it has become rare.[107] Cats were not common in a baronial household. Alexander's friend might have had a tamed wolf.

Both in warfare and in peace the men and women of the baronial class made considerable use of tents. When Lanval was led to the tent of his fairy mistress, he found it handsome and well pitched; a golden eagle appeared at the summit of the principal pole. Marie does not estimate the value "of the ropes nor of the pegs which hold the sides."[108] Often valuable material, brocaded silk, for instance, was used for the tent, in green, red, blue, and violet shades.[109] The "pommel," as the figure or knob on the top of the pole was called, could be gilded or actually made of gold.

Some special variety of tent is indicated by the word *alcube*, and since this form is of Arabic origin we can assume that it was Oriental: "King Louis caused his tent [*tref*], his *alcubes*, and his *brahanz* to be set up."[110] Similarly in the *Prise d'Orange* there is this passage: "The others are left at the tents [*tres*] and the *brehanz*."[111] It is customary to translate *brahant* by "tent," but I am inclined to interpret it as a "shelter," since I associate it with the Arabic word *barbahhane*, which is supposedly the source also for *barbican*.[112]

Intermediate between house and tent were the shelters or "loges." These were open structures made of poles, with an awning or a roof of thatch. "There where the tourney was to be, there were some large wooden loges, because the Queen would be there and the ladies and the maidens. . . ."[113] For this same tourney Chrétien de Troyes mentions that the overflow of knights were taken care of in tents and in loges. The more favored ones were housed in lodgings in the town, and, of course, the most favored lived at the king's palace.[114] Nicolette made a loge at a crossroad, with her own hands. She constructed it out of oak branches and leaves and lined it with flowers and leaves. It is quite possible that in addition to the upright poles and the roof there were branches intertwined along the sides of a loge to shade the occupants from the sun.[115] The word loge has a different meaning also. It can refer to a gallery open to the street, but part of a house, as in the *Yvain:* "One could not spend a single evening with the other without turmoil and quarreling, but in a small house of several parts, where there have been constructed loges and rooms, the thing can be."[116] Further on: "Hatred went to the loges facing on the road, because she wished to be seen. . . ."[117] Apparently in the place of a closed room a gallery with window arches might be built on any one of the floors of a house. The colonnade before a church was undoubtedly called a loge.

The twelfth-century man loved a party, and the grandest occasion of all was when a wedding was held. During this century the custom of having the two parties concerned exchange formally their *verba de futuro* had been re-established.[118] This was considered more binding than a simple betrothal, although the authorities, Gratian and Peter Lombard, differed on this point. On the following day, or whenever was convenient, the exchange of vows—the *verba de praesenti*—was held. Most canon lawyers insisted that this was the binding factor in the sacrament of marriage, although Gratian had held that the actual consummation was the most important act. After this exchange of vows a nuptial Mass was heard, and then the party went off to dinner.[119] After the meal the minstrels were encouraged to "do their stuff," and young men and young women would dance their caroles, but not together. After supper, which came at Vespers, the priest or bishop blessed the marriage bed, and then the crowd of guests were ushered out of the room. The bride's mother and her attendants undressed her, and the groom came to bed also. At dawn the next day all went to Mass, and then there was polite conversation.

After dinner, till None (three o'clock), there were more caroles and more minstrels. A moderate wedding could break off at this point. One that was celebrated at great expense might drag on in this way for days; but on a third day it was customary to provide some exercise, such as hunting and fishing, for the men in the party.

Other events could be celebrated in elaborate fashion. The visit of King Arthur is cause for similar festivities at the castle of Yvain and Laudine. Rugs are laid in the streets; the walls of houses are hung with silks; curtains are stretched across, from house to house, as awnings over the roadway. Horns and bells make the air ring. Acrobats perform. The ladies gather near the minstrels who play on *vieles*, flutes, and drums. On just such an occasion a *ludus theatralis* could have been performed. This celebration lasted a week. The guests visit the estates of their host; they hunt and fish and call at the castles within four or five leagues (a league was two and a half miles). Above all, there is feasting.[120]

But a still finer feast is that described by Wace in his *Brut*, where he gives details on a celebration held by Arthur.[121] Servants come and go. Lodgings are commandeered from their owners, who move out to accommodate their noble guests. The walls are hung with curtains, and bedchambers and upper rooms are cleared. The *mareschals* are the officers who attend to this clearing of lodgings. For some of the visitors loges are constructed and tents are set up. An observer would see many a squire leading palfreys and war horses. Stables are erected, and tent pegs are driven in. Horses are being tied, curried, and watered. Grain, hay, and grass are brought. Boys (*vallez*) and chamberlains run about hanging up mantles, folding them, and carrying *peliçons* of vair and gris. The knights are playing at the targets, showing off their horses, fencing, throwing stones, hurling darts, and wrestling. Ladies watch from the walls. Some are playing at chess, others at dice. These gamesters sit two at a table, and the dicers are constantly borrowing from those who stand by, allowing twelve deniers in repayment for eleven received. Some are taking off pieces of clothing for wagers, and some of the players are almost stripped. The minstrels are ever present: acrobats, singers, and instrumentalists (*estrumenteurs*). This high feast begins on a Sunday morning and continues in this way through Tuesday. On Wednesday the King gets down to serious business and passes out fiefs and honors.

We will close this chapter on a more mundane note. We will give a description of the farmyard litter which could clutter up the courtyard of a castle. In Alexander's own words, such a court usually was filled with farm utensils and birds:

> In the granary or storehouse there should be a strickle, a *corus*, a *modius* or *mui*, a winnowing fan, a *batus*, and various other measures of wheat, barley, rye, winter wheat, oats, and darnel. There should be kept also, for the use of birds in the court, straw, husks, darnel, and avens. The birds of the court are: chickens, hens, fatted capons, cocks, ducks, geese, swans, herons, pheasants, cranes, coots, doves, divers, kingfishers, woodcocks, and peacocks or Juno's birds.

Then he takes us outside the courtyard:

> In the stable should be a manger, a cowshed, a pigstye, a trough, currycombs, bridles, bits, wheelbarrow, halters, and harness for a horse which I have enumerated elsewhere.[122]

In order to evaluate the mediaeval measures I offer the following tables:[123]

LIQUID

1 pinte	.931 liter (modern)
4 pintes	1 lot
8 pintes	1 sestier
2 sestiers	1 double-sestier
36 sestiers	1 mui
3 muis	1 tonne

DRY

1 sestier	.96 pint (modern)
2 sestiers	1 quart or batus
8 quarts	1 mui
4 muis	1 boisseau
15 boisseaus	1 corus

The *corus* is a measure of corn occurring in the Bible. It is doubtful that it was used by a European farmer.

Apothecaries' weight had 1 *maille* equal 10 grains, or barleycorns; a filbert is 120 grains; 1 nut is equal to 9 filberts.

account, he commented upon the painted and carved ceiling beams of that room, which were remarkable. After supper, which was certainly eaten in the main hall, or *salle*, on the first floor, to the left of the entrance vestibule, he was given a tour over the place. They started with the west side and visited successively the little buildings which surrounded the house. There was first a *phala*, or small barbican tower, where the weapons were stored. This was of wood, and it was from there that the defense would be initiated in case of attack. It probably had only one floor and a half-basement. The lances were kept in racks. The next building, as they passed along, was the library, a storehouse for books. No description was given of the furnishings, but we can be sure that it contained some chests of books and a scribe's writing chair. Probably elementary school instruction was given to the children there. Following this was a building that contained chapel, guesthouse, and infirmary. After this came a storehouse, then a barn adjacent to an open space where carts were kept. They had now completed the circuit of the western side of the court. Adam and his guides then passed to the eastern side. There they found a laundry, with a running stream, the stables, another storehouse for baskets and such, the outdoor oven, and the kitchen which contained also the pantry. This brought them once more to the entry of the manor house proper. Adam comments upon the lower floor of this house. To the right as one entered was a room where the women of the household did their work—at the loom, sewing, and so forth. Immediately adjacent to this, leading out from it, was a little room where chests of clothing were placed. One chest had only headgear, and so on. Adam does not describe the big room which must have been on the left-hand side of the lower floor, except to refer to it as the *palatium*. When he first entered the house, he found a household "fool" or jester in this room who provoked considerable mirth by his awkward rising. A jester usually carried a small toy club or *maçue*.[3]

A well-to-do peasant did not have to be a *maire* to occupy a house similar to the one just described. This was the typical house for a prosperous farmer, whether he be knight, *serjant*, or peasant, granted that he was not the military overlord of the region, in which case he was obliged to maintain a fortified castle.[4] The description of a house which we gave earlier, in the words of Alexander, was really intended to illustrate a country house.[5] Alexander spoke of aromatic spices which were hung outside the east window, in gourds, to improve the quality of the air. He spoke of a maid who was in charge of upstairs arrangements. We omitted the particulars concerning the downstairs or kitchen maid, which we will now proceed to give. First we will repeat what is said of the dress of the upstairs maid, by way of contrast:

> Now let her exclude the intemperate air with a *cote*. A band or a hair net should restrain her flowing hair. She should have a necklace, and a brooch by which she can fasten the neck opening of her *cote*, or fustian, or shirt. She may have bracelets and earrings. There should be also a serving maid who will place eggs under the sitting hens and will give maslin [mixed rye and wheat] to the geese, and who will feed the ailing lambs with milk from a ewe other than the mother, in her gentleness. She will keep the calves to be weaned, whose teeth are few, in an enclosure near the barn. On holidays her clothing should be a cast-off *pellice* and a wimple.[6] It is her practice to give the swineherd, plowmen, and other herdsmen whey, but to the master and his friends, clabber in cups, and to offer in the evening bran bread to the dogs in the pen.[7]

No mention of spinning is made by Alexander. One of the two maids must have participated in this; perhaps they both did, along with their mistress and her daughters. A spindle and a distaff were used. The distaff was held in the left hand (unless the woman were left-handed) and the unspun wool or flax was drawn from it. With the other hand the spinner operated the spindle or top. The length of wool to be united with another was fastened at one end through the hole in the spindle, and then, as the top turned, this was allowed to twist around another length of wool grasped in the fingers of the right hand. Wool intended for warp thread was spun to the right; that intended for weft thread was turned to the left.

Here is Alexander's description of the requirements of an average peasant, whose house may not have been as fine as the one we have just portrayed:

A peasant spending his life in the country, wishing to provide for poverty and old age, should have many kinds of baskets [*corbes*, *calathi*, *cophini*, *sportes*] and beehives of willow wands.[8] He should have also a fishing fork shaped like a hook that he may get himself fish. Nor should he be without a willow basket for pressing clabber, in which milk saved from the milking, pressed frequently, may be transformed into cheese with the whey well extracted. The whey should be kept for young children to drink.

The container used in milking resembled a large chalice. It was probably of wood.

Afterwards the cheese in its fresh state should be kept in a cheese-box of paper or of marsh reeds, wrapped in leaves and covered against the attacks of flies, mice, stinging flies, locusts, and such. Also he should have straw and coarse grains, which are fed to hens, ducks, geese, and birds of the kitchen yard. He must have also bolting cloth and a strainer, so that he can sift flour with them; he can clarify beer with them too. He must possess a sword, a guisarme, a spade, a threshing sledge, a seed bucket for sowing,[9] a wine strainer basket, a wheelbarrow, a mousetrap for mice, and a wolf trap. He should have also stakes or pales, frequently sharpened and tested in the fire. He should have a two-headed axe for removing thorns, thistles, brambles, spines, and bad shoots, and holly wood for tying and renewing hedges in order that, taking advantage of carelessness, no thieves may enter into the livestock enclosure and take animals. He should have a large knife also by which he may cut grafts and insert them into trees if there should be need. He may have hoes for removing tares, chicory and bennet grass, vetch, darnel, thistles, and avens. Some of these, however, are eradicated better with a curved implement than with a hoe.

He needs a herdsman and a shepherd because of the treachery of wolves, and he must be provided with a fold in order that the sheep placed there may render richer the land with the wealth of their dung. The shepherd must have a hut in which a faithful dog shall pass the night with him. The sheepfold ought to be moved frequently in order that all the area of the field can feel the benefit of the urine as well as of the dung of these animals.[10] Our peasant should have also a cow barn and mangers: one manger for horses, one for cattle, and, if prosperity smiles a bit and Fortune is kind, he should get an ass and a stallion for a stud.[11] He will need also sheep, goats, oxen, cows, heifers, bullocks, wild oxen (?), wild asses, asses, rams, ewes, wethers, bull calves, and mules. He must have boxes, nets, and long lines to trap hares, does, kids, stags, hinds, and young mules. This is the equipment of the peasant. He will require also brachet hounds, *levriers*, and mastiffs.

The account goes on:

He should have a plow which can produce the necessities of life, in the middle of which is a huge piece of oak, which we call a beam or pole.[12] This, widening into two prongs, forms twin ears or earthboards whereby the furrow is made wider. A certain kind of plow has only one ear. This oaken beam curves into the back end which is known as the tail of the plow . . . [more false etymology]. The plow handles, to which grips are fixed and by which the plow is directed, should go up obliquely. There are three kinds of grips [*capuli*]: that in the handle of a sword, the kind attached to a funeral bier, and the kind which the plowman holds with his hands. But a plow is difficult to control when it is opposed by hard earth and rough or clay soil, where the yoke of the draft animals or the willow bands are broken. A share beam should be added, to which a plowshare is inset. I pass over willingly the hedge, harrow, nails, bars, cords, and knife.[13] I leave to those who understand such things to develop and elucidate how the fields should be manured,[14] cleared off, or renovated when Sirius or Procyon is in the ascendant, or when "houses" are falling; also how to burn off when the stalks have been left, or level off with a cylinder [*chilindrum*],[15] or cover the sown land with a drag, or put the seed in the ground in order that the inert seed may burst into green; how it is necessary to reap, to beat on a threshing floor, to send the bundles or stacks to the granary, to clean with a rake, to cleanse with the winnowing fan,[16] afterwards to grind with the millstone, to sift the flour through the holes of a sieve, and by the art of baking transform it into bread. I omit for the present a goad, drag, scarecrow, and a lecherous representation of Priapus, not from ignorance but because I do not recall them precisely.[17] I have discussed many of these in my other writings, and repetition does not please me as much as it does so many others.[18]

Peasants were supplied with required wares by traveling merchants who carried their packs from farm to farm.

The peasant at work is represented faithfully in the many sculptured versions of the Labors of the Months, a familiar scene in twelfth-century ornamentation. In these scenes the peasant appears in the acts of digging, pruning, reaping, pressing grapes, sitting by the fire, threshing with a flail, killing hogs, hoeing, driving oxen, and riding. The version of these which has been preserved from the Duomo at Ferrara (Italy) is unusually clear.[19] The costume of the peasant is represented in excellent detail: the working shoe with its very heavy sole (probably of wood) and separate heel, the snood cap fastening under the chin, the hair long at the nape of the neck, the leather belt with some kind of hooked clasp (to be distinguished from the more elegant tie-belt worn by gentry), and the wrapped leg coverings. These figures are so lifelike that they seem to be moving before our eyes.

In the fireside scenes found in the Labors of the Months it is evident that a stool was used which had elaborate rungs and knobs. A few seemed to have claw feet, and a cushion on the seat. Some of them are carved; some have a low back. We presume that the stool would be kept in the chimney corner for the master of the household, if he were the occupant of a prosperous manor house. Apparently such a stool was used in the castles also and could be pulled away from the hearth and placed next to a bed (used as a couch) during polite conversation.[20] A common variety of chair used by everyone was the *faldestuel*, or folding chair, which resembled closely a modern *pliant*.

We have mentioned in an early chapter the *plaissié*, or detached farmyard, which was a stockade some yards away from the house. Chickens were kept there. Apparently the farmer's wife would lay out her newly pressed cheeses there to dry.

[Tiecelin the raven] saw thousands of cheeses which had been put out to sun. The woman who should have watched them was gone into her house. . . . [He grabbed one.] The old woman ran out into the street; she saw the raven and threw at him pebbles and stones, and cried out, "Young man [*vassal*], you'll not carry it away." Tiecelin saw that she had little sense; [he answered,] "You'll not get this one back, I'll have my mustaches shaved first. . . . I risked getting it because it is tender, somewhat yellow, and of good savor. I am so fond of it, if I can get it to my nest I will eat it quietly as though it were boiled meat or a roast.[21]

This begins the *Roman de Renart* version of the well-known tale about the Fox and the Raven. A *plaissié* would hardly offer protection against a still more troublesome enemy of cheeses than Tiecelin, namely, the flies. The twelfth century was troubled with them also; witness this: "You are filthier than a fly which people swat in summer."[22]

The trials of a peasant housewife are aptly illustrated by an English writer:

And what if I ask besides, though it may seem silly, how the wife stands, that heareth, when she cometh in, her child scream, sees the cat at the bacon, and the dog at the hide? Her cake is burning on the stone, and her calf is sucking all the milk up. The pot is boiling over into the fire, and the churl her husband is scolding. Though this be a silly tale, maiden, it ought to deter thee more strongly from marriage, for it seems not silly to her who trieth it.[23]

A detail on the method which she used in sweeping is perhaps a commonplace, but it is worth repeating:

When the poor widow would cleanse her house, she gathereth into a heap, first of all, all the largest sweepings, and then shoveleth it out; after that she cometh again and sweepeth together all that was left before, and shoveleth it out also; again, upon the small dust, if it is very dusty, she sprinkleth water, and sweepeth it out away after all the rest.[24]

But marriage had its compensations, even for the peasant girl, because it brought her children whom she could love and play with: ". . . as the mother with her young darling:

she flies from him, and hides herself, and lets him sit alone and look anxiously around and call "Dame, dame!" and weep a while, and then she leapeth forth lightly with outspread arms, and embraceth and kisseth him, and wipeth his eyes."[25] A trick which is still used to comfort a little person who has bumped himself was employed then: " . . . and if a child stumble against anything or hurt himself men beat the thing that he hurteth himself upon, and the child is well pleased, and forgetteth all his hurt, and stoppeth his tears."[26]

The twelfth century, like every other period in the history of man, had games and toys for children. Yvain in his brief period of mental illness found a boy "who held a bow and five barbed arrows which were sharp and broad."[27] Although it is not specifically stated, we get the inference that these were "boy's size." We know that the boys played ball. In the *Hortus deliciarum* manuscript there is a miniature which is frequently reproduced.[28] It shows a boy and a girl standing over a table, manipulating two jointed figures of knights with swords. By agitating the strings which they have in their hands, they make the figures clash against each other. Similarly, children used to take plantain spikes (the spike is a stalk bearing the fruit or minute green flower) and strike them together, pretending they were knights. The one which struck the flower off the other was proclaimed winner.[29] Petronilla, the wife of Arnoul d'Ardres, was a simple young lady of childish tastes: "She would apply her youthful self to children's games and dances, and similar amusements among the maidens, and very often to dolls."[30] She had another habit, considered rather scandalous, of bathing in the fish *vivarium* in the kitchen yard, clad only in her shirt, on a hot day, in front of the knights as well as the girls. We might think of this young lady as the inventor of the swimming pool. When children played by the sea, they had the same pastimes that they have today. Giraldus says that his little friends used to build castles in the sand; but he showed his future aptitude by building sand churches and monasteries.[31]

While we are speaking of children, we note this amusing statement in a farcical work (of the thirteenth century, to be sure):

> I have never cared for children, little, medium-sized or big: the little one is hard to rear and does not let the people sleep at night; the middle-sized one runs down the street and must be kept from horses and carts; the big one battles with father and mother to get rich estates, and he has to be brought back continually from the taverns.[32]

We have said that cats were not very popular in baronial households; but they were certainly a favored pet among lesser folk. The anchoresses are told in the *Ancrene Riwle:* "Ye shall not possess any beast, my dear sisters, except only a cat."[33] Apparently the cat in the Middle Ages was of the same breed that we have today and enjoyed the same antagonism to rats and mice. A somewhat gruesome find was made recently in the Southwark area of London. Buried in the ground, underneath a spot where sixteenth-century woodwork had been subsequently built, there came to light the mummified remains of an ordinary house cat engaged in combat with two large rats.[34] It is presumed that the animal met its fate in the fifteenth century, or earlier. Very striking is the action displayed in both the figure of the cat and that of the rat which it holds in its mouth. We can only assume that some cave-in of soil must have buried the animals instantly.

We have been writing about peasants who held a manor with its surrounding lands from a feudal lord. There were many shades of wealth and poverty among the peasants.

Some were stewards, or *maires*, holding *censes* (or *curtes*), estates which were in turn subdivided into lesser holdings. A few manors and small castles were in the possession of knights who owed knightly service and no other rent; these were both *chasez* and *aloués*.[35] The free peasant, or villein, held land under two types of contract: *bail à part de fruits* and *bail à ferme*. The first meant payment of rent with a certain per cent of the produce; the other signified a lease at a fixed yearly sum (say, four to six deniers per *arpent*). The sum might be stipulated as so much cash and so much produce.[36] Very little actual labor service was demanded of a free peasant in the late twelfth century. A week's work on the lord's demesne at harvest time might be required, but this was not the rule. At times the lord gave himself a good laugh by leasing on the terms of *droits ridicules*.[37] On rent-paying day a peasant might pay the smoke of a roast chicken, or he might be obliged to take a bath—in public, you can be sure—etc. These were entertaining jokes, but they did not bring in any income. A free peasant was not able, ordinarily, to sell his land to another without the consent of the lord's *maire*. Some military service, as a *serjant*, might be included in a peasant's rent. The whole system became more complicated when a rich peasant held lands which owed a knight's fee to the lord's estate. In that case, of course, scutage had to be paid to the lord, or a knight had to be hired to perform the requisite service.

A lower class of peasant was that of the serf. The amount of labor which he owed to the demesne was much greater. In addition, he had to pay certain vexatious fees if he wanted to be ambitious and move around; for instance, to get the privilege of marrying a wife who was not on the estate he had to pay *formariage*. If he wished to live somewhere else, he was required to pay chevage. There were other arbitrary tailles. When he died, all the property that he had accumulated belonged to the lord.[38] In the Paris area much of this was beginning to be softened. Many serfs had bought their freedom or received it as a gift. In many cases the lord preferred to forget the serf status of a useful individual. He would allow complete freedom of movement, would even contribute to the serf's education, and might allow him to become a member of the baronial class—but in this case the man's technical status as a serf continued in the background and influenced him in remaining loyal, and perhaps subservient. A fine example of this is that of the seneschal of Henri de Champagne who counseled his lord against excessive generosity.[39] He was strongly rebuked by Henri in view of his status as a serf. It was convenient also to give a local benefice to a cleric who was of serf origin. But not all the nobles were venal. Many were glad to have their serfs make enough money to purchase freedom, and they often allowed *main morte*, which means that the serf could leave his money to anyone at will, so long as that person lived on the estate.[40] Eighteenth-century writers, and later ones too, have made much over the *jus primae noctis*. There is some evidence of this practice, particularly in the south of France; but if you look at the matter impartially, having in mind social conditions of the twelfth century, the abuse does not seem very great.[41] If an overlord were sufficiently interested in a girl of the serf class to demand this favor, she probably did not make herself difficult on that night or a previous one, provided she was compensated in some way. (I do not want to seem heartless in a statement of this kind. What I am stating is that standards of morality were, on the whole, lower at the time than they are now in the society that most of us frequent.)

There was still another type of peasant, the *hôte*.[42] A

hôtise was a parcel of land granted by the lord's *maire* to a squatter, a person who was willing to put up a shack of some kind and work for better times. In the literature of the twelfth century we occasionally come upon a man of the knightly class who is reduced to farming under the most miserable circumstances, like the good knight in *Rapularius*. Perhaps he was tilling a *hôtise*. There were certain common lands on a demesne—forests, meadows, and marshes—which were not leased to any individuals. The peasants insisted that they had certain rights there and were frequently in dispute on this subject.

The poorer peasants, including serfs, liked to have their get-togethers on a long evening where they danced and sang. A peasant in the *Roman de Renart* has a *viele* which hangs from a peg in his one-room hut: ". . . every night all his neighbors came together with him. He gave a lot of pleasure to his children with it."[43]

Smaller nobles, and some of the greater ones, did not have a private chapel or church, but attended one nearby, in their village or in the country. A small chapel would be served by a single priest, assisted by one clerk, a boy. There might be a choir of laymen, perhaps consisting of two boys and two men who sang from behind a partition near the chancel. The young clerk slept in the bell loft or some similar place. He rang the bells, cared for the property, and assisted at Mass and the other offices. We have taken this description from the *Flamenca*.[44] Alexander Neckam lists the contents of a church:

> The furnishings are these: a baptismal font, a crucifix, a Little Mary, and other images; a lectern of some kind, a ewer, a small ewer, basins, a chair, the chancel, an elevated seat, a stool, candlesticks, the piscina or lavabo, the altar stone, a case for images, cruets, and pyxides. Let there be a bier for the dead,

a hand towel, a face towel, and a fine cloth [on the altar]. There should be gilded vessels, a thurible,[45] gilded columns and bronze veneering with silver and marble bases. . . . There should be books: Missal, Breviary, Antiphonal, Gradual, Processional, Manual, Hymnal, Psalter, Troper, and Ordinal. The priest's vestments are surplice, silk cap,[46] cincture, headband, baldric, stole, maniple, and chasuble. [In the ceiling] there should be beams of maplewood or oak, crosspieces where the roof adheres to the beams or to the leads. Wooden pegs and iron nails are required where the tiles and roof siding are suspended. Small bells, immense bells, and little bells must be hung in the tower. A cupola, tower, and bell tower are the same thing. A weathercock can be placed on top. Bent bars, bolts, hinges, and locks should be there [on the doors]. There should be an entry vestibule for temple, or church, or monastery, or oratory, or chapel. . . . Let there be a tabernacle in which the Eucharist may be kept most worthily, the salvation of faithful souls, for he who does not believe cannot be saved.[47]

The *Chronicle of Jocelin* gives still further details.[48] The abbey church of Bury-St. Edmund's had a great beam which crossed over the altar. From this hung the crucifix, with the Little Mary on one side (probably the left) and the image of St. John on the other. The reserved Sacrament was often placed inside the Little Mary. There was also a reliquary suspended from this same beam. The altar was concave in shape. The walls could be draped with curtains or tapestry, like any other room. A pulpit was not essential, but Abbot Samson placed one in the church for ornament and because there were many who liked to hear him preach. In this abbey church was a big sheet of metal (*tabula*) hanging from an upright, which was struck as a gong *pro mortuo*, or to give warning in an emergency. The abbey had also a water clock, with dropping weights so attached that they fell and roused the guardian of the vestry at the proper hours, as before Matins.[49]

Large and expensive chandeliers could hang in the nave

Peasant wearing the "snood" cap, long linen *braies* tucked up at the knee, and a *gonne* open at the side for freedom of action
Courtesy Curia Arcivescovile, Ferrara

Jongleur and female dancer, detail from the Limoges casket
From A Guide to the Mediaeval Antiquities
Courtesy British Museum

of a church. St. Bernard condemned this usage, but Baudri de Bourgueil took delight in such a *corona* or *rota*, ornamented with figures and gems.[50] These Latin words describe the designs. The chandelier hung by iron chains.

Cupboards were placed in the apse, behind the high altar, in many churches. Vestments, sacred vessels, and even offerings of food (wrapped in cloth) that had been received were stored there. Jocelin records that the fire at the Shrine of St. Edmund started from a source similar to this.[51]

The service books which were required offer an interesting list.[52] In addition to the Missal, or Mass book, we find the Breviary, which contains the canonical hours of prayer; the Manual, or collection of miscellaneous offices—baptism, marriage, burial, visitation of the sick, extreme unction, the Asperges, blessing of salt and water, and purification of women—and a calendar. Next comes the Processional, which gives the litanies and the processions for special feasts. The Hymnal could contain as many as 132 Latin hymns, beginning with *Ad cenam agni* and ending with *Vox clara ecce*. We would hope to find in it the *Ave maris stella*, the *Eterne rerum conditor*, the *O lux beata Trinitas*, and the *Vexilla regis prodeunt*. The music was often recorded in the Hymnal. The Psalter contained the Psalms, a calendar, the Canticles, the Athanasian Creed, and the Litany. Certain of the Psalms there would be followed by one or more antiphons. The Antiphonal, Gradual, and Troper were music books. The first provided the music for the Breviary; the Gradual gave the music for the Mass. The Troper furnished music for the *farsuras* or interpolated introits and offertories, and for the Kyrie, Gloria in Excelsis, Sanctus, Agnus Dei, and Ite, missa est. The Ordinal gave rubrical directions and details on the proper offices during the course of the year.

Other Church books which Alexander could have mentioned, but which he did not, are the Collectarius or collection of Collects, the Epistle book, the Gospel book, the Martyrology, the Legenda or Lessons book, and the two books which belonged to a bishop, the Pontifical and the Benedictional. The Gospel book had a specialized use other than for the reading of the Gospel at the Mass. It was employed on many occasions for administering oaths. The *Evangiles* which is so frequently mentioned for oaths was this Gospel book. The bones of a martyr were used for the same purpose. The Compotus gave tables for calculating the golden numbers, regulars, and epacts. The Venerable Bede introduced the practice of using the palm of the hand and the finger joints for this kind of computation. A Compotus based on this was called a Compotus manualis. Another book not included by Alexander in his list is the Customary, or Consuetudines Chori, which gives ritual directions.

There did exist a Mass book for the laity, in Anglo-French, as early as 1150–70, but its use must have been very limited. The common devotional book used by the laity was the Psalter (previous to the late thirteenth century, when the Prymer or *Livre d'heures* came into use). The penitential psalms and the litanies were recited from the Psalter.

Those receiving the Blessed Sacrament came forward and stood before the altar with their hands held before them, palms touching, and with one knee bent slightly forward. They did not kneel.[53] Those who made an offering did so by placing it on the altar, in proper wrapping, if necessary.[54] The congregation knelt, and perhaps sat at times, on the floor of the nave. The pavement could be quite chilly, so the ladies, at least, must have formed the habit of bringing cushions and low stools with them. They stood for the Gospel, and at other parts of the Mass, as people do today.[55] It was customary to pass around pax among the congregation. At the proper moment the clerk, or altar boy, brought the Gospel book opened at a special page, and each member of the congregation kissed it as he said *Pax vobiscum*. Between the congregation and the chancel, insane people were sometimes tied to the rood screen, in order that they might be improved by attendance at Mass.[56] They must have made a strange sight, frequently with the sign of the cross cut into the hair on the tops of their heads.[57]

The choir in a small chapel such as we are describing would not attempt any elaborate music. They would probably sing the canticles from memory, but in case a music book was needed this would be a large parchment manuscript, set on a reading stand, which could be seen by all in the choir. Not all music at the time was in unison. In a branch of the *Roman de Renart* where the Fox and Tybert the cat attempt to hold Vespers it is specifically mentioned, in satire, that Renart sang the *Benedicamus* in organum.[58] In parallel organum two parts move a fifth or a fourth apart. In free organum they can move about, separated by any desired interval. A chorus of nonsolo singers commonly stuck to one-part music. Soloists performed organum in groups of two or more on each part.[59]

The Cloisters Museum, in New York, has set up a Romanesque chapel, a small church interior of the twelfth century.[60] The stone of the nave comes from Notre-Dame-du-Bourg at Langon. Here, as is often the case, the carvings are not limited to religious themes. It is believed that one of the capitals shows portraits of Henry II of England and his queen, Eleanor of Aquitaine, sculptured in 1155. The altar is not strictly twelfth century, so we will pass it by. There is a crucifix suspended over it (Spanish make) which is thought to retain some of its original paint. The body is in flesh tint; the hair and beard are black; the loincloth is blue, bordered with gold. There is a gold diadem studded with green and red stones. The cross itself is dark green with a gilded border, and it too is studded with gems.

A huge baptismal font of black basalt is preserved in the cathedral at Winchester (England). It has in bas-relief the miracle of the three marriageable daughters who are given dowers by St. Nicholas. The size of the font is explained by the fact that baptism was commonly by immersion at that time.[61] Infant baptism was, of course, the only usual kind. Baptism of adults was limited to Jews and pagans who had been converted. Mass baptism of pagans was more common in the *chansons de geste* than it was in real life. On these occasions, according to the *chansons de geste,* tubs were brought and placed near the font. Those about to receive the sacrament were stripped to the *chainse* and dipped in the tubs.[62] In all baptisms it was the godfather who lifted up the child from the water in the font, and so the verb *lever* gets the meaning "to serve as godparent," in Old French.

In England, and probably with little difference in France, the average layman went to three services on Sunday and other holy days. He went to confession early in Lent, and perhaps again just before Easter. Although he was expected to receive Communion three times a year, the minimum was once a year—at Easter. Matins, Lauds, and Prime were said together, in a parish church, at Prime. Terce and a procession preceded the High Mass, at Terce. The priest said Sext and Nones after this Mass, usually without a congregation being present. Vespers were sung at the appointed time, and Compline could follow this directly.[63] Presumably a devout cleric with simple tonsure, as well as a devout layman, would go to church every day at Prime, if this were feasible.[64]

The country chaplain was often of the serf class. After returning from the schools, and after his ordination, he took charge of the chapel while tilling his glebe land in person and occasionally doing a little work on the lord's fields.[65] This picture appears in various places, notably in the *Roman de Renart*. There the village priest, who is Danz Martin d'Orliens, spreads his fertilizer with a pitchfork, like any peasant, and while doing this he is in a position to take a swipe at Bruin the bear who is in flight.[66] Renart tells Tybert that this priest has a great store of wheat and oats and is therefore much troubled by mice. Renart goes on to say that the priest has many chickens in his courtyard. In reality he has only two hens and a rooster. He has also a female companion and a son, which was one of the types of irregularity often encountered in the twelfth century.[67] At times the chaplain was obliged to attend a synod, called by his bishop. From an Old French proverb we know that some attended unwillingly.[68]

We have promenaded Alexander Neckam sufficiently over the country lands of his baronial host. Perhaps he was accompanied over parts of the estate by a forester like Sire Lanfroi in the *Roman de Renart*. No special entertainment was planned at the castle for Alexander, but supper, coming at Vespers, was an occasion to look forward to. No one was hurried after an hour at the table. It was pleasant to sit around the fire, telling tales, stewing fruits, and on many occasions listening to a minstrel.[69] People sat around the fire even in fairly moderate weather. If it was too warm, the gentlemen removed their *cotes* and *chainses* and sat around in their *braies*. The ladies were in the habit of coming downstairs for this meal, and they too would relax, although they stayed fully clothed.[70] Cushions of some kind, low stools, and small rugs were brought out to make the rush-covered pavement of the floor a little softer. As the quinces and pears simmered over the fire, the company prepared to listen to a minstrel who was about to chant them a short lai. This would consume an hour or a little more.

This particular jongleur had arrived earlier in the day. Like many of his fellows, he had studied for a little while at the schools and was a former clerk. He rode a very respectable horse which had been given to him somewhere along the line by an enthusiastic patron. His *viele* was in a case attached to the *culière* behind his saddle. When he appeared at the gatehouse he was no stranger, having made a brief stay at the castle some months before, and he was admitted immediately. Jongleurs were paid very little respect; they were received with amused deference. But the barons knew that they got about all over the place and that they were a constant source for the spread of gossip. They inspired some fear, therefore. Alexander's host made a point of receiving this guest in private, while Alexander was touring the estate, and in this way he learned the latest public and private news of his neighbors. Such kitchen news was apt to be more enlightening than the tidings of Church and State which Alexander brought with him from the city of Paris. At the supper table the minstrel was seated fairly low, but his host saw to it that he got a good meal. He was asked about his repertoire, and he might have replied as Renart did when he pretended to be an English minstrel: "I know good Breton lais of Merlin and of Noton, of King Arthur and of Tristan, Marie's *Chievrefueil*, and the *Voyage of St. Brandan*."[71] This was the repertoire of an English minstrel. The continental jongleur knew also many *chansons de geste*, as we know from the high celebration at the court of Archimbaut de Bourbon, which is told in detail in the *Flamenca*.[72] Biblical lais (now lost) and contes adapted from the *Metamorphoses* of Ovid were popular, as we know from that same source. The minstrel would take his place facing the guests and begin. He sat on a stool, or perhaps on a cushion. If the selection was a Breton lai, without refrains, he performed unaided throughout the entire piece. He struck on his *viele* the notes of his first melody of one or two lines and then chanted to this for a while, probably without continuing to play. When the structure of his piece required it, he changed over to a second melody, perhaps playing it first on his instrument. After a while he went back to the first tune, and so on, until he had completed the performance. At certain high moments he may have accompanied the melody, in unison, as he chanted. If he had been performing a *chanson de geste* which had a recurring refrain, such as in the *Chanson de Guillaume* and the *Chanson de Roland*, he would have sung a line every now and then to a melody which we will call his "refrain tune." Immediately the audience would have taken their cue and would have come in, perhaps with proper handclapping, chanting a refrain which did not vary throughout the piece.[73] This audience participation was exceedingly popular, but to perform a *chanson de geste* in its entirety was a long proposition. I doubt that the *Chanson de Roland* could be executed in this way in less than five hours' steady going. This meant that two, and maybe three, sessions were needed to perform it.[74]

After some days, when his welcome was getting cooler, or when his wanderlust came to the fore, the minstrel would announce his desire to depart and would receive the lord's *congié*.[75] He would be given some payment. To prevent any grumbling about him at the minstrel's next point of call, the baron might be excessively generous. *Largesce*, or excessive generosity, was an important element in a baron's code of life. Although moderation (*mesure*) was preached for everything else, it was not considered a virtue in the giving of gifts or rewarding for personal services.[76] As a traveling minstrel could not be expected every week in the year, I imagine that some of the people in the castle tried to supply this lack. If they could not sing and play, they narrated in prose form, but very often there must have been a young man, or an old one, who had a knack for repeating some lai that he had heard.

For the professional minstrel the touring of castles could be fatiguing. He would attend school from time to time, during the coldest months, and would thus increase his repertoire. Undoubtedly some instruction in reading and writing the French tongue was given in these jongleur schools. Some of the barons, such as the Count of Ardres (near Calais), took great pleasure in increasing the spread of vernacular literature. They paid clerks to translate, and they gathered small libraries of works in French. This was a kind of jongleur school, although it may not have passed under that name. Renart, posing as a minstrel, pretended that he had studied at Besançon: "And I know a very good song that I was taught at Besançon."[77] At times a jongleur was attached permanently to a lord's court, but that was likely to be the case only when a baron fancied himself as a poet.[78] After all, it was rather undignified for the master of the household to pick up his *viele* and sing, but when he could teach his verses to his domestic minstrel, that was something else indeed. Minstrels could be hired just to sing praises. William of Longchamp, bishop of Ely and chancellor of Richard I of England, was accused of bringing over from France "singers and jongleurs" whom he attracted with rich gifts. These professionals were to sing about him in public places. Apparently they inserted his name into existing songs. "He bought flattering lyrics and emended songs."[79]

We mentioned in the previous paragraph the patronage of jongleurs by some of the barons. This is so signficant a matter that it would be wise to give some details. Ebles II, viscount of Ventadour, must have had such a group gathered around him. On the other hand, we have positive evidence about Count Baldwin of Ardres, and his son Arnoul de Guines. Baldwin caused the Song of Songs to be translated into French, also sermons, a *Life of St. Anthony*, part of a medical treatise by Godefroi de Latin, and the work of Solinus. These items could not, of course, be sung by minstrels, but the activity is indicative. The chronicler goes on to say that "in *chansons de geste* or in the past deeds of barons, and even in tales of ignoble characters," the knowledge of the Count was equal to that of the most notable jongleurs. He had a layman in charge of his library, and this layman had received his learning from another layman.[80]

We are informed further that Arnoul, the son, was a gay young gentleman, free with money. He loved tourneys and was constantly surrounded by amusing associates, including young people of his own age. He had a few older intimates who could narrate for him "fables and stories and past events of our ancestors." There were three of these men: a knight, Robert de Coutances, who charmed his ears with tales of the Roman emperors, of Charlemagne, Roland and Oliver, and Arthur of Brittany; another, Philippe de Montjardin, who knew about Jerusalem, the siege of Antioch, the Arabians, the Babylonians, and deeds beyond the seas; and finally, his brother-in-law, Gautier de l'Ecluse, who could tell about the tales of the English, Gormont and Isembart, Tristan and Yseut, Merlin, Marcolfus, and the early history of the Ardennes. On one occasion, when the court was obliged to remain indoors for two days because of a violent storm, this Gautier de l'Ecluse sat down before them all, and placing his right hand against his beard, combing it in and out, he told (in prose?) about the history of the Ardennes.[81]

It is evident that certain feudal courts, and undoubtedly some monasteries, contributed much to the spread of vernacular literature. The Richard who wrote the extant Old French Crusade epics omitted all mention of his patron, Count Baldwin of Guines, because he was not satisfied with some payment that he had been given; but that was earlier than the date which we are now considering.[82] Young Arnoul de Guines was knighted by Philip of Flanders in 1181, and had spent much time at Philip's court.[83] It is evident that this is the same milieu in which the great Chrétien de Troyes found himself. The *Conte del Graal* was composed, or rather begun, at the behest of this same Philip of Flanders.

These jongleurs used French as their principal language. Those who were native English speakers and Celts had their language difficulties. In the *Roman de Renart*, and elsewhere, there is much fun being poked at the broken French of an English jongleur. Marie de France certainly learned a little of the Breton speech, presumably from a singer who interlarded his recitations with it. When minstrels passed on down into Italy, some of them adapted their material into an artificial Franco-Venetian jargon, formed by using Italian vowels with French consonants. The V7 manuscript of the *Chanson de Roland*, and other epics, are in this kind of language. I am of the opinion that a northern French speaker and a speaker of Provençal, at this time, could understand each other, although some critics recently have been making statements the other way. It is quite probable also that Spanish and Italian were intelligible to a Frenchman of the twelfth century, and that the Spaniards and Italians understood French. This would mean that the public that could appreciate French poetry was quite extensive. The Goliardic minstrels, who were also moving about, sang in Latin for clerical audiences. They may have had some difficulty in making themselves understood in other lands because the pronunciation of Latin varied from country to country.[84]

There was much profit for a minstrel along the pilgrim routes. The most important of these led to St. James of Compostela in Galicia. Thousands of pilgrims were on the road, in the better seasons, headed for that shrine. A pilgrim dressed for travel. He carried a wallet (*escrepe*) around his neck, and a staff (*bordon*) of ash wood. Like many travelers, he wore a hat with a brim somewhat broader than usual, similar to that the peasant might wear in the fields. He had a *chape* with a hood. The wallet and the staff were the tokens that identified his purpose to passers-by.[85] Pilgrims journeyed on foot, on assback, and on horses. If they were doing special penance, it was usual to find them on foot. They stopped at night at the many hospices which were maintained for them along the routes. There they were bedded down in large rooms with straw on the pavement. This was an ideal setting in which the minstrel could perform. The evenings were long, especially in the summer months. The travelers were naturally fond of the *chansons de geste* which told about heroes who had given up everything for the cause of the Faith and had driven back the Saracens. Joseph Bédier taught that the monks who operated the hospices had much to do with the encouragement of the *chansons de geste*. Perhaps we should not be so sure about that today, since these hospices did not stand to gain much by the extra crowds which flocked around the singer. The pilgrim audience was there in any case. Probably the demand preceded the *chansons de geste*.[86]

Some of these pilgrims were on their way to Rome, and a very few were headed for the Holy Land, a journey requiring five months.[87] Those of the second category wore a cross marked on the right shoulder. They traveled to Italy with pilgrims who were going to Rome. Travelers to the Holy Land continued on to the south of Italy, to Brindisi or Bari, or perhaps to Sicily, and there they bargained for passage by sea.[88] In 1185 the Pope, Urban III, was resident in Verona and was not actually in Rome. It was in 1188 that the Pope, then Clement III, returned to the Lateran Palace. When the popes were in residence at the Lateran, the principal church of Rome was Santa Maria Maggiore. It was there that the Pope said Mass on special occasions.[89] In the year 1185 many of the pilgrims must have gone on to Rome for their pilgrimage to points of devotion in that city, after a visit to the Pontiff at Verona. Passage over the Alps was usually made by the Col de Mont-Cénis, which lies on the road from Lyon to Turin.[90] This was a dreary journey, accomplished at a rate of fifteen to twenty miles a day, but the company was interesting. The twelfth-century man was not altogether impervious to the beauty of the scenery, either.

We will now return to Alexander Neckam for our final glimpse of him. He was a person who tended to be scornful of others. We read how he dismissed the details of farming with the remark that those who knew about them could tell more.[91] In the *De naturis rerum* he makes adverse comments on the knights and barons. He accuses some of abandoning their comrades in battle under a secret understanding with the enemy which would enable them to share in the ransom money. He claims that some of the haughtier barons were descended from female *histriones* (minstrels or actors), while legitimate heirs of their fathers were excluded from the estates.[92] He rails against the insincerity and flattery that are required at court. "How much vanity in spectacles, in empty conversations, in cynical detractions, in blandishing adulation [cf. the *losengier* of vernacular literature], in detestable voluptuousness, have they experienced who, in their penance, are beheld by Divine Mercy." He goes on to say that "adulation is a poisoned honey." He insists that "flatterers should be condemned along with those who detract unduly."[93] He thinks that flattery should be "left to those who are exposed to theatrical spectacles."[94] On various occasions Alexander refers to *ludi theatrales* and *spectacula*. He seeks to give the impression that he scorns these things as part of the Devil and all his works; but it is evident that these *ludi* and their *histriones* offer some attraction for him.[95] He was, of course, familiar with the ecclesiastical dramas presented inside the monasteries and churches at certain seasons of the year. There was a tradition for such presentations at his school in Dunstable. Geoffrey of Gorham, a Frenchman from Maine, founded the Dunstable schools and had on one occasion borrowed certain vestments and other accessories from the monastery at St. Albans in order to present miracle plays at Dunstable. The day after the performance his own house, in which the borrowed vestments were stored, burned down.[96] This event took place quite early in the twelfth century.

But Alexander has in mind performances of a different kind when he speaks scornfully. There must have been a class of jongleurs who put on monologues and dialogues of a more worldly kind, outside the churches. The *Jeu d'Adam* could have been performed before the church door; I am inclined to believe that the *Jeu de Saint-Nicholas* could never have been performed inside it, because there are scenes there that could not have been represented within ecclesiastical precincts. In his description of a room Alexander referred to a *canopeum scenicum.* I shall have to leave this problem to historians of the theater. Remember, also, that Giraldus accused the monks of Canterbury of making comic gestures like those of *histriones.*[97]

With this grave problem about the comic drama unsolved, we will take our leave of Alexander Neckam. He returned to Dunstable in the following year (1186).[98] In our next and final chapter, we will take up certain details and artistic matters which it has not been possible to weave into our framework.

Chapter IX

"To Talk of Many Things"

MEN AND women in twelfth-century Europe were not tall in stature. J. C. Russell is my authority that a tall man at that time was about five feet ten inches; an average short man was some five feet two inches in height. Women averaged shorter than men, as is always the case.[1] The strain of Germanic blood was somewhat more prominent in the upper level of English and French society than it is today. The ideal type of feminine beauty scarcely varies from romance to romance: blond curly hair, gray (*vair*) eyes set wide apart, straight nose, white skin, very red lips of Cupid's-bow design, long neck and waist, slender and firm breasts, and long, shapely fingers.[2] A perfect set of teeth and good breath are occasionally mentioned. The ideal male matches this description rather closely, allowing for masculine differences. He too must have the curly blond hair and broad forehead, but he should be broad in the shoulders and small in the waistline. Some will argue that these were ideal types, seldom found in actuality; but I do not agree. There must have been a considerable number of people of this description. Listeners identify themselves with the protagonists in a romance, and they would not prefer unusual types. Usamah, when speaking of the Franks in the Holy Land, stated that tall, thin knights were considered preferable.[3]

Granted that he had grown past childhood, a man could expect to live to his thirties; if he survived the thirties, his expectancy was for the late fifties.[4] The prevailing causes of death, aside from violence and the chance of meeting a pneumococcus or a typhoid germ, were brought on by circulatory trouble.[5] Apoplexy, coronary occlusions and thromboses, and angina pectoris carried off most of those who lived their lives sheltered from accidents. Meat and alcohol were consumed in great quantity, particularly during the cold months of the year. Fortunately, at this time everyone lived a very active life, which made it possible for such food to be assimilated. The element which was most lacking from the daily menu was vitamin C. Citrus fruits were known, but they were curiosities in northern Europe. Vegetables served at table were always boiled or stewed, and vitamin C is soluble in water. It is true, however, that some vegetables, including onions, might be eaten raw away from the table. All this means that there was a scorbutic tendency in the offing. Under normal routine this did not become serious because of the eating of fresh meats, the occasional taking of whey and clabber, and the consumption of fresh fruits such as cherries, currants, and apples. But abnormal conditions increased now and then, so that thinness, bad gums, bloody dysentery, ulcers, etc. were by no means unusual. The mediaeval man understood the efficacy of chicken broth in cases of weakness. This is a good tonic against scurvy. Very few men and women of the time had satisfactory teeth. These must have fallen out of poor gums more often than they were pulled because of painful cavities. Good teeth and a sweet breath were highly prized, however, and deemed most desirable.[6]

Women were a poor risk because of childbirth. Any sort of abnormality or complication resulted in death, as there was no expert knowledge of labor beyond what a practiced midwife would know. If a woman survived her childbearing period, she was more apt to live to a ripe old age than was her husband. Take the case of Eleanor of Aquitaine, who died in 1204 at the age of eighty-two. She had lived an intensely active life and had borne nine children. Her two husbands had died many years before, both of them as a result of circulatory conditions.

We repeat here what has already been said, that the diseased and handicapped people were in evidence everywhere. Edged weapons were employed in daily sport. This meant many scarred faces, disfiguring scalp wounds, and mutilated arms and legs. There were no institutions that cared for the mentally handicapped; so these were turned loose on the community, often furnishing entertainment. A limited amount of care for the violently insane was provided in monastic institutions. The prevalence of skin diseases, scurvy, ulcers, and bad teeth in an average mediaeval crowd would be very distasteful to us moderns (if a time machine could enable us to see them). On the other hand, the remark which we made about the people of London should not be forgotten. In every age there are people who care for cleanliness and neatness, and there are others who are careless. Today the former class predominates in most of the society which we see. In the twelfth century the careless group were more conspicuous and predominant; but cleanly folk *did* exist.

Elementary education consisted of instruction in reading and writing, and in the rudiments of counting. It is probable that an *eschequier* or counting table was explained, although the fingers made an excellent abacus if the countings did not go high. Daude de Pradas says that seed pods strung along a stick could be used for adding small sums.[7] Boys who were destined to be clerics received instruction in a nearby monastic school or from their parish priest.[8] Teaching began with the alphabet; then the common beginner's reader was the *Disticha Catonis*, which was read and copied *ad nauseam.* The *Eclogue* of Theodulus was used in the same way, while Donatus was the Latin grammar. The students carried wax tablets on which they wrote with an ivory, bone, or metal stylus.[9] The tablets were held on the right knee. At times there were so many boys beginning letters that it was profitable for a clerk to start a small school and not limit himself to private instruction. There is a fascinating picture of such a class given by Guibert de Nogent:

> Once I was beaten in school; the school was only one of the rooms in our house. Of those whom the teacher accepted I alone had been free from discipline. My careful mother had exacted this from the teacher by increasing the fee and conferring the honor of her patronage. Therefore when at one evening hour, the class having been dismissed, I came to my mother's knee soberly, having been beaten harder than I deserved, she began to ask as usual whether I had been whipped on that day. In order not to betray the teacher I denied the fact completely, but she, willy-nilly, lifted up my undergarment, which is called a shirt, and found the ribs somewhat discolored by the blows of the rod, and the skin covered with welts. When she had grieved from the depths of her heart over this excessive cruelty endured by my tenderness, she stormed and wept, exclaiming: "You shall never be a clerk, and you will not endure punishment in order to learn letters." I answered her as reproachfully as I could: "I would rather die than to stop learning and not be a clerk." But she promised me that if I would wish to be a knight she would give me arms when I had reached the proper age.[10]

This charming passage was written during the first half of the twelfth century. Alexander himself declared that the master should use only a ruler on the palm for minor offenses. A rod might be employed for graver "sins," but under no condition should a scourge be used.[11]

As students of literature we are concerned to know about the laity, whether they too could get the rudiments of an education. We have noted above that the librarian of Baldwin of Ardres was a layman. It is likely that many of the daughters of upper-class groups learned to read and write, and doubtless some young boys who intended eventually to be knights got elementary instruction in letters at an early age. Guernes of Pont-Sainte-Maxence says, "All those other romances which have been made about the Martyr, written by clerks or laymen, monks or ladies, I have heard many of them lie."[12] Some girls went even further and received some advanced education in Latin literature. Marie de France was one of these; Giraldus writes a poem to a "learned lady";[13] Baudri de Bourgueil addressed the learned Emma.[14] Examples of just plain reading ability can be multiplied.[15] Gaimar says that Dame Custance read the *Life of Henry of England* in her private chamber.[16] In the *Yvain* a young girl reads from a romance to her father and mother.[17] We are not puzzled that common minstrels should know how to read because many of them had had clerical instruction and they continued to attend jongleur schools.[18] We wonder a little about the shipmaster in *Huon de Bordeaux*. Huon is given a letter addressed to the seaman Garin, who sails out of Brindisi and who is guardian of that port:

They find the sailor seated in a chair, on two cushions. There was an awning over him to protect him from the sun, that it should not harm him. Huon sees him and dismounts to the ground, for he thought the sailor was lord of the region. . . . "You are wrong, Sire," said Garin, "when you get off your horses. I am surely not lord of this place. I am a sailor and that is how I earn my living." . . . "Sire," said Huon, "look at this letter." He took the letter and broke the seal; he read the letter, for he knew enough to do so, and he saw well what was written there. . . .[19]

It is rather strange to find a sailor who can read.

The method of instruction which was used was the phonetic system.

A priest once wished to teach a wolf to read. "A," said the priest. "A," said the wolf, who was very sly and clever. "B," said the priest. "Say it with me." "B," repeated the wolf; "I grant that." "C," said the priest; "go on and say that." "C," said the wolf. "Are there so many of them?" The priest answered: "Say them by yourself."[20]

The wolf could think of nothing but "B," which of course signified "lamb" for him and remained an *idée fixe*. If a wolf could find a private instructor, we might expect that a girl could easily find one also.[21] This instruction probably included more French reading and writing than was given in such a class as the one attended by little Guibert de Nogent. The girl would continue with her private instruction until she tired, which might mean that she could advance as far as the trivium. As soon as a boy had learned to read with facility in his class, or under private tutoring, he asked to receive the simple tonsure from his bishop, and he was then able to move to the higher schools. His age would be eleven or twelve at that time. Two years would be consumed with the trivium, perhaps more, and then he would be ready to think of higher things, at the age of fourteen or fifteen. He might specialize further on some phase of the trivium, as Alexander continued to do, before going on with the quadrivium, law, and medicine.

It is doubtful that any of these mediaeval students ever attained to a superior degree of reading ability. Their facility could not have exceeded that of a modern court reporter when he is reading from stenotype notes. A page did not stand out at a glance as it is accustomed to do for us moderns. This is a factor which is seldom taken into account. Silent reading was not the rule, even when there was no one else in the room. Lips continued to form the words. In the correspondence of everyday business and legal matters, a clerk had to become proficient in translating from Latin into French and vice versa.[22]

We have already stated that men and women of the baronial class were constantly accompanied by birds and animals. A hall in a castle would have reminded us somewhat of a zoo.[23] Those who were fond of hunting had their favorite birds on their wrists, and some of these were placed, from time to time, on a T perch which stood in the room. The hunting birds had soft leather thongs or jesses on their feet, and they might have their eyes hooded. A bird of this kind loses balance occasionally and gives a few flaps with its wings. The one who holds it makes an upward swoop with his arm as though to increase the support. We can picture such flappings and arm movements distracting the attention of a group of barons at frequent intervals. Not all the birds carried were hunting birds. There were some popinjays or parrots, which had been imported from the Middle East. An occasional tame raven may have been set on the floor or on the perch. We have mentioned the three breeds of dogs that walked at their masters' heels. They moved about on the rush-littered paving, and many were not house broken. There were sure to be a few monkeys. A tame badger or weasel could be present in the hall. At table the food thrown on the floor would be picked up by the dogs. Puppies were amusing, even when they got up on the tables and benches. There is an attractive picture of a peasant playing with his dog in Marie's fable "De l'asne ki voelt juer a sun seignur." Although the lion is a frequent character in their literature, I doubt that a twelfth-century man had ever seen one, unless he had been to the Holy Land. Information on the habits of the king of beasts could come from Pliny. In the *Yvain* Chrétien gives the impression that a lion was no bigger than a large dog, capable of being carried on his master's shield, and of lying with him in a bed.[24]

The role played by the hunting bird is emphasized by Alexander Neckam when he describes a bedroom. "There should be present also a perch on which can rest a sparrow hawk, a kestrel, a goshawk, a gerfalcon, a tercel, a peregrine falcon, an osprey or 'serpent eagle,' a saker, a crane falcon or hobby, a mountain falcon, and a lanner."[25] These are the usual varieties. Alexander fails to mention the various kinds of merlins. The important event in the lives of these birds was the molting season. Daude de Pradas (born late in the twelfth century) says that a bird should not be used for hunting much in March.[26] Eight days before the end of that month the molting preparations must be carried out. The cage or mew should be set in the direct sunlight, covered with reed matting. At the start, certain medicines are to be given on various days. The perch must be made soft. This period of molting continues for four months, and the bird's health is attended to as though the bird were a human being. Daude insists that a man who is handling a hunting bird should wash, change clothes, and dine before holding the bird. When the hunt is begun, the hood is removed from the eyes and the bird is tossed off the hunter's wrist against the wind. This is done when the prey becomes visible. A properly trained bird will return and give up the prey to the huntsman without a struggle, and will once more take its place on the wrist. The pleasure in falconry lay in watching the bird perform—a pleasure unlike that derived from shooting with an arrow, where the hunter's marksmanship is all important, or from hunting the boar with a lance, where the element of personal danger is exciting.[27]

There was no organized system of carrying letters and parcels in this period. If the sender were important enough, he made use of a private messenger, a *courlieu.* John of Salisbury mentions using a monk in this capacity.[28] In the fabliau *Del fol chevalier* a group of seven knights deliver a message for their lord. Lesser folk had to wait until someone whom they knew was going to the desired destination and they could impinge upon his good will. As letters were very stereotyped at that time, except when written by learned men, it is doubtful that they gave much comfort to either sender or receiver. They could, of course, impart valuable news on the safety or danger of an individual, and they could recommend the bearer. A letter was written on parchment, one side only, as a rule. This was folded, slashes were made with a knife, and a cord was passed through. The two strands of the cord were then connected with a seal of wax or of lead. Wax was, of course, the common material for most people. Probably Villon's description of the procedure of sealing was true also at this earlier date.[29] The sealer took a wafer of wax, chewed it in his mouth, and then flattened out the resulting wax ball with his thumb, on the desired spot. He took a seal, usually on a ring, and made an impression. If this seal remained unbroken, and if the cord was not cut, the addressee understood that the message had not been tampered with. At the same time he recognized the seal of the sender and was assured that it really came from him.[30]

At various intervals we have mentioned the vocal music of the twelfth century: the plain chant, used invariably by larger groups of singers; and parallel, free, and melismatic organum, which could be performed by small groups of trained singers. It was at Compostela and at Limoges that the melismatic organum was devised and soon grew into popularity. In this type of singing the tenor or *cantus firmus* (lower part) goes slow, with whole notes (to use a modern term), while the upper part or *duplum* weaves about. It soon became convenient to use fewer words, particularly in the slower *cantus firmus*. Short *clausulae*, such as *Benedicamus domino*, *Deo gratias* were sufficient, if repeated over and over, for a whole vocal production.[31] The choir school at Notre Dame Cathedral in Paris had great influence on secular as well as ecclesiastical music. The *Magnus liber* of Leoninus offered appropriate music for the whole Church year. By 1183 there was a new organist and choirmaster at Notre Dame who was still more exciting. His name was Perotinus.[32]

Musical instruments were still not used effectively.[33] One might be employed at times to carry a single part in an organum. (Perotinus had introduced still another vocal line—the *triplum.*) Instruments were used also to accompany dancers. We have the instrumental *estampie*. Horn combinations were possible.[34] It is probable that a jongleur accompanied himself occasionally, in unison with the voice. The commonest instrument was the *viele*. This was a flat-bottomed fiddle, slightly triangular, which had no sound post in its interior. It might have three strings, tuned in fourths or fifths, and it was held flat on the upper left arm, close to the chin. The bow was a little awkward to handle because it was concave. The *gigue* was a tenor *viele*, the ancestor of the *viola da gamba;* it seems to have been set on the left knee and played in cello fashion. It could also be held in front of the chest and chin, horizontally rather than vertically. The harp was a small instrument of seven or twelve strings, held on the knee. A *rote* was a zitherlike harp of five strings.[35] The *mandore* was a kind of mandolin, played on the lap. A *monicorde*, or organistrum, was ordinarily played by two people. It was a long, guitar-shaped instrument. The single string was varied by changing metal contacts, and the music was produced by another musician who turned a hurdy-gurdy handle at the end. The psalterion was a zither; it was held in front of the chest and the strings were plucked. It is not easy to distinguish between the small reed instruments because they were still in an immature stage of development. The *frestelles* were Panpipes: two or more pipes of different lengths, tied together in descending scale. The *flaute* was a kind of flageolet, with eight holes. The *chalumele* was a rustic oboe. The *estive* and *muse* were varieties of bagpipes. The chanter of such a bagpipe also was named a *chalumele*.[36]

The horns had no valves, as yet, which meant that they could blow only the fundamental tone, the octave, the third and fifth, and one other note. The *buisine* was a large, crooked horn with turned-up end—the Roman *buccina*.[37] We are assuming that the *graile* was a long, straight horn.[38] The *cor*, or hunting horn, was usually a cow's horn, but it could be made of an ivory tusk, imported from Asia Minor.[39] The *tabour* was a small drum, suspended from the neck, and beaten on each end by the player's fingers.[40] The *clochetes* were a series of small bells, strung on a rod, and played with a hammer from a sitting position.

We have reserved for the place of honor among these instruments the organ.[41] It had great possibilities in the training of a choir because the playing of it was easy and the notes were steady in pitch. A large organ in the twelfth century might have two players seated at the one keyboard, and from two to four men occupied with the bellows. Each of the players operated a single rank of pipes, consisting of from ten to twelve pipes. These were not graded—that is, they had the same diameter throughout their scale—the variation was in length only. As a result the upper tones were more shrill than the lower. The keys, called *lingulae*, were slides that were pulled out and pushed in. Each one was stopped with a small copper-headed nail to prevent it from sliding all the way out, and often the key had a small knob which the player could grasp as he pulled it out. Each key had its note letter scratched on it. The bellows were constructed of plane-tree wood, with pleated sides of heavy linen fastened to the wood with casein glue. A canopy was lowered over the organ from the ceiling by means of a pulley, to keep out the dust. We cite an appreciation of organ music from Wace's *Brut:* "Much would you hear the organs play and clerks sing and chant in organum—their voices going up and down, the songs rising and then falling. Much would you hear the knights coming and going in the churches, as much to hear the clerks sing as to view the ladies."[42] Probably each of the two players at the keyboard took one of the parts of the organum in unison with the singers.

This book of ours is no place to discuss musicology, but we can say a few words about scales and notation. I have in my possession a fragment of a musical manuscript written in France in the latter part of the twelfth century. A staff of four lines has been ruled with a scratching instrument, not with ink. The movement of the music up and down the staff is marked on these four lines by the usual neumes (shown below).[43]

Given *c*, *d*, and *e* as any three successive tones, the neumes (in the order shown) can be expressed by the following combinations: *c*, *c*, *cd*, *dc*, *cdc*, *dcd*, *cde*, the same, *edc*,

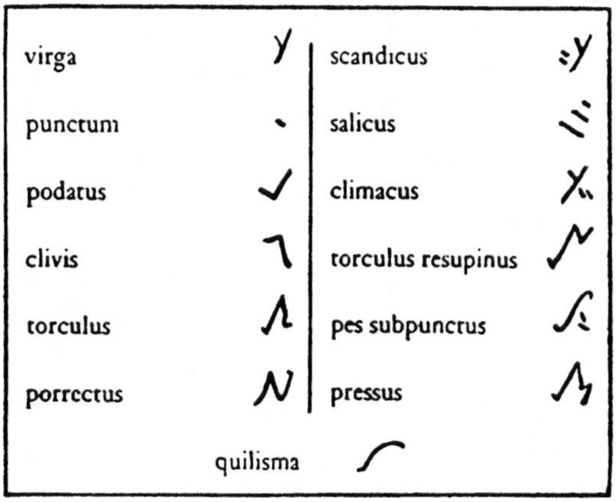

cdcd, *dedc*, a sustained tone, and a portamento. There are a few more neumes than these, but I am mentioning only those which I have noted on my musical fragment of the period. All music at this date was fond of the octave, fifth, and unison. Thirds occur usually as glide notes only. The Early Church modes took the place of scales. B-flat was the only accidental.

At this point we will hint at the concept of aesthetics, or the understanding of Beauty, as it was analyzed in the twelfth century.[44] There were four constants: symbolism, allegory, proportion, and brilliance of color. The Essence of Beauty is the Invisible becoming visible (Scotus Erigena). Symbolism is a personal intuition, an aesthetic expression of our share in Existence. Allegory, on the other hand, expresses the principle that inner forms and eternal beauties can be foreshadowed in outer forms. The great principle in color was considered to be luminosity. Light is a little of God; God is Pure Light. A man or woman was thought to be beautiful not because he or she was well proportioned; rather because the concept of the ideal human being shows through. Quantitative proportion was thought of as very important. Musical tones and visual harmonies should be in numerical relation. Beauty was thought of, therefore, as a sort of arithmetical progression: musical tones should be related on the scale of 12–8–9–6. In plastic art perfect squares were arranged two on two or three on three. Rectangles in which the long dimension surpassed the shorter by one unit were preferred. Boethius, Scotus Erigena, and St. Augustine were authorities in all this. The ancients held the same aesthetic theories as the man of the Middle Ages, but their application was mostly from observation. The mediaeval man wanted to make syntheses of all the texts at his disposal and to generalize on them.

At this point the reader might expect us to turn to the visual arts. Sculpture and painting in the Middle Ages were so closely allied with the industrial crafts, however, that it will be more logical for us to come to them after further consideration of the trades.

The superstition of the time was a complicated matter. John of Salisbury mentions that his early teacher was more concerned with divination than he was with anything else.[45] Monday was at all times an unlucky day on which to begin any enterprise.[46] The unlucky days varied with localities, but here is a typical set:[47] January 1, 2, 4, 5, 10, 11, 15; February 1, 7, 10; March 2, 11; April 16, 21; May 6, 15, 20; June 4, 7; July 15, 20; August 19, 20; September 6, 7; October 6; November 15, 19; and December 6, 7, 9. When one of these was a prominent saint's day it was, of course, made lucky. To see birds on the left side was still considered a bad omen. This is satirized in the *Roman de Renart* where Tybert the cat, as he approaches Renart's house, sees the bird of St. Martin (a kite) on the left, between an ash tree and a spruce.[48] To hear thundering (on the left?) and to leave the house by a step with the left foot were also ominous.[49]

Astrology was founded upon the belief that the planets (according to the Ptolemaic system)—Moon, Mercury, Venus, Sun, Mars, Jupiter, and Saturn—had constant influence upon our bodies and upon the treasures of the mineral world. These planets gave the appearance—and still do to the uninitiated—of moving along an imaginary belt (16 degrees wide) which goes slantwise across the heavens. This is the zodiac. Along this belt are twelve fixed constellations more or less well spaced. They are Aries, Taurus, Gemini, Cancer, Leo, Virgo, Libra, Scorpio, Sagittarius, Capricorn, Aquarius, and Pisces. Capricorn and Aquarius are called the houses of Saturn; Sagittarius and Pisces belong to Jupiter; Scorpio and Aries are for Mars; Leo is the house of the Sun; Taurus and Libra house Venus; Mercury has Virgo and Gemini; and the Moon owns Cancer. This series will explain how a planet could be in its own house. Saturn and Mars tend to be evil; Jupiter, Sun, and Venus are held to be favorable; and the Moon and Mercury are a little of both. The first hour of the day was supposedly governed by the planet after which the day is named. The second hour was thought to be controlled by the next planet, and so on in order. A planet was in the ascendant when it appeared just above the eastern horizon. It had meaning also when it was in conjunction, or proximity, with another heavenly body.[50]

To continue with other superstitions, the Monge de Montaudo mentions that it was unlucky to see a cripple or a blind man, especially first thing in the day.[51] The minerals in the earth were believed to have absorbed virtues from the planets, and thus all sorts of gems and minerals were considered magic-workers. Alexander did not dispute these.[52] He mentions that the agate renders the wearer eloquent, amiable, and powerful. The *allectorias* (a pebble from a rooster's craw) gives victory in combat; the lodestone, when placed on a sleeping woman's head, tells whether she is chaste.[53] There are many of these legends, circulated mostly from the Latin lapidary of Bishop Marbod, which was composed early in the twelfth century. The belief that a perfectly pure substance would purify a base substance with which it came into contact was also a basis for the alchemy of the time. A few people were seeking that perfectly pure substance which would turn base metals into the perfectly pure metal—gold. The catalyst that would perform this transformation was sometimes called the "philosophers' stone," but it was referred to by many other terms. This sort of thing was more highly developed among the Arabs and the Mozarabs (Arabicized Christians) in Spain. Toledo was thought of as the true center for the study of magic and the black arts.[54] Wistasce li moines goes to Toledo for such study and, in a later branch, Renart the Fox puts in an apprenticeship there. (These sources are a little late, but they reflect a belief that must have been current earlier.) Perhaps those who knew something about Spain were impressed strangely by the Spanish calendar, which added thirty-five years to the traditional Christian dating; this looked as though the Spaniards dated from a heathen tradition.

An uneducated man's superstitions (which were more often than not shared by the educated) were not very deep, but they were extremely active and varied. He believed that there were *folets* or goblins, who could be friendly.[55] There was a good witch named Abunde who flew around at night. Bad witches were apt to be demons who had taken on the human forms of certain individuals. Such a witch, when caught, should be branded with the key of the church door; burning on a pyre was the ultimate fate.[56] There were birds that came from Hell.[57] There were also demons—incubi and succubi.[58] These were presumed to cohabit with mortals on occasion, when they had taken on beautiful or handsome human forms. Merlin was the result of one such cohabitation.[59] The dead could appear as ghosts.[60] On one occasion a man bewailing his dead wife saw her with a group of supernatural dancers; he snatched her away and she returned to live with him, bearing him more children. The story of Edric Wilde, who cohabited with and married a lovely supernatural lady, and who lost her only when he reproached her with a reference to her sisters, is narrated by Walter Map. These stories bear some evidence of Celtic folklore. The Welsh and Irish were predisposed to believe such things.[61] There were many superstitions of various kinds. It was thought that the wound of a murdered man bled when the murderer drew near.[62] In a birth of twins some held that two men were responsible.[63] Children were supposed to be marked by the physical mutilations of a parent. A child, thereby, could be born without an ear, or without a nose.[64] Some—perhaps I should say many—folk were prone to have unorthodox religious ideas. The people were somewhat free in canonizing "saints." This tendency is mocked by the author of the first branch of the *Roman de Renart*, in his usual bitter way. People were also ready to accept as authentic many unauthenticated "miraculous" cures. They believed in changelings.[65] Divination of the future was quite common.[66]

An educated man had his ideas on the marvelous magnified by what he read in Solinus and Pliny. He considered Vergil a magician. Alexander discusses Vergil in his *De naturis rerum*.[67] He repeats the tale of Vergil's golden leech which saved Naples from a plague when it was placed in a certain well. Centuries later when that well was cleaned and the golden object removed, there was no longer any protection against the plague. On another occasion the butchers in Naples were disturbed by the rapid spoiling of their meat. This too was corrected by Vergil. It was accepted that Vergil, in his Fourth Eclogue, had prophesied the coming of Christ. Vergil was said to have constructed a huge palace in Rome, containing images with warning bells. When asked how long this building would stand, he was supposed to have replied: "Until a Virgin shall bear a Child." Alexander trusted also in the Prophecies of Merlin, which were the work of Geoffrey of Monmouth and were incorporated into his *Historia Regum Britanniae*.[68] Alexander cites one of these prophecies as evidence that the schools at Oxford will one day be transferred to Ireland. Above all, it was believed that dreams had true portent.[69] This, of course, found support in the story of Joseph in the Bible.

The offspring of crossbreeding were accepted with little hesitation. We know today that two species of animals will not mate unless they are closely allied, but Giraldus and his contemporaries believed that a combination of dog and monkey, cow and stag, etc., was entirely possible.[70] Spontaneous generation of bees, beetles, wasps, and other insects was commonly believed in.[71]

We now turn to a survey of art in smaller and larger forms. The common materials for lesser objects were oxhorn, *cuir bouilli*, and ivory. Both oxhorn and ivory could be pressed into plates after being heated with moist heat. These plates were carved, sometimes with exquisite skill, and then nailed into position on a wooden base. I have before me a photograph of a twelfth-century box lid, preserved at the Cluny Museum. It shows a representation of Our Lord in a central medallion, with the four Evangelists in the four corners. The border and the center dividing lines, as well as the figures, are beautifully carved. There are three large clamps and many small nails which hold the ivory pieces in place. Many ivory chessmen and draughtsmen, in the round, have been preserved. I fancy that some of the pieces which we think were used in playing draughts were actually counters, in use on the *eschequier* or counting board. Horn was the material for commoner objects: spoons, pen cases to be carried at the belt, handles, cases, combs, and so on.[72] It was only when superior artistry was to be displayed that these everyday objects were carved from ivory. The *flabellum* was a fan to be used at the altar of a church; it often had a handle of carved ivory.[73] A common type of walking stick at this date was a wooden stick with a T handle. When carried by an abbot, as a badge of his office, the stick was referred to as a tau cross and the handle was of carved ivory. "Triptychs," or panels folding into three, were placed at the back of small altars. These triptychs were nearly always carved ivory plates set onto wood. *Cuir bouilli* can be made by heating thick leather in oil to a degree just short of the boiling point.[74] When this has cooled and dried, it becomes a very hard, bony material which can be carved. This material is sufficient unto itself and does not have to be mounted. It was used, therefore, for articles such as knife cases, which were subject to hard wear.

In 1175 the Church Council of Westminster decreed that chalices should be made of gold or silver.[75] Some of the poorer churches continued the use of pewter for sacred vessels.[76] Pewter, an alloy of tin and lead, was not in common use in the average household in the twelfth century.

Thin plates of the various metals were nailed to a wooden base and handled in much the same way as ivory. There is an evangeliary, made in the Rhineland in the period 1150–1200, which can be compared with the ivory binding that I have described above. The binding is of wood, covered with leather, on which silver-gilt plates have been nailed. The Blessed Virgin is in the center with the Infant Jesus on her knee. The four Evangelists are in medallions located at the four corners.[77] Where metal was involved the goldsmith nearly always incrusted on it some cabochon gems (roughly bruted). These are sprinkled rather profusely, without much taste for color or size. Moonstones, sapphires, garnets, agates, and amethysts are commonly met with—also jaspers and chrysoprases.[78]

If the metal object was solid, or made of thick plates, the twelfth-century artist liked to add enamel. The design was first gouged out. This would be filled with powdered glass containing the desired coloring matter. When fused in a furnace this produced enamel. This is *champ levé* work, as opposed to *cloisonné*. In the British Museum there is a beautiful enameled plaque showing the figure of Bishop Henry of Winchester and his brother King Stephen. The usual base for enamel was copper. If the whole surface of the metal is coated with enamel and an elaborate design is made, this is called "painted enamel." Limoges was famous for its enamels.[79]

We have spoken of bookbindings in ivory and metal plaques on a wooden background. Such binding was rare and was employed for expensive books only. The average book was bound in wooden boards without any design. Leather was often glued over the surface, but it remained plain and untooled. There are some forty exceptions to this, made in England. Because the same metal stamps were used on them, we judge that all of these come from the same bindery, probably a monastery which developed this novel idea and later abandoned it.[80] One of these books is the Oxford manuscript Rawlinson C163, of which I have a rubbing in my possession. The book is a copy of the *Sententiae* of Peter Lombard. The front and back have both been repaired. Not many stamps were used. They are geometric or they represent fantastic birds and animals. One is a kind of griffin which has its tail curled high over its back.

The British Museum has a collection of finger rings which were discovered some hundred years ago. The collection was found with some coins contemporary with Henry II of England.[81] There is a friendship ring, clasped hands and no stone. There is also one which has filigree in black on an enamel *chaton*. The others show the following stones: sapphire, amethyst, and colored glass with a painted foil at the back.

Although pottery was not popular, this does not mean that baked clay was not used for other things. Floor and roof tiles were very important. It is difficult to date surviving floor tiles. A common type was a rough yellow design on a red clay background.[82] The design might be bird, beast, or geometric figure. There were many variations. The art of mosaic was practiced, but the surviving specimens are largely Italian, sometimes on a French design. The Cluny Museum has some of these. One of them shows a workman filling a wine cask from a bucket, with the aid of a funnel.[83] Another has a sort of griffin, similar to the stamp on the tooled binding, with its tail curled over its back.[84] Roof tiles have not survived from this period. Their position was too vulnerable.

The most realistic art from the twelfth century is certainly that which is found in bas- and high reliefs, usually in tympana and on the capitals of columns. The Church of Saint-Ursin in Bourges has a splendid tympanum of this kind.[85] There is a scroll border; then three rows of figures. The upper row shows Renart the Fox, a goose, two hens drawing a two-wheeled cart in which Renart rides, and a tree. The middle row is a boar hunt, with lances. There are fine details of costume, including a sort of legging fastened with a garter band at the top. The *levriers* are there, with their short ears. The lowest row displays the common theme of the Labors of the Months. The villein tends a fire, prunes, hoes, wields a scythe, measures, winnows, picks grapes, puts wine into casks, slaughters, eats, and cooks over a fire. For the month of April there is a representation of a gentleman in a *chape*. The realism of these figures is excellent. The famous tympanum over the Porta della Pescaria of the cathedral at Modena (Italy) is in bas-relief.[86] On the arch it has a representation of an Arthurian scene. The lintel over the door shows Renart the Fox who is being buried by two hens, and who then revives and carries them off. This Renart scene resembles the one at Saint-Ursin, in Bourges, where the hens are drawing Renart in a cart.

The capitals found in the cloisters of the twelfth century are remarkable. The Cloisters Museum in New York City has some fine examples. As Mâle has repeated, it is possible for a botanist to recognize many of the vines and plants thus depicted.[87] A capital in the cloister of Saint-Guilhem has beautiful acanthus leaves. Another shows the heart-shaped leaves of the bryony vine. There is the Hell capital which pictures sinners being brought in chains to the mouth of Hell. The Massacre of the Innocents, and the Presentation of Christ in the Temple are the subjects of others. The capital from Langon, which we have mentioned already as being in the Romanesque Chapel, shows two heads which may be those of Henry II and Eleanor of Aquitaine. The capitals of the Cuxa Cloister are more rudely done. There the human heads, animals, birds, acanthus leaves, grapes, and so forth are stylized and conventional in design, with little attempt at realism. The few capitals preserved from Pontaut are well executed leaf forms, rosettes, etc., and birds picking grapes.[88]

Fresco painting was done on wet walls with colors mixed with lime. For instance, flesh colors on this surface were made with ocher, cinnabar, and lime.[89] In painting wooden objects, such as a crucifix, or painting on leather, a linseed base was used, and the resulting finish was then varnished with linseed and sandarac gum. A painter at this time used a sort of fixed palette: flesh tints were made from white ceruse (white of lead), yellowed ceruse, cinnabar, and a little green added.[90] Half-shadow flesh tint used more green, ocher, and cinnabar. Then there was a deeper combination for full shadow, and there were also prearranged palettes for rose, darker rose, high light, and so on. Wrinkles, nostrils, and the area around the eyes took the half-shadow.

Not all fresco work was religious in theme. Marie de France refers to a painting of Venus casting Ovid's *Remedia amoris* into the fire.[91] Baudri de Bourgueil mentions secular themes on the wall of a bedroom.[92] Peter Pictor complains that he has to paint goddesses all day long.[93] Henry II of England caused many frescoes to be made in his palace at Winchester; among them was one symbolizing the rebellion of his sons. Time and damp have eliminated nearly all such work.[94] The place to find painting best preserved is in surviving manuscripts. We have been depending on these illuminations for many of our details in this book. The figures in these miniatures are stiffer in pose than those in the sculptured reliefs. The proportions of the human figures are awkward. Perspective is clumsy or missing altogether. Some of the work is better than others. The medium used was tempera.[95] After sketching his design with a lead, the illuminator ground his colors and mixed them with white of egg, perhaps also with the yolk. The red was red lead or minium; the white was ceruse; the blue was ultramarine or lapis lazuli (a valuable material which illuminators occasionally stole by concealing it in their mouths); the green could be copper verdigris; the yellow was usually orpiment or realgar, but it could be yellowed ceruse; the black was lampblack, or perhaps burnt vine twigs. Gold leaf was applied in richer illuminations where yellow was demanded. This was applied on a white-of-egg base and then burnished with a deer tooth, or boar tusk. There were some simple drawings made in both black and red ink.

A scriptorium did not have to do afresh every set of miniatures, where these were used a number of times. An original set could be made to serve as a model. The English Psalter in the Morgan Library has illuminations which were multipled in this way. A piece of vellum or parchment was laid under an illumination, and the outline of the figures was punched into this with a pin. This newly formed pattern would be laid over a fresh page on which the miniature was to be reproduced. A pouncing bag of cloth, in which fine charcoal had been placed, would be rubbed over the perforated vellum and the dark outline would come through on the surface to be painted. A pouncing bag was used also to transfer designs to a wall, from a previously prepared pattern.[96]

Architecture was the major art of the twelfth century. Many serious and considered constructions of secular buildings were made in the early reign of Philip Augustus. There were the market halls at the Campelli, new city walls, civic buildings, and many others. But architecture as a decorative art applied primarily to ecclesiastical buildings. Northern France and England, around 1180, were thrilled by the possibilities of the new French style (which we call Gothic).[97] The principal element in this style is the support of ceiling vaults with intersecting ribs known as ogives. Ogival ceiling vaults occurred in Evreux as early as 1120. In Durham (England) the cathedral had them in 1093, and the cathedral at Gloucester used this type of support in 1104. In Lombardy, St. Ambrose (Milan) was vaulted in this way as early as 1075, and so was Saint-James at Corneto in 1095. It would seem that the Lombards began this style, copying it perhaps from ancient Roman models, and that it spread from Lombardy to England and northern France. As a result of this new distribution of stress in the ceilings, the architects began to employ more and more the pointed fish arches which are commonly supposed to be the chief characteristic of the style. The ogival ceiling vaults and the pointed arches threw more stress onto the outer walls, and thus flying buttresses became necessary. These were dissimulated at first, as ambulatories. Sculptured decorations began to alter also. The Romanesque architect liked fancy moldings: the billet, the square billet, the nailhead, and beakhead designs. In the new style the ornamentation was more illustrative of the play of light on curved surfaces. After 1175 the transition stage was over and simple Gothic had won the day, except in Auvergne and central France where the advance was slower. It was the great Basilica of Saint-Denis, near Paris, the creation of Abbot Suger between 1140 and 1144, which gave the chief impetus to the spread of the new style. That is why Gothic is rightly called the French style, as opposed to Romanesque. The cathedral at Chartres (1144–53) and the one at Bourges also were copied extensively elsewhere. Where Romanesque structures continued to be built, they were modified in some ways by the Gothic or new French design. Many modern readers who admire the diabolical gargoyles of Notre Dame de Paris imagine that these are part of the original design. That is not true. Most of them are creations at the hands of Viollet-le-Duc, the nineteenth-century architect. Most twelfth-century buildings had no gutters. Where gutters did occur, the end-spouts (or gargoyles) were geometric in form as at Fontenay in Côte-d'Or. The convent church of Saint-Pierre on Montmartre, built after 1147, had a firmer and better reinforced roof structure. This also was copied rather widely and became standard for the Gothic style.

For those who are not familiar with the simple plan of a mediaeval church building, a few remarks on this might be helpful. The larger churches were designed in the form of a cross with the intersection approaching close to one end. The main body of the church, where the congregation gathers, is the nave. The aisles on each side of the nave are the ambulatories, separated from the nave by columns and their arches. The part of the building which intersects is called the transept. As a church in those days always had its altar at the east, there is a north transept and a south transept. The space beyond the transepts is devoted to the chancel or choir, the sanctuary containing the altar, and usually a space behind the altar where a shrine or chapel is placed. The ambulatory, or side aisles, usually continue around the choir section, passing through the chapel or shrine in the apse. Many churches have an atrium or vestibule inside the front doors, at the west end, which is partitioned off from the body of the nave. The reader will understand that the roofs of the ambulatories do not need to rise as high as the roof over the nave. This makes possible a series of windows high up along the two sides of the nave. That area is called the clerestory.

So ends our sketch of the twelfth-century crafts and arts. It would be pleasant to close on this note, but there remain certain matters of a different kind which we must summarize. Among these are law and justice, taxation, and money. A layman was responsible to the court of his feudal lord. If his lord was an abbot or some other ecclesiast, the *avoué* or lay baron of the church lands administered lay justice. A churchman was forbidden to spill blood.[98] Petty barons did not always have the right of high justice (life and limb) over their vassals, and in such cases serious offenses were handled by the overlord of the small baron. A lord who administered high justice was said to have the right of "ban."[99] In northern France and England the law in force was custom law, which varied somewhat from area to area. There was a *Coustumier de Normandie*, and so on. Where custom law proved inadequate, an enlightened baron pieced out its defects with the Roman law, and for this purpose a clerk who had been trained in civil law at Bologna, or elsewhere, was much in demand. A lord when administering justice was assisted by his barons, and presumably by his clerk who was trained in the law. Usamah noted this procedure among the Franks in the Holy Land: "The king said to six, seven knights, 'Arise and judge this case for him the defendant.' The knights went out from the audience chamber, retired by themselves, and consulted together until they all agreed upon one thing. Then they returned to the audience chamber and said, 'We have passed judgment to the effect. . . .' Such a judgment, after having been pronounced by the knights, not even the king nor any of the chieftains of the Franks can alter or revoke."[100] This is not strictly true; but for the lord to override the verdict would have provoked much dissatisfaction among his vassals. The defendant and the plaintiff were required to appear in person at this date. If the case could not be settled immediately, the lord would demand pledges. Friends of the defendant would come forward and pledge their estates as guarantee that they would produce the defendant in court when this was required. In the romances and *chansons de geste* many arbitrary rulings are made by the lord. He could cause those who gave the pledges to be hanged along with the defendant if he so desired.[101] It is questionable that such procedure could actually have been followed with impunity. Philip Augustus, and even Louis VII, his father, were much concerned over the administration of justice in such baronial courts. They were encouraging important cases to appear before the *Curia Regis* in Paris. The procedure of appeal was in its infancy. St. Louis in the following century made the needed reforms.

In the twelfth century it was still a common thing for a defendant to prefer trial by ordeal or combat. Female defendants, particularly in cases where honor was involved, were apt to prefer the ordeal. Women could have recourse to trial by combat. In that event they were permitted to find any champion who could be persuaded to fight for them. The theory back of these trials was that Divine punishment would be meted out to the perjurer. Before combat or ordeal, the defendant took solemn oath on the Gospel book, or on a reliquary containing saints' bones, that he was not lying; the plaintiff did the same. After they attended Mass, the trial was held. Women of higher rank preferred the ordeal with the hot bar of iron. They walked with this in the bare hand before many witnesses. If the burn healed in a specific length of time, the defendant was adjudged innocent.[102] A serf who was accused was usually given the ordeal of water.[103] A huge cask was filled and a wooden board was set across the top. The victim undergoing the test was bound with a rope attached to his shoulders. If innocent he was supposed to sink; if guilty he would float. Men of lower rank were allowed to have trial by combat, making use of cudgels, with or without a shield.[104]

A feudal lord could have spent a large amount of his time holding court and administering justice to petty offenders. Many turned such duties over to their viscount or sheriff, or to some other deputy. If a person thought that he was wronged by some act that was in the process of accomplishment, he could stand at the spot and call "Haro." This was equivalent to placing an injunction upon his adversary. As soon as the justice arrived, a decision could be made then and there.

There was considerable laxity about the administration of the death penalty. When a court was functioning efficiently, it was customary to allow a young offender, his first time up, to get off with a warning or a flogging. He might on the second, or even the third, occasion receive a mutilation: loss of an ear, a hand, etc.[105] This was a very severe penalty. If the offense were repeated over and over, the defendant would eventually be hanged or blinded. Among those who had financial position a fine was very often assessed, and exile was meted out to offenders of all kinds.[106] If the court desired, the accused might be put to the torture. Application of fire and drawing of teeth were common forms.[107] Usually a mediaeval author says that the victim was *gehenné* without mentioning the specific form. Hanging was apt to be by strangulation, without the breaking of the neck. The guilty party had a rope placed around his neck and was then pulled up to a high limb of a tree, or to a beam on a specially constructed gallows. In *Wistasce li moines* a young man is told to hang himself, which he does.[108] For treason or sacrilege the terrific penalty of being burnt at a stake, or being drawn by four horses, might be exacted.[109]

The cleric was not subject to the civil courts, although Philip Augustus hoped to arrange it so that in an affair in which both civil and clerical parties were involved the civil court alone would have jurisdiction. The bishops had their own *serjanz* and knights, who maintained order. The bishop's court could not administer the death penalty, but it could excommunicate and fine. It could also incarcerate, and that was not a light punishment.

Strange to relate, murder and personal violence did not always provoke the hand of Justice. Matters of that kind were too often left to the victim's family to avenge. The family of the victim would demand justice from the court, and the murderer or rapist might get off with a money payment. Some families, however, took justice in their own hands, and the subsequent killing was looked upon as justified.[110]

We have already mentioned the values of the coins which were in circulation. A number of mints were authorized to issue money.[111] Under Louis VII there were royal mints in Paris, Mantes, Etampes, Aquitaine, Bourbonnais, Langres, and Saintes. There were semiroyal mints at Laon, Angoulême, La Marche, and Périgord. Certain dukes, lesser lords, bishops, and even abbots were permitted to strike their own coinage. Here is a partial list of the places: Brittany, Anjou, Touraine, Blois, Chartres, Châteaudun, Perche, Châteauroux, Issoudun, Sancerre, Vierzon, Celles, Nivernais, Auvergne, Limousin, Turenne, Toulouse, Saint-Gilles,

Narbonne, Béziers, Anduze, Rodez, Provence, Vienne, Lyon, Saint-Etienne de Dijon, Bourgogne, Auxerre, Champagne, Provins, Meaux, Reims, Amiens, and Beauvais. No wonder there was work for the money-changers on the Grant Pont and elsewhere. The money-changer was primarily interested in the amount of good silver in the coin. The English deniers were *esterlinc* (sterling) and their composition was very good. Under Philip Augustus the mint at Tours, which produced the *deniers tournois*, became exceptionally trustworthy. The king's deniers minted at Paris were known as *parisis*. Punishment for counterfeiting money was rather heavy if it were done by an ordinary thief. The barons got away with all sorts of irregularities, such as reducing the amount of silver and clipping. A merchant on accepting payment, if he noticed anything suspicious or a strange mintage, could satisfy himself by taking a bite with his teeth. Base metal was softer than silver. Letters of credit were yet to be devised, in Italy, some centuries later; but I dare say this simple device existed in a haphazard way as early as the twelfth century. If a Paris merchant went to London, he might be accommodated with *esterlinc* by a professional acquaintance over there. That same Englishman, on going to Paris, would not have to take so much silver with him, as his associate could reciprocate the favor. Money, valuable silver, gold objects, and jewels were kept at home in those heavy chests bound with iron which we have already observed in the treasure room of a castle. They were so heavy that they could not be moved quietly, which was the basis of their security.[112] When a wealthy man first got the habit of leaving large sums with a money-changer, that was the key moment in the history of banking. We do not know whether this happened at so early a date as the twelfth century.

The amount of money in circulation was not enough to take care of the daily economy of a community. For there was much hoarding and laying away in chests, which caused deniers to disappear from circulation. Workmen were often paid in kind. Here are the wages of Gilbert, a carpenter, who worked for the Abbey of Saint-Germain-des-Prés: per diem, two white and two dark loaves of bread, a half *sestier* (four pints) of wine, usually with beans, and meat on special days; annually, a half *mui* of wheat and one frock (*tunica*) to the value of five sous. In the season of winepressing, when he was binding casks, he got each day, extra, a denier and the old hoops and pieces of wood that could not be used. Last of all he was granted the *terram de Vaus*. The document which notes this arrangement is dated 1180. The reader will note that the real payment which he received was the use of a small piece of land; he could not have supported himself without this. Poole says that palace servants in England received only one denier per diem.[113] Like Gilbert, the carpenter of Saint-Germain-des-Prés, they doubtless received other perquisites, and perhaps the use of a bit of land.

The question of taxation is too vast for our present discussion. It involves, first of all, an understanding of the degree of relationship between the feudal lord and the groups of men on his fiefs. By the last quarter of the twelfth century, more and more French towns were recognized as communities of free men, and they received increased economic and political privileges from their overlords.[114] If the taille could not be abolished entirely, the bourgeoisie sought to regularize it; they did not wish to leave the lord the right to levy on them at will. In some cases, by agreement, a fixed sum, such as twenty-five livres per family, was levied each year; in others, the tax paid was proportionate to the income. In still other instances, only extraordinary contributions were demanded; the marriage of the lord's daughter, the knighting of his son, travel abroad, invasion, and enthroning of a new abbot (on ecclesiastical fiefs) were the occasions.[115] The knights who held fiefs were subject to these *aides extraordinaires*. The bourgeoisie felt somewhat elevated when their obligations were similar to those of the knights. It was often specified that voluntary contributions would be gladly accepted. In Paris there was a *taille abonnee*, or annual tax paid to the royal provost on a proportional income basis. This was in effect by the end of the twelfth century. Unfortunately, we have no Paris tax roll dating earlier than 1292. This particular document that we have is most interesting. The very rich paid as high as forty livres a year, and the poor paid very little, not more than two sous in many cases.[116]

The tax paid by peasants again brings us into the complicated domain of feudal taxation. Rents have already been mentioned above. Extraordinary *aides*, *taille abonnee*, and arbitrary tailles could be exacted, depending upon local conditions. The lord had also his invisible taxes in the form of *banalités* or monopolies: the oven, wine press, and mill. The right of lodging and special exactions of labor could be levied.[117]

Despite these various tailles, an industrious peasant could usually make a good living, and so could a bourgeois. It was the baron who was constantly faced with economic ruin. The great pull on his resources was from *fole largesce*, or excessive generosity.[118] In addition there were the tithes and the maintenance of benefices.[119] Instead of granting lands and income to monasteries, cathedral chapters, and hospitals, it had become customary to grant tithes from a given area.[120] As this money was levied on lands, it was paid by barons and peasants according to their holdings. When land was given to an ecclesiastical foundation, it was frequently given in "frankalmoigne"—that is, the clergy gave payment through their prayers.[121]

In closing, we will add a few words on the heretical or non-Catholic sects. These were increased at a later period in the Middle Ages. Walter Map records what they were in the twelfth century. The Waldensians had their Bible (not complete) in the French tongue. They were directed by lay preachers who sought to obtain from Alexander III the right to preach. Walter says that he was one of their examiners. He expresses amusement at them because, being untutored in theology, they admitted to him that they believed in God the Father, God the Son, God the Holy Ghost, and the Mother of Christ, making a Godhead of four persons instead of the Trinity. They were finally excommunicated, in 1184.[122] Another sect, mentioned by Walter, were the *Brabançons* or *routiers*. We should not take too seriously the statement that these formed a heretical sect. They were a group of banditti first organized in Brabant. They were "fugitives, false clerks, runaway monks, and deserters of God of every sort."[123] Both William of Newburgh and Walter Map speak of the *Paterini*.[124] They did not accept the Gospel of St. John, and they held a view of the Holy Communion similar to that taught by Zwingli in the sixteenth century. They were an ascetic group coming first to England in 1160. They were condemned at the Council of Oxford in 1166, and they recrossed to Normandy. Strangely enough, Walter Map says nothing about the Albigenses, who were waxing strong in southern France in his day. Their chief strength was at Albi (Tarn). This group had strong connections with coreligionists in Italy and Bulgaria. They rejected most of the Catholic dogma, including the

Mass. Their leaders called themselves perfecti, and their ideal was one of extreme asceticism, which had an appeal to the masses in the twelfth century. They believed in two coequal powers: God and the Devil. One was the Spirit of Light, and the other was the Lord of Darkness.[125] Only by eschewing the carnal pleasures of the world could one approach purity. Unfortunately, most of the Christian virtues such as truth were not required, and that made it very difficult to trace the movement, since none of its practitioners felt obliged to tell the truth when under oath.

Notes

Maps Appearing as End Sheets

In drawing the map of twelfth-century London, I began with the one reproduced in Sebastian Münster's *Cosmographia*, which, to judge by the costumes of a group of figures engraved thereon, can be dated in the late sixteenth century. I corrected this map from John Stow's *Survey of London* (first published in 1598) and from other available sources. I have compared my map with that given (p. 16) by William R. Shepherd in his *Atlas of Medieval and Modern History* (New York, 1932). Allowing for the fact that Shepherd is reconstructing the London of 1300, while I am attempting to sketch the city as it was in 1178–80, there are still a few major differences that need explaining. Chief among these are the locations of the four streams which flowed in the city or just outside. Stow says of the Old Bourn that it broke out of the ground "about the place where now the Holborn bars do stand, and it ran down the whole street till Oldborne bridge, and into the river of the Wells, or Turnemill brook" (p. 15). I have drawn the burn in this way; but Shepherd merely labels a section of the Fleet River (previously the River of the Wells) above the Holborn Bridge with the name "Hole Bourn." The next controversial matter is the position of the Langbourn. By virtue of its name we can assume that this burn had a long course. Stow says of it: "Langborne water, so called of the length therof, was a great stream breaking out of the ground in Fenchurch street, which ran with a swift course, west, through that street, athwart Gra street, and down Lumbard street, to the west end of St. Mary Wolnothes church, and then turning the course down Shareborne lane, so termed of sharing or dividing, it brake into divers rills or rillets to the river of Thames. . ." (p. 15). If this description is correct, how does Shepherd find authority for running the Langbourn into Walbrook at Lombard Street? Furthermore, his map indicates that the burn ran alongside and not through the center of Fenchurch Street.

In addition, the Shepherd map cuts Watling Street through from Newgate direct to the London Bridge. I do not know where to substantiate this. Surely the sixteenth-century map would retain some trace of such a street cutting through the city. That section of London preserved much of its early lines until the Great Fire of 1666. In the accompanying map I do not profess to sketch in all the streets. This would be impossible archaeologically.

In the map of Paris I have followed for general contours the one prepared by M. Halphen. It was necessary to modify his plan, since he, like most of those who reconstruct Capetian Paris, begins with the walls of Philip Augustus. For the area contained within that early wall on the right bank, of which the very existence is a mystery to many mediaeval historians, I have been guided by Marcel Poëte. Constant use has been made of the published cartularies of the city, of Notre-Dame de Paris, and of the Hôtel-Dieu. In tracing the actual lines of the streets, I began with the excellent scale maps of Gomboust (1652) and Jouvin de Rochefort (1675). Some use has been made also of the notes of Abbé Leboeuf, especially where he comments on the *Rues de Paris* of Guillot de Paris.

I have added a small touch which may seem useless to the reader. Where a house is specifically mentioned in the various cartularies as existing in a given place during the period 1150–80, I have placed a small line in approximately the correct position. It is not possible to determine this exactly, of course—we do not know on what side of the street to place it—but these small marks will give an idea of where some of the houses were changing hands.

The Rue des Sept Voies seems to have been the principal street of the Bourg Sainte-Geneviève. It is mentioned in a document of 1185. To judge by the appearance of this street in the later maps, it got its name because seven roads actually joined it. At so early a date as 1178, when the greater part of the hillside was still in vineyards, most of these streets would have had dead ends, as I have tried to show.

Preface

1. John of Garland was born in 1180 and came to Paris in 1195. His appellative was derived from that Rue de Garlande which led from the Orléans road to the Place Maubert.

2. Fr. Gabriel, of the University of Notre Dame, tells me that he has located some more manuscripts of this, in addition to those listed by Manitius.

3. *Jahrbuch für romanische und englische Literatur*, VIII (1867), 60–74, 155–73. Wright printed the Cottonian MS (Titus D. xx) and gave collations from B.N. lat. 7679 and lat. 217.

4. Frederick Tupper and Marbury B. Ogle (tr.), *Master Walter Map's Book De Nugis Curialium* (London, 1924), pp. 75, 197. Hereafter referred to as W.M.

5. *Roman de la Rose*, vv. 4543–44.

6. *Metalogicus*, III, 4. It is in Migne, 199, col. 900.

Chapter I

1. Cf. Urban Tigner Holmes, *A History of Old French Literature* (New York, 1948).

2. For details on this political history, and the brief statement on economic conditions which follows, consult the references in L. Paetow.

3. *Polycraticus*. This political theory is summed up by John Dickinson in *Speculum*, I, 308–37.

4. R. W. Linker (ed.), *Yvain* (Chapel Hill, 1940), vv. 650–55.

5. *Ibid.*, vv. 65–85.

6. The best reference on Alexander Neckam is Max Manitius, *Geschichte der lateinischen Literatur des Mittelalters*, III, 784–94. We are aware that occasionally in the *De nominibus utensilium* Alexander is quoting verbally from earlier authors: Isidor, Juvenal, and Horace. This does not affect the value of his evidence for contemporary matters, for such quotations would be meaningless if his own age did not have the equivalent. This same principle applies to passages in the *Roman de la Rose*, such as the statement found there that a gentleman should have a good tailor. Perhaps Ovid did suggest this to Guillaume de Lorris, but a similar belief doubtless prevailed in the thirteenth, and in the twelfth, century or it would not have been repeated. M. Esposito in the *English Historical Review*, XXX, 461 ff. is our source for information on the authors quoted in the *De nominibus*. C. H. Haskins argues for Neckam's authorship of the *Sacerdos ad altarem* and gives excellent information on this mediaeval grammarian. Cf. Haskins, *The Renaissance of the Twelth Century* (Cambridge, Massachusetts,

1927) and *Studies in the History of Mediaeval Science* (Cambridge, Massachusetts, 1924).

7. Du Boulay, *Historia Universitatis Parisiensis*, II, 725.

8. Pp. 7–61.

Chapter II

1. The facts on Dunstable are in every encyclopedia.

2. Sir W. Dugdale, *Monasticon Anglicanum* (6 vols., London, 1846), II, 187.

3. These figures on the amount of mileage covered, and the time, can be checked in *Blonde d'Oxford*, ed. Le Roux de Lincy (1858), vv. 5205, 5268, 5271, 5283; above all, in Montaigne's account of his voyage to Italy, where he gives full data on the stages and the ground covered. In expressions of time, the word *haute* means "well advanced" and *basse* signifies "just after." Cf. *tresque la basses nune* in the *Pèl. de Charl.*, ed. W. R. Lansberg (Chapel Hill, 1939), v. 571.

4. It is probable that he had only the simple tonsure, which is equivalent to acceptance only as a candidate for orders. Today the "tonsure" is usually given the day before the service at which the four minor orders are conferred together. A clerk in minor orders could marry, but a married cleric could not teach in the schools. See G. Paré, A. Brunot, and P. Tremblay, *La Renaissance du XIIe siècle. Les écoles et l'enseignement* (Paris, 1933), pp. 62–63.

5. Alexander did not esteem very highly the qualities of a mule. See Thomas Wright (ed.), *Alexandri Neckam De naturis rerum . . . with the poem of the same author, De laudibus divinae sapientiae* (Rolls Series, London, 1863), p. 266. Hereafter referred to as *N.R.* There is an excellent picture of a twelfth-century headstall in the single sheet of twelfth-century illumination (English, about 1170) which is in the Morgan Library in New York City. This is usually called a sheet from the Winchester Bible. See Ricci and Wilson, *Census*, No. 619.

6. Thomas Wright (ed.), *A Volume of Vocabularies* (privately printed, 1857), p. 99. Hereafter referred to as Wright. The Heidelberg MS 112 of the German *Roland* has excellent illustrations showing saddles and the saddle cloths. In *Floire et Blancheflor*, ed. Du Méril (Paris, 1856), p. 40, there is this description of equipment: the *sousele* is of checkered cloth, the pommel and cantle *(arçon)*

are of blue and red ivory with gold inlay, and the top cloth is *d'un brun paile de Castele toute florie a flors d'orfrois.*

7. In the *Cid* a difference is indicated between *siellas coceras,* "light riding saddles," and *siellas gallegas,* which were the heavier kind used in warfare.—*Cid,* ed. Menéndez Pidal (Madrid, 1916), vv. 992–93. The custom of fastening a bag to the *culière* or crupper strap is illustrated vividly by Alexander: *Simia vero, locum manticae tenens* pushed the jongleur, his master, off the horse.—*N.R.,* p. 210.

8. John of Garland, in Wright, p. 123, says: *Sellarii vendunt sellas nudas et pictas. . . .* The provost Estienne Boileau stated that saddlers were required to sell their saddles undecorated. A preacher of the twelfth century complained about the clergy who maintained "painted saddles, spurs, and gilded bridles."—L. Bourgain, *La chaire française au 12e siècle* (Paris, 1879), p. 278.

9. The Monge de Montaudo remarked: *Et enoia'm e no'm sab bo de sella quan croll'a l'arço.*—*Enueg,* vv. 77–78.

10. The bells hanging from the *peitrel* are mentioned very often. A specific reference can be found in *Gui de Bourgogne,* ed. Guessard and Michelant (1859), vv. 2334–35. Enide rides a *sambue* all through her adventures in the company of Erec. See *Erec und Enide,* ed. W. Förster (1911), vv. 2810ff. In the *Aiol,* ed. Normand-Raynaud (1877), vv. 8313–14: *et de sambue de brun paile A fleurs d'argent fet a entaille.*

A woman's saddle is portrayed at Autun in the Cathedral of Saint-Lazare.—Deschamps 36 B. The lady sits sideways, with a back- and footrest. A quilted cloth covers the seat and footrest. In the *Chanson de Guillaume,* vv. 1549–50, stirrups are mentioned as associated with the *sambue.*

11. Wright, p. 99. This type of short, hooded cloak is frequently seen in art of the period. There is a sculptured relief in the Romanesque Hall of the Louvre which shows peasants in the field at the Annunciation. One of these wears a short *chape* very plainly. The Monge de Montaudo could not get along without one: *Ancor i a mais que m'enoia cavalcar ses capa de ploia.*—*Enueg,* vv. 73–74.

12. The *revelin* is so named and described in Chrétien's *Conte del Graal,* ed. A. Hilka (Halle, 1932), vv. 1176ff. In the Reichenau Glossary, No. 423, the word *ocreas* is explained by *husas.* The tympanum of Saint-Ursin at Bourges (which can be seen on p. 29 of the Bédier and Hasard, *Histoire de la littérature française*) illustrates various styles of leg covering. A peasant sometimes wears coarse, loose sacking draped around his legs. See also Webster, Plates 31, 31a, and 42. These leg cloths, like stockings, were fastened

by a garter band just below the knee. A well-dressed man prided himself on his leg covering. In the *Cid* the Count of Barcelona is annoyed because he is defeated by men who are *malcalçados* (v. 1023). He is referring to the Cid's men who wore *huesas sobre calças* (v. 994). The following passage is interesting: *Par tel vertu a le planchié passé Rompent les hueses del cordoan soller.*—*Charroi de Nimes*, ed. J. L. Perrier (1931), vv. 56–57. Apparently the puttees extending up from the *soller* were called *hueses*, and they broke under the strain.

13. On black clothing for clerics: *Non dicas opprobrium Si cognoscas morem, vestem nigram clerici, comam breviorem.*—"Debate of Phyllis and Flora," No. 52 in the *Oxford Book of Mediaeval Latin Verse*. The cleric was seldom bearded: *E enoia'm capellan e monge barbat.*—Monge de Montaudo, *Enueg*, v. 8. Further: *Cuida que tuit proveire fussent . . . Kar tuit erent tondu e res.*—*Rou*, ed. H. Andresen (1877), Part III, vv. 7119ff.

14. The description of the Scot has been lifted from Jocelin, pp. 77–78. Samson, before he was abbot, traveled in Italy disguised as a Scot. Nigel Wireker remarks that the English are *largos* while the French are *tenaces.*—*The Anglo-Latin Satirical Poets and Epigrammatists of the Twelfth Century*, ed. Thomas Wright (Rolls Series, 2 vols., London, 1872), I, 65. Hereafter called *S.P.* This custom of observing national and racial traits has long been practiced. Giraldus says of an Italian legate: *cui ille caput et humeros more suae gentis avertendo.*—*Giraldi Cambrensis Opera*, ed. J. S. Brewer (Rolls Series, 8 vols., London, 1873), II, 345. Hereafter referred to as Giraldus.

15. For the term "commun language" see *La vie d'Edouard le confesseur*, ed. Södergard (Uppsala, 1949), vv. 2016ff.

16. *Ibid.*, vv. 1–10.

17. The quality of being *fier* is very frequently mentioned. Typical is a description in Marie de France's *Yonec*, vv. 519–20: *Que c'iert li mieudre chevalier Et le plus fort et le plus fier*. See the *Lais*, ed. E. Hoepffner, (1921).

18. *Venit equo residens sua cantica voce resultans More viatorum sic breviabat iter.*—*Rapularius*, ed. K. Langosch (1929), I, 317. A fine view of a man on a horse is in the frieze of the Cremona Cathedral.—James Carson Webster, *The Labors of the Months* (Evanston, Illinois, 1938), Plate 25.

19. For verse structure see Gustave Reese, *Music in the Middle Ages* (New York, 1940), p. 387; also Archibald T. Davison and Willi Apel, *Historical Anthology of Music* (Cambridge, Massa-

chusetts, 1947), I, 16–17, 216. The *Descriptio Kambriae* (Giraldus, VI, 189) mentions the Scottish habit of singing a second part. Giraldus describes Welsh harmony also. He says of those north of the Humber that one voice is "murmuring in the bass, the other warbling in the treble."

20. E. Martin (ed.), *Roman de Renart* (Strassburg, 1882–87), Branch II, vv. 45–46.

21. All this description is imitated from Branch I of the *Roman de Renart*, but in the *Chanson de Guillaume*, vv. 3410–13, also a *bordel* or peasant house is described. It is made with piles driven into the ground. These are provided with *fourches*, or angle pieces, at the top and then a ridgepole is added.

22. In England, land was held for these types of service: knight's, *serjant's*, and socager's. A socager paid rent in kind or money only. A serf, called also a cotter or bordar, was obliged to give labor, and the merchet fee for the marriage of his daughter.—Austin Lane Poole, *Obligations of Society in the XII and XIII Centuries* (Oxford, 1946), Chapters 1–3.

23. John Stow, *A Survey of London*, with Fitzstephen in the Appendix (London, 1908), p. 502. Hereafter referred to as F.S.

24. This picturing of the relative location of sites and buildings is made from various sources. See note to London map, above. A solicitor of Gray's Inn, with whom I had the pleasure to talk recently, confirmed my opinion of the distances in Holborn. He has walked over these streets countless times. Fitzstephen says of the palace at Westminster: ". . . the royal palace rears its head, an incomparable structure, furnished with breastworks and bastions, situated in a populous suburb at a distance of two miles from the city" (p. 502). In 1184 the Templars abandoned their tower in Oldborne and moved down to the bank of the Thames.

25. The earlier name for Westminster was Thornley. The abbey church, adjacent to the royal tower, was dedicated to St. Peter, but by the mid-twelfth century the designation "West minster," as contrasted with St. Paul's, the minster within the wall of London, was far more common. Cf. on all this *La vie d'Edouard le confesseur*, vv. 1499–1500 and *passim*.

26. A significant painting from twelfth-century England has survived. This is "The Ladder of the Salvation of the Soul and the Road to Heaven," recovered in the parish church of St. Peter and St. Paul at Chaldon (or Chalvedon) in Surrey, not far from Westminster. The background is in red and the figures are in lighter red, pink, yellow, and white. See *The Victoria History of*

the County of Surrey, ed. H. E. Malden (London, 1902–12), IV, 191–93. There is a reference to the murals at Westminster in the accounts of Henry's grief over the rebellion of his sons in 1173-74. —Giraldus, VIII, 295.

27. F.S., p. 45.

28. Dugdale, VI, 626–27.

29. The description of Smithfield or "Smoothfield" continues from F.S., pp. 506–507. Jocelin describes the stalls in a market (p. 209).

30. ". . . it is a common saying, 'From mill and from market, from smithy and from nunnery, men bring tidings.' "—*Ancrene Riwle*, ed. James Morton (London, 1853), pp. 88–91.

31. Naturally we can only imagine the appearance of the wall of London. A city wall and gate are illustrated in a Cambridge MS, Trinity College R.17.1, dating about 1150. The gate is there flanked by two towers with three upper stories to each tower. The crenelated top of the gate is higher than the walk on the top of the wall. See Dorothy Hartley and Margaret M. Elliot, *Life and Work of the People of England* (New York, 1931), I, Plate 20e.

32. The description of wooden houses is elaborated from Bayeux Tapestry, No. 48, in Eric MacLagan, *The Bayeux Tapestry* (London, 1945).

33. J. P. Bushe-Fox, *Old Sarum. Official Guide* (London, 1934), p. 12.

34. I cannot give my exact references for this impression of the houses of the time. It is a conglomerate of personal impressions acquired over some years from visiting extant houses in England, France, and Italy, combined with a study of illustrations and reading in texts. Some details will be easily traced. Houses at Chartres show the ornamental windows on the principal floor. In *Aucassin et Nicolette*, ed. R. W. Linker (1948), there is mention of the small pillar of stone in the center of such a window: *le noua au piler de la fenestre* (§12).

35. The Assizes of 1189 established certain housing ordinances. The text from which we are quoting is that given in Thomas Stapleton's *De antiquis legibus liber* (Camden Society, No. 34, London, 1846), pp. 206–11. The greater part of the city had been built of wood previous to the fire of 1135–36 which destroyed from the Bridge to St. Clement's Dane (p. 210). To encourage construction in stone the Assizes gave many privileges to the owner of a stone house, over his less affluent neighbor. If anyone should have a stone wall on his own land to the height of sixteen

feet, his neighbor must make a drain and receive in it, on his land, the water shed from the stone wall and carry it across his land, unless it can be brought into the King's street, and nothing must be constructed by him on the aforesaid wall when he builds near it. If he does not build he must continue to receive the water shed from the stone wall, without damage to the owner of the wall (p. 208). A common stone wall cannot be altered without the consent of both parties. *Garde-robe* pits, not walled, must be dug five and a half feet away from the neighbor's boundary; if walled, the pit can be only two and a half feet. A window facing upon a neighbor's land can have its view cut off by subsequent building unless a specific agreement forbidding this has once been made. One who is building is forbidden to make a *pavimentum in vico regio ad nocimentum civitatis et vicini sui injuste* (p. 211).

36. "On the west are two castles strongly fortified. . . ." F.S., p. 502. Marie de France wrote of two such castles, side by side, divided only by a single curtain wall, in her *Laostic*, vv. 35-44.

37. *N.R.*, p. 209.

38. Stow lists these docks in F.S. Queenhithe is still in existence.

39. The Bayeux Tapestry, Nos. 43–45, shows these weird figureheads on ships.

40. For the two bridges consult Stow in F.S., p. 23. Jehan Bodel has a few words on bridge building: *Faisoit alignier ses granz mairiens qarrez, Faire trox et mortaisses.—Saisnes*, ed. F. Michel (1839), II, 49–50. The bridge was all important: *A sun batel en va amont Dreit a Lundres, desuz le punt, Sa marchandise iloc descovre.—Tristan*, ed. J. Bédier (SATF, 1902–1905), vv. 2647–49.

41. Wace, *Brut*, ed. Ivor Arnold (SATF, 1938–40), vv. 3207ff.

42. F.S., p. 502. Thomas says: *Al pé del mur li curt Tamise. . . . —Tristan*, v. 2659; and further: *Par une posterne del mur qui desur la Tamise. . .* (vv. 2792–93).

43. The cookshop is in F.S., p. 504.

44. *Brut*, vv. 11191–204.

45. V. Gay and H. Stein, *Glossaire archéologique du moyen âge et de la Renaissance* (Vol. I, Paris, 1897; Vol. II, Paris, 1928), under Huissier.

46. *N.R.*, p. 141.

47. U. Nebbia, *Navi d'Italia* (Milan, 1930), Plate. See also Bayeux Tapestry, Nos. 5–6.

48. F.S., p. 43.

49. Dugdale, V, 85–104.

50. F.S., pp. 506, 508–509.

51. Bayeux Tapestry, No. 4.

52. Gaimar, *Estorie des Engleis*, ed. Thomas Wright (London, 1850), vv. 5981–98. Similarly in *Ille et Galeron*, ed. Löseth (Paris, 1890), vv. 4100–4102.

53. As in the *Tristan* where Iseut receives such treatment from King Marc.

54. F.S., p. 503.

55. Such was certainly the case in the thirteenth century. Crowds gathered around the Earl of Gloucester in London, and the Earl of Oxford was greeted in the same way in Boulogne. See *Blonde d'Oxford*, vv. 2458 ff., 5484 ff. Those who have received Ille's charity crowd about him as he passes through the streets.—*Ille et Galeron*, vv. 3788–99.

56. Scheludko in *Archivum Romanicum*, XI, 278.

57. *Die Exempla des Jakob von Vitry*, ed. Joseph Greven (SMLT, 1914), No. 97.

58. We are projecting into the past, present conditions of navigation on the Seine River. See George Millor, *Isabel and the Sea* (New York, 1948).

59. "A poon [*sic*] peddler, who carries nothing but soap and needles, shouteth and calleth out clamorously what he beareth, and a rich mercer goeth along quite silently."—*Ancrene Riwle*, pp. 152–53.

60. It was in 37 Edward III (1363) that the bells of Our Lady at Bow were substituted.

61. Herbert de Boseham, *Materials for the History of Archbishop Thomas Becket* (Rolls Series), III, 20–21.

62. *N.R.*, p. 213. The knights made up a smaller proportion of the population than is commonly believed. Poole estimates a maximum of seven thousand knights in England at this time, out of a total population of three million.—*Obligations of Society*, p. 36. The knight had two principal duties: war service (usually forty days every August and September), and garrison or ward duty. These could be commuted by payment of scutage, a fine. Knights on garrison duty had the work of police officers, sometimes that of detectives.—*Obligations of Society*, pp. 38–39, 40, 55. In the *Quatre fils Aymon*, ed. F. Castets (Montpellier, 1909), v. 9854, and elsewhere, exaggerated numbers are given. This is typical of the *chansons de geste*.

63. Margery Bassett in *Speculum*, XVIII (1943), 234, argues *ex silentio* that Newgate was not used as a prison before 1188. The jail at Ludgate (later the Fleet) was in existence in 1189.—F.S.,

p. 348. I am inclined to believe that both these gates were used for prisoners for some years previous. The Tower of London also was an ordinary prison. Richard d'Amble was retained there in irons.—F.S., p. 11.

64. The tendency was growing to take an amercement or fine in the place of physical punishment. Poole, pp. 81, 104, 106. This was imposed after the accused had thrown himself on the king's mercy.

65. *Boz i ot et culovres, don ert esmaiés.—Floovant*, ed. Guessard and Michelant (1859), v. 845; *Prise d'Orange*, ed. Katz (1947), vv. 1230–31.

66. E. P. Leigh, *Historic Exeter* (n.d.), pp. 35–37. In the *Prise d'Orange* there is a *bove*, or underground tunnel, extending from the tower to the river Rhone (vv. 1173 ff.). There is a *bove* in the *Quatre fils Aymon*, vv. 13751 ff.

67. *N.R.*, p. 326; Giraldus, IV, 86, where the men are of gold and ivory. Cf. Fritz Strohmeyer's "Das Schachspiel im Altfranzösischen" in the *Tobler Festschrift*, pp. 381 ff.

68. The board on low trestles which was used for the game of chess was called an *eschequier*. By extension this term was applied to other low, light tables. In the tavern portrayed in the *Jeu de Saint-Nicolas*, ed. A. Jeanroy (Paris, 1925), vv. 942, 1079, 1086, 1162, the dicers sit at an *eschekier*. The counting board was another light table surface which also shared in this common name. On the counting board there was a "tree"—a long line crossed by a series of lines, regularly spaced, alternately long and short, for units, fives, tens, fifties, hundreds, five hundreds, and so on. It was from the word *eschequier* applied to the ordinary counting board that the term *exchequer* came into use. Most lexicographers, including the authors of the *NED*, seem mixed on this. They imagine that a table top resembling a chessboard in its checkered squares was used for counting the royal revenues!

69. *Chevalerie Ogier le Danois*, ed. J. Barrois (Paris, 1842), vv. 3122–91. In the same way Louis slays Gibert in the *Anseÿs de Mes*, ed. H. Green (Paris, 1939), vv. 297–302. See also *Quatre fils Aymon*, vv. 1938–41.

70. *Aspremont*, ed. L. Brandin (1923–24), vv. 6161–64. Also *Floovant*, vv. 2393–94, and *Roman de Renart*, Branch II, vv. 205–206.

71. *Rou*, Part III, vv. 2339–40.

72. O. M. Dalton, *A Guide to the Mediaeval Antiquities and Objects of Later Date* (London, 1924), p. 100.

Chapter III

1. *Hist. Archb. Th. Becket*, II, 81.
2. *Ibid.*, II, *xxx*, 96.
3. *Ibid.*, II, 134: *In multorum quoque confractorum operculis specula mulierum invenimus.*
4. L. C. Lane (tr.), *The Chronicle of Jocelin of Brakeland, Monk of St. Edmundsbury* (London, 1907), p. 120.
5. *Red Book of the Exchequer* (Rolls Series), II, 715.
6. The best reference that I have encountered for the early history of Dover is Samuel P. H. Statham, *The History of the Castle, Town, and Port of Dover* (New York, 1899). Less useful today is John Lyon, *The History of the Town and Port of Dover and of Dover Castle* (2 vols., 1813–14).
7. Statham, pp. 42–43.
8. *Hist. Archb. Th. Becket*, III, 476–77.
9. *Enueg*, vv. 59–60: *et enoia'm estar a port, quan trop fa greu temps e plou fort.*
10. Statham, pp. 210ff.
11. Dugdale, IV, 530.
12. Bayeux Tapestry, No. 28.
13. *Brut*, vv. 11205–28.
14. See G. T. Zoëga, *A Concise Dictionary of Old Icelandic* (Oxford).
15. *Prothesilaus*, ed. F. Kluckow (1924), Version I, vv. 1424–25.
16. *Anseÿs de Mes*, vv. 3427–41. We read in *Huon de Bordeaux*, ed. Guessard and Grandmaison (Paris, 1860), vv. 2812-15: *Dedens ont mis bescuit a grant plenté, Et pain et car, et vin viés, et claré; De iaue douce i fait asés porter. Aprés i font lor biax cevax mener.* In this vessel boarded by Hue there are two sailors, one boy to watch the horses, and thirteen passengers (vv. 2824–28). In the Channel vessel boarded by Jehan in *Blonde d'Oxford* there are twenty sailors.
17. Wright, pp. 114–15; p. 230, n.49.
18. Certain classes of persons were exempted from the *teloneum* or tax, but Alexander was not yet in that class. See *Red Book of the Exchequer*, II, 723–24. For the cost of the passage consult *Wistasce li moines*, vv. 2183–84.
19. *De expugnatione Lyxbonensi*, tr. C. W. David (New York, 1936), p. 61.
20. Nine hours were taken by Jehan to go from Dover to

Wissant (twenty miles) in *Blonde d'Oxford,* vv. 2044–46. The distance from Dover to Boulogne is thirty miles.

21. Alexander speaks of seasickness in a few lines of the *De nominibus utensilium* which are not in the edition published by Wright: "*Nausea* is from *navis* because vomiting often happens in a passage, where there is *nausea.*" Elsewhere Alexander says: *Immo longe majoris temeritatis censendi sunt qui hodie mari se committunt, nisi articulo urgentissimae necessitatis.—N.R.,* p. 140. See also *Neptuni numquam sit tibi tuta fides* in his *De laudibus sapientiae.—N.R.,* p. 402.

22. Our chief reference on early Boulogne is A. d'Hauttefeuille and L. Bénard, *Boulogne-sur-mer et la région boulonnaise (Ouvrage offert par la ville de Boulogne)* (1860), p. 716.

23. At this date, 1178, the little Countess Ida was about to embark on her first marital venture. Eventually she was married five times. The scandal of her father's marriage to her mother, a nun at Ramsay, England, had had repercussions that were still being felt. The Archbishop of Canterbury had denounced this marriage in no uncertain terms, and the Count of Boulogne felt hostility to English clerics as a consequence. Philip of Flanders was actually in control of the Port of Boulogne. See *Boulogne-sur-mer,* pp. 83 ff.

24. *Ipomedon,* ed. Kölbing and Koschwitz (Breslau, 1889), vv. 1621–22. "And he bore a letter-case around his neck in which were contained the letters of his monastery."—Jocelin, p. 29. See Camille Enlart, *Le costume* (Paris, 1916), pp. 416–19.

25. John of Salisbury was excused the customs fee at Calais by special privilege.—H. Denifle and E. Chatelain, *Chartularium Universitatis Parisiensis* (Paris, 1889), No. 19. References are to letters in the Pars Introductoria, Ab Alexandro Papa III usque ad Annum MCC, pp. 3–56. Hereafter *C.U.P.*

26. The reader may ask at this point what sort of accommodation a layman could expect who was not of the upper class. In the *Boucher d'Abbeville,* ed. Montaiglon and Raynaud, *Recueil général et complet des fabliaux* (6 vols., Paris), vv. 62 ff., the butcher prepares to stop for the night and is directed to the priest. He says: *Biaus sire, que Dieus vos aït. Herbregiez moi pour charité, Si ferez honor et bonté.* The answer is *Preudom, Dieus vous herbert!* This is a refusal. The priest says that he cannot entertain a layman, that the traveler should go farther into the village. Eventually the priest does give him shelter, but at a price.

Unquestionably a fee was charged in every case except where the traveler was the guest of a noble or of an abbot. We assume that

Alexander paid his lodging at each of the hostels where he stayed. We have no reason to believe that a layman such as the butcher of Abbeville would not have been received into a hostel maintained by monks—in fact, it is quite certain that he would have been. An individual cleric, however, might have consented to take only a brother churchman.

27. Alexander was not important, so we suppose that he traveled light. Giraldus traveled with considerable baggage on one of his continental journeys. Once his chamberlain, who carried the bags, went astray. These contained goods to the value of forty marcs ($280): cups, spoons, clothes, a box full of letters, writing tablets which had on them accounts of his journeys and which had not been copied—and, last but not least, the palfrey also was valuable.—Giraldus, I, 82–83.

28. John of Salisbury had several horses with him, but he was traveling in more style. He complained to Thomas Becket that he had managed to scrape together only twenty-four marcs ($168) for his journey and that most of this money was spent for equipment before leaving Canterbury.—*C.U.P.*, No. 19.

29. This is the itinerary which was followed by the travelers in *Blonde d'Oxford.* John of Salisbury, when traveling some fifteen years previous to this journey on which we are accompanying Alexander, went by the Calais route. After landing at Calais, he went on to Saint-Omer, then to Arras, Noyon, and Paris. His association with the Archbishop made him an interesting person, as he was known to have first-hand information on the quarrel which Thomas had with the King. He was given hospitality in the baronial castles, except at Arras, where, because of the absence of Philip of Flanders, he stayed at the monastery of Saint-Martin. *C.U.P.*, No. 19.

30. The English had a reputation for being heavy drinkers. See John of Salisbury in Migne, *P.L.*, 199, col. 72; *S.P.*, I, 63. Gaimar, in *Estorie des Engleis*, vv. 3811–15, describes the wassail procedure in detail. Cf. also *Brut*, vv. 6953–82. A Cluniac variant of the wassail is in Giraldus, IV, 209.

31. Ten sous are in the priest's purse in *Du prestre teint*, v. 121. Wistasce mentions fifteen sous in a full purse and sixty pounds in a belt.—*Wistasce li moines*, vv. 940–42. In the latter reference (v. 61) it is recorded that an evening's drinking cost the host three sous.

Et ceinture et aumosniere Qui fu d'un riche seigneri brocadé.—*Karrenritter*, ed. W. Förster (1899), vv. 1891–92.

32. From a document recorded by Sidney Painter in his *The Reign of King John* (Baltimore, 1949), p. 94.

33. Baudri de Bourgueil describes a handy set of writing tablets: eight leaves threaded together, making fourteen pages, the whole fitting into an embroidered sack.—*Baudri de Bourgueil*, ed. P. Abrahams, No. 47.

34. Such a pick-up meal is in the *Yvain*, vv. 1046ff. In *Li vileins fols*, vv. 64ff., a meal of a lighter kind consists of cakes, *flaon*, salt mackerel, and claret.

35. *N'i ot sonmiers a cofres de dras troussez en male.—Berte aus grans piés*, ed. Urban Tigner Holmes (Chapel Hill, 1946), v. 734.

36. In northern France the ox was going out of style as a draft animal for carts.—J. H. Clapham and Eileen Power (eds.). *The Cambridge Economic History of Europe*, Vol. I, *The Agrarian Life of the Middle Ages* (Cambridge, 1942), p. 132. Carts are represented in the Bayeux Tapestry. In the *Karrenritter*, Chrétien de Troyes makes it evident that to ride in a peasant's cart is a great disgrace for a knight. Excellent representations of carts are in Webster, Plates 33a–b, 34a–b, from the eleventh century.

37. Wright, pp. 107–108.

38. The traffic on these roads is commented upon by Louis Halphen in *Paris sous les premiers Capétiens* (Paris, 1909), p. 15. On the regulation against building see Robert de Lasteyrie, *Cartulaire général de Paris*, I, 193. The presence of the milestones is recorded in Walter Map, p. 276.

39. The remains of the temple were still visible to H. Sauval, *Histoire et recherches des antiquités de la ville de Paris*, I, 349–50.

40. Here are the actual words of Nigel Wireker: *Hac in valle situs quis locus esse potest? Haec est Roma, puto, magnis circumdata muris! Urbs ita turrita quid nisi Roma foret?—S.P.*, I, 77. The city is, of course, Paris. The turrets and great walls must have reference to the Roman wall around the island, as well as to the Grant Chastelet, the Royal Palace, and perhaps the fortified parapets of the Grant Pont.

41. *Hist. Archb. Th. Becket*, III, 446. Perhaps a permanent gibbet was already set up at the foot of the hill. Montfaucon was already a designated place for this: *Carles pendi son frere au puis de Montfaucon.—Quatre fils Aymon*, v. 7072.

42. The two kings met there in 1169. See reference in the preceding note.

43. The very existence of this stockade previous to the wall of Philip Augustus is not realized by many. The evidence for it is

accumulated by Marcel Poëte in *Une vie de cité: Paris* (Paris, 1924), p. 94, and by Halphen, pp. 11, 71. See also the article by A. Berty, "De l'enceinte du faubourg septentrional de Paris antérieure à celle de Philippe Auguste et de la possibilité d'en retrouver des fragments," in *Revue archéologique* (1854-55), pp. 516-17.

44. The field of the Holy Innocents was drained and walled in 1186.—Halphen, p. 17.

45. Early in his reign Philip Augustus bought out this fair and united it with the market at the Campelli or Champeaux.

46. The Chaussée crossed this gulley over the Pont Montmartre, which is not mentioned in the text. For the Passellus see Br. Krusch in *Forsch. zur deutschen Gesch.*, XXVI (1886), 170–71.

47. St. Martin's was busy reclaiming the marshlands which lay there. Much good farm land was constantly being cleared at this time. The director of such an operation was called a *locator*. Clapham and Power, pp. 278ff. Maugis and Renaut de Montauban spend a night *el porche del mostier saint Martin.—Quatre fils Aymon*, vv. 4877–79.

48. See n. 43 above.

49. The Templars are located there in *Archives de l'Hotel-Dieu de Paris*, ed. Brièle, Léon, and Coyecque (Paris, 1894), p. 290.

50. Giraldus, III, 27–31. This reminds us of a similar procession in the late fifteenth-century *Jehan de Paris*, ed. E. Wickersheimer (Paris, 1923).

51. On the Grève see Lasteyrie, I, 103. Dung heaps and pigs were once quite common there. W.M., p. 285.

52. The Campelli, beside the Church of the Holy Innocents, were given permanent warehouses and walls by Philip Augustus in 1183, three years before he drained and walled the churchyard. —Halphen, p. 17. The Campelli market dates back to 1138. *Es rues de Paris se prist a eslaissier Parmi les portes s'en vait tot .i. sentier, Entresci c'as Campiaus ne se volt atargier.—Quatre fils Aymon*, vv. 5010–12.

53. Poëte, I, 86; Estienne Boileau, *Règlements sur les arts et métiers* (Paris, 1837), p. *xxvi*.

54. Poëte, I, 85.

55. *Et nos certe panem habemus et vinum et gaudium.* This remark from the lips of Louis VII is reported by Walter Map, p. 281, and Giraldus, VIII, 318. It was admitted also that there were extra vices and temptations.—*C.U.P.*, No. 22.

56. This description of the Grant Pont is drawn from many sources; views of the bridge in Renaissance maps give some idea

of the spans and the length. See also Lasteyrie, I, 380, 391, 497. John of Garland is our authority that leather merchants and goldsmiths were there in his day.—Wright, pp. 124, 128; Poëte, p. 87.

57. There is a fine representation of such a balance on a capital at Vézelay.—*Vézelay. Editions TEL* (Paris), Plate 32.

58. In November, 1180, a new English coinage was put into circulation to oppose the existing counterfeits. William of Newburgh (Rolls Series, No. 82), p. 225.

59. For the Porte de Paris see Lasteyrie, I, 286, 380, 497, 566.

60. *C.U.P.*, No. 15 (commentary).

61. This was the principal, and probably the only, hospice at the time serving the suburb on the right bank. Sainte-Opportune, at the Porte de Paris, opened its lodginghouse in 1188. Giraldus visited the new chapel dedicated to St. Thomas Becket which had been constructed in the vicinity of Saint-Germain l'Auxerrois, in the district known as the Louvre. Giraldus, I, 49.

62. For the sources of our information on the streets of Paris see the notes to the map.

63. For the synagogue see M. Guérard, *Cartulaire de l'Eglise Notre-Dame de Paris*, I, 38–39. It was changed into a church (Sainte-Madeleine) in 1183. When the Jews were exiled at that time, the drapers asked for the twenty-four houses which had been confiscated from the Jews. E.B., p. *lxix*. In 1179 the Third Lateran Council forbade Christians to live with Jews, which must have meant, of course, that they were doing so.—Rolls Series, No. 82, p. 213.

64. Lasteyrie, I, 181, 184, 250, 464.

65. The tolerance and kindliness of Louis VII were frequently described, as in Giraldus, VIII, 131–35. Walter Map was less friendly to him.—W.M., p. 283. The same may be said for John of Salisbury, who, although he spoke of the King's humility in not allowing his foot to be kissed, yet called him a *baculus arundineus*. —*C.U.P.*, No. 19.

66. The cloister was at the eastern end of the island, separated from the streets here mentioned by a wall. *C.U.P.*, No. 55 is our authority that space in the cloister could not be rented to students. It was in 1127 that the schools were moved out of the cloister itself.—Poëte, p. 101.

67. Albert Lenoir, *Statistique monumental de Paris* gives a description of this sixth-century church.

68. The Dix-huit Clercs were granted meager *bourses*.—*C.U.P.*, No. 50.

69. On this bridge see Lasteyrie, I, 535, 578, and Poëte, pp. 92, 101–102. See also the remarks of the anonymous canon in Bouquet, *Recueil des historiens de France*, XVIII, 798: *Sed et habet exedras per quas speculantur Et latentem fluminis fundum perscrutantur. . . . Alii natatibus quoque delectantur Et aestivis solibus usti recreantur.* I have estimated the number of houses from the Truschet-Hoyau map of 1552, allowing for the *exedras.*

70. Poëte, p. 102.

71. This *epicausterion* was probably a basin or pot containing live charcoal. It was used in southern Europe until very recent times.

72. Pictured and described in Jean Destrez, "L'outillage des copistes du xiiie et du xive siècles," in *Geisteswelt des Mittelalters*, or *Festschrift Martin Grabmann*, pp. 19–34.

73. Theophilus describes the manufacture of ink. Bark of thorn wood (surely he means oak) was gathered in April and soaked in water for eight days, at most. The water was then boiled until the decoction thickened; pure wine was next added, and the whole was left to stand until it thickened once again. The resulting ink was stored in bladders or in sewn parchment bags. Before being used, the ink was mixed with vitriol (sulphate of iron).—Robert Hendrie, *An Essay upon Various Arts, in three Books, by Theophilus, called also Rogerus* (London, 1847), pp. 50–51, 75.

74. Black cloth placed in the windows is advised also in the *Ancrene Riwle*, pp. 50–51: ". . . the black cloth does less harm to the eyes, is thicker against the wind, more difficult to see through, and keeps its color better." Such curtains, bordered with orphreys, are mentioned in *Girard de Roussillon*, tr. P. Meyer (Paris, 1884), §74.

75. Wright, pp. 116–17.

76. If Alexander wrote the vocabulary known as the *Sacerdos ad altarem*, as the late C. H. Haskins believed, we have an excellent variant for this description of the scribe's materials:

"The copyist, who is commonly called the scribe, shall have a chair with projecting arms for holding the board upon which the quire of parchment is to be placed. The board must be covered with felt on which a deerskin is fastened, in order that the superfluities of the parchment or membrane may be more easily scraped away by a razor. Then the skin of which the quire is to be formed shall be cleaned with a mordant pumice and its surface smoothed with a light plane. The sheets shall be joined above and below by the aid of a strip threaded through them. The margins of the quire shall be marked on either side with an awl in even measure so that by the aid of a rule the lines may more surely be drawn without mistake. If in writing any erasure or crossing out occurs, the writing shall not be canceled but scraped off. . . ."

Note the use of a lapboard, padded and covered with deerskin, instead of a writing stand.

This translation, with a few modifications, is that of Haskins in his *The Renaissance of the Twelfth Century*, p. 134. The Latin original is in his *Studies in the History of Mediaeval Science*, p. 361.

77. *Chaitivel*, vv. 231–33: *Issi fu li lais comenciez, Et puis parfaiz et annonciez.*

78. *Estorie des Engleis*, vv. 6438ff.

79. Giraldus, VI, 155.

80. Guernes, *Vie de Saint-Thomas Becket*, ed. E. Walberg (Lund, 1922), v. 162.

81. *C.U.P.*, No. 19. John of Salisbury says that he paid twelve pounds for a year's rental of his room. This would be a dreadful rent. A whole house on the Rue neuve Notre Dame rented in the year 1200 for sixty sous (thirty dollars) annually. *Arch.H.D.*, No. 54.

82. He quotes from the Hebrew Bible: *Be resiz bara Eloym ez ha samain vez ha arez.—N.R.*, pp. 7–10. Robert of Saint Frideswid, Exeter, also knew some Hebrew.—Giraldus, VIII, 63.

83. Letters of this sort are published in the *C.U.P.*, Nos. 33–39. No one was ever refused admission who came to see Louis VII.—Giraldus, III, 32.

84. This complaint is repeated by Poëte, pp. 102–103. Saint-Victor was an important center. *Sonnent cil saint de par toute la ville De S. Victor et des autres eglises.—Amis et Amiles*, ed. K. Hofmann (Erlangen, 1882), vv. 1349–50.

Chapter IV

1. Poëte is still the best reference for this.

2. J. Quicherat, "La rue et le château de Hautefeuille à Paris," in *Mélanges d'archéologie et d'histoire*, I (1886), 450–55. In the *Chronicle of Guillaume de Nangis*, ed. H. Géraud (2 vols., 1843) this is referred to as *olim ibi fuerat palatium sive castrum quae nunc adhuc habentur. Altum Folium vocabatur.* Further information can be found in an article by L. Delisle, in the *Bull. Soc. Nat. des Ant.*

de France (1867), pp. 176–77, and in a discussion by R. de Lasteyrie in *Mém. Soc. Hist. de Paris et de l'Ile de France*, IV (1877), 270–301. People still knew of this pile of stone as late as 1366, although its usefulness as a building was destroyed, first by the wall of Philip Augustus in 1211 and then by the abbey of the Dominicans. It may have been the capitol of Lutetia, erected A.D. 100.

3. F.-G. de Pachtère, *Paris à l'époque gallo-romaine*, pp. 80–85, Plate 7.

4. This was under the jurisdiction of the Abbot of Sainte-Geneviève.—Clapham and Power, p. 312. Vineyards were planted and cultivated under *complanteur* arrangement. Land would be feued to a peasant for five years. He planted and tilled it. At the end of that period one half of the vineyards went back to the lord's direct control, and the other half was rented by the planter. For the Thermes see Halphen, p. 27. There was a grain barn there.—*Arch.H.D.*, No. 41. Several houses are also mentioned. Although this Roman building was fed by an aqueduct, the arrangement of its rooms and the small-sized pools make it unlikely that it was built for a public bath. In all probability it was a villa of some kind. It was called a *palais* after 1268.

5. In the *Quatre fils Aymon*, v. 1850: *De Paris sont parti, sor Saine vont és prés* where they do some tilting. See also *Amis et Amiles*, v. 1458, and Poëte, p. 115. The only spot beside the Seine which lent itself to such exercise was the Pré-aux-clercs.

6. In the *Chaitivel* of Marie de France, vv. 107–108, the lady watches the tournament from her tower. In *Amis et Amiles*, vv. 1461–63, Belissant calls to Hardré in the Pré-aux-clercs from the palace window on the island.

7. By 1210 some expensive, noble mansions—almost palaces—had been erected in the Burgum Parvi Pontis. *Les Narbonnais*, ed. H. Suchier, (2 vols., SATF, 1898), vv. 1987–88, 2110. In one such description forty knights sit on a carpet in front of the fine house, playing chess and draughts (vv. 1996–99). In another passage: *A Petit Pont un grant palés trova. Fors le Charlon mellor n'a, Estables longues et grant celier i a* (vv. 2111–13). Note the reference to the stables in this last. Apparently, for a great house in a suburb these were in a long loge or wooden outhouse.

8. Such guards (mercenary *serjanz*) at Saint-Omer received much of their pay *in avena et caseis et in pellibus arietum.* They could claim something extra at Christmas.—Jean Gessler, *Textes diplomatiques latins du moyen-âge* (Collection Lebègue, Brussels, 1948), p. 63.

9. E.B., p. *xxii.*

10. Clapham and Power, p. 316; E.B., pp. *li–liv*. In *Solomon et Marcolfus*, ed. W. Benary (SMLT), Chapter 19: *Cum autem venisset extra civitatem invenit furnum unum et intravit in eum.*

11. There is a kind of pancake mentioned by Platearius. It can be used to enclose medicine.

12. A basket of these pasties is pictured very well in Hartley and Elliot, Plate 14c.

13. Wright, p. 127 (John of Garland).

14. Wright, p. 126.

15. E.B., p. *lxiv*. Alexander Neckam is our authority that the soft fruits—cherries, mulberries, grapes, and apples—may be eaten on an empty stomach, whereas pears and quinces are better after a meal.—*N.R.*, p. 175.

16. Mahaut, wife of Simon de Poissy, left a *crierie* or *clamatoria* and its profits to the Hôtel-Dieu in 1089.—*Arch.H.D.*, p. 14. The bowl is mentioned in E.B., p. *lxi*. The bowl and beating with a stick are in the *Jeu de Saint-Nicolas*, vv. 616–20.

17. Philip K. Hitti (tr.), *An Arab-Syrian Gentleman and Warrior in the Period of the Crusades* (New York, 1929), p. 165. Hereafter referred to as Usamah.

18. By Frederick Tupper, in *Carleton Brown Essays and Studies*, p. 50, from *Architrenius*, III, 1, in *S.P.*, I, 275 ff.

19. Tupper, *ibid.*, p. 46.

20. *S.P.*, I, 63.

21. *En mi la sale ad fait sun lit parer.—Chanson de Guillaume*, v. 2861.

22. *Arch. H.D.*, pp. 2–3.

23. Thomas, in his *Tristan*, vv. 1235 ff., gives the duties of a chambermaid as: to prepare beds, remove them, sew clothes, wash heads, prepare other things.

24. The scissors of the period were of the spring type, similar to our grass-cutting shears in mechanism. See the illustration reproduced in Hartley and Elliot, Plate 3c.

25. Wright, p. 100.

26. *Li reis en sa chambre a conduite sa fille; Portendue est trestote de palies et cortines.—Pèl. de Charl.*, vv. 705–706.

27. Jules Guiffrey, *Histoire de la tapisserie* (Tours, 1886), pp. 14–15.

28. Galeron remains hidden between curtain and wall.—*Ille et Galeron*, vv. 1768–69.

29. *Guillaume de Palerne*, ed. H. V. Michelant (SATF, 1876), vv. 7843–46.

30. Beneeit de Saint-More, *Chronique des dus de Normandie*, ed.

Fr. Michel (Paris, 1838), vv. 25994–97. Also in the *Yvain: Qui estoit cielee a clos, Dorez et pointes les meisieres De boene oevre et de colors chieres* (vv. 964–66). *Entre el palais pavé de lambre* (*Ille et Galeron*, v. 967) is not so clear.

31. *La duchesse s'en entre en sa chambre de mabre, Qui fu trestoute peinte a oisiaus et a brames.—Doön de la Roche*, ed. P. Meyer and G. Huet (SATF, 1921), vv. 3594–95. Keeping in mind a statement by Dr. Lister in 1699, that the English were fond of rooms paneled with wood, while the French preferred plaster and stone walls, we wonder whether the same distinction did not prevail in the twelfth century.

32. *Pèl. de Charl.*, vv. 124–27.

33. *Yvain*, vv. 2755–56.

34. *Baudri de Bourgueil*, No. 196; F. J. E. Raby, *A History of Secular Latin Poetry in the Middle Ages* (2 vols., London, 1934), I, 282.

35. In the *Vie de Saint Thomas Becket*, vv. 3926–30, Guernes mentions *chaalit quiriez* (a bed frame with leather cord) and a quilted mattress with rushes piled loose on top of it, topped by expensive sheets. The soft *coutes* (or *coiltes*) are covered over with a silk cloth in *Li Biaus Desconeus*, ed. G. P. Williams (Paris, 1929), vv. 2365 ff. Such luxury is the opposite of *Qu'estroiz ert et la coute tanve, Coverte d'un gros drap de chanve* in the *Lancelot* or *Karrenritter* of Chrétien, vv. 5551–52. In *Floire et Blancheflor*, p. 36, the coverlet is mentioned as decorated with *tors* or spiral twist. In the museum of the cathedral at Autun (Saône-et-Loire) there is a Romanesque relief of the Dream of the Magi which illustrates such a coverlet in magnificent detail. It resembles a braided rug. The border has five parallel rows of beaded embroidery.

A simpler bed frame is illustrated in Br. Mus. Add. MS 39943, fol. 17b, where there is only a bare frame with legs. The legs of the bed could have simple knobs at the top. *Vézelay. Editions TEL*, Plate 31.

36. In the fabliau *Du prestre teint*, vv. 136–37, the mistress and her guest make a special point of sitting on the bed instead of the floor. In the *Yvain*, vv. 1040–41: *Sel mena seoir en un lit Covert d'une coute si riche.* This mattress or *coute* could be set on the floor for use as a seat: *Sor une grant coute vermoille Troverent la dame seant.—Yvain*, vv. 1951–52. In the manor house belonging to the family of Adam dou Petit Pont the whole upper floor had beds which, presumably, were kept standing.—Barthélemy Hauréau, *Notices et extraits de quelques manuscrits latins de la Bibliothèque*

Nationale (Paris, 1891), III, 207. A *coute* could be placed on a stretcher for a wounded man.—*Ille et Galeron*, v. 1119.

37. *Mort Aymeri*, ed. Couraye du Parc (SATF, 1884), vv. 138ff.

38. Beds could be curtained in time of labor or of illness: *Comme dame en gecine fut bien ancortinez.—Floovant*, v. 727. There was a limited use of bed curtains where the arrangement was of a permanent nature: *En son lit jut e la roine Entur els out une curtine.*—Gaimar, *Estorie des Engleis*, vv. 3941–42. Also in *Huon de Bordeaux*, vv. 4312ff.

39. *Orson de Beauvais*, ed. G. Paris (SATF, 1899), vv. 104ff.

40. A *chandoile* was a small tallow candle (costing a maille, in the *Jeu de Saint-Nicolas*, vv. 696–97. The *cierge* was a large wax candle which gave out more light: *Si con cierges antre chandoiles, Et la lune antre les estoiles.—Yvain*, vv. 3247–49.

41. Here is the description: *mensam auream de longitudine duodecem pedum, et de latitudine pedis et dimidio, et quoddam tentorium de serico magnum adeo quod ducenti milites in eo simul possint comedere; et duos tripodes aureas sub mensa aurea, et viginti quatuor cuppas argenteas et viginti discos argenteos.*—Benedict of Peterborough (Rolls Series), II, 133. Also in Richard de Devizes (Rolls Series), III, 396.

42. Vv. 1043ff.

43. *Vie de Saint Edouard le confesseur*, vv. 3963–64. The word *dois* (from Latin *discus*), like German *Tisch*, could mean sometimes a permanent table at the end of the room. I assume that such a table was of stone. *Erec et Enide*, v. 4744.

44. Some of the utensils set on the table are mentioned in the *Yvain: Mes del mangier ne fu deduiz, Qu'il n'i ot pein ne vin ne sel Ne nape ne coutel ne el* (vv. 3468–70). See further: *Et desus les tables assises Et les salieres et li pains. Lavé ont, si se sont assis. Del sanglier mangierent au poivre Et del cerf firent bons lardez Et des capons firent pastez.—Roman de Renart*, II, v. 65. *Et le menger fut moult riche apresté. Assis sont, quant chascuns ot lavé.—Aquin*, ed. Joüon des Longrais (Nantes, 1880), vv. 2378–79. *Et Ysengrims devant euls taille, Qui lor apresta lor vitaille.—Roman de Renart*, II, p. 321.

45. This buffet is portrayed in a carved capital at Vézelay.—*Vézelay. Editions TEL*, Plate 25.

46. *Tot maintenant fu l'eve demandee, La veissiés tant toaille ovree, Et tant bacin o chaainne noee.—Aspremont*, vv. 10920–22. *Jordain enmainent en la plus maistre sale; Au lavoir vait Jordains,*

ses mains i lave, Oriabel li tendit la touwaille.—Jourdains de Blaivies, see ed. of *Amis et Amiles,* vv. 1509–11.

47. It annoyed the Monge de Montaudo to sit at a long table when the towel was short: *E enueia'm, si Dieus mi vailla, longa taula ab breu toailla.—Enueg* vv. 55–56.

48. There is an illumination, a little later in date, showing a servitor kneeling and cutting a loaf which he holds in his left hand.—Hartley and Elliot. Three kinds of bread were served at supper in the house of Adam dou Petit Pont: *azimis, infungia,* and *placenta,* which would mean ordinary raised bread, unleavened, and perhaps dumplings.—Hauréau, p. 208.

49. We assume that such a roast is the *lardez* which is so frequently mentioned.

50. Wright, pp. 101–102. A similar ecstasy over wine is registered in the *Jeu de Saint-Nicolas,* vv. 649–51. Adam dou Petit Pont mentions specifically that raisin and mulberry wine and *lorea* (?) were missing at his family's table.—Hauréau, p. 208.

51. For example, *Pèl. de Charl.,* vv. 411, 835, also in *Prise d'Orange,* vv. 174, 552. Professor Sisson of the University of London is my authority that the peacock was listed as food in the Chancery records of sixteenth-century London.

52. *Ancrene Riwle,* pp. 324–25.

53. See S. Glixelli in *Romania,* XLVII (1921), 1–40.

54. *Chanson de Guillaume,* v. 2617.

55. In the *Asinarius,* ed., along with the *Rapularius,* by K. Langosch (SMLT), p. 214: "Breaking bread, cutting pasties, he lifts the cup and offers to drink, and holds the napkin while the girl drinks."

56. While Richard was with Philip Augustus *singulis diebus in una mensa ad unum catinum manducabant.*—Roger de Hoveden (Rolls Series), p. 635. The fact about the Young King and his father is *ibid.,* p. 619.

57. *Que tote jor devant nos taille Mouffles chauciees no vitaille, Dont il tert son nes et sa bouche; Espoir en plus ort leu l'atouche Quant il fet le vilain afaire.—Roman de Renart,* II, p. 323. The Monge de Montaudo says: *E enueia'm hom qu'ap mas ronhozas tailla.—Enueg,* v. 55. In the *Ancrene Riwle:* "Thou washest thy hands two or three times in a single day" (pp. 324–25).

58. *Rou,* III, v. 1871.

59. In the *Flamenca,* ed. P. Meyer (Paris, 1865), vv. 944–46. The custom of using snow for cooling drinks would depend upon the nearness to mountains and upon other variable factors.

60. The shape of a *gastel* is assumed from *Le pauvre clerc,* a

fabliau, in which the cake is compared with a rock in shape. See Montaiglon and Raynaud, V, 132.

61. V. 8352. The yeast which was used was liquid.

62. *Roman de Renart*, I, vv. 512 ff. The average peasant ate much better than this. At a marriage feast, in the fabliau *Du vilain fol*, vv. 230–34, there is a boiling cauldron in which pork flavored with pepper and juniper savory is simmering. The guests sit around the fire.

63. *Vie de Saint Grégoire* (unpublished), ed. J. Hutchinson, v. 1692. The *morterel* and the *composte* are described in the fabliaux of Jehan Bodel.

64. Our description is drawn from many visits to surviving houses of the period. In Saint Nicholas' Priory in Exeter the position of the *garde-robe* pit beside the kitchen fire is well illustrated; also in a thirteenth-century house at Exeter, now used as a haberdashery, this is visible.

65. For this I am drawing on the seventeenth century. Samuel Pepys describes the emptying of the *garde-robe* pit in the cellar up through the house. Doubtless they were not more fastidious about this in the twelfth century. Dr. Lister, in 1699, is our authority on the quality of the Paris water.

Two kinds of wells are illustrated from the twelfth century. One has a windlass which draws up a bucket. The other has a counterweight at one end and a bucket at the other. The second kind could have been used where the water was near the surface. See Hartley and Elliot, Plates 4b and 5b.

66. A *vivarium*, or fish pool, could be large enough to permit swimming.—*Lambert d'Ardres, Historia Comitum Ardensis et Ghisnensium*, ed. *MGH*, XXIV, *Scriptores*, 629. It was caulked with grease and pitch.—Brunetto Latini, *Tresor*, ed. Carmody (Paris, 1948), p. 128.

67. Such a cupboard is pictured in a thirteenth-century illumination. It has double doors, with large wrought-iron hinges. There is a cornice along the top, overly ornate. Shelves are inside. Hartley and Elliot, Plate 4b.

68. We know that dishes were frequently washed in hot water, but the sink was not the scene of the action. See Wright, p. 132 (John of Garland).

69. In the fourteenth century, fish could be baked in bread crumbs and then grilled on hot coals, or they could be cooked in a broth savored with spices. *Gawain and the Green Knight*, ed. Tolkien and Gordon, vv. 891–92.

70. The pantry, or *dispensatorium*, was an important room under

the care of those who waited on table. *Serjanz* ate in the pantry.—*Escoufle*, ed. H. Michelant and P. Meyer (SATF, 1894), vv. 5754–55.

71. A lantern had a glass covering in *Blonde d'Oxford*, vv. 1143–44.

72. Baskets were of many shapes. One with a handle is mentioned in *Du prestre teint*, v. 78.

73. Wine could be kept in jars, in a cupboard in a cellar (Hartley and Elliot, Plate 4b) or in big casks placed lengthwise on the floor. There is a mosaic preserved in the Cluny Museum which shows such a cask very clearly. See also Hartley and Elliot, Plate 5a, and Bayeux Tapestry, No. 40. Wine was kept in skins which might hold as much as five *sestiers* or gallons apiece. *Del fol chevalier*, vv. 193 ff. A skin was brought directly to the persons drinking.

There is a most interesting picture of a table stand, or buffet, having two shelves below, each holding a *henap*. This is at Vézelay.—*Vézelay. Editions TEL*, Plate 25. Bread is being broken on the top by two people. In front of this piece of furniture there is a very low stool on which two wine jars (with small ears) are placed.

74. Cupboards, chests, and hampers all had keys.—Jocelin, p. 61.

75. Wright, pp. 100–101. The *Charroi de Nimes* (vv. 775–77) names these utensils: pots, pans, cauldrons, tripods, andirons, sharp hooks, and tongs.

76. *Vézelay. Editions TEL*, back cover. Paul Deschamps, *French Sculpture of the Romanesque Period* (Florence, 1930), Plate 38d.

77. Gay and Stein, p. 749.

78. *Et tret le feu d'un chaille bis, Si l'a de seche busche espris.*—*Yvain*, vv. 3463–64. It is my personal experience that for this operation the tow must be charred or it will not ignite.

79. *Ille et Galeron*, vv. 3122 ff.

80. *Vie de Saint Grégoire*, vv. 1302–51.

81. See Chapter 2, n. 35.

82. *Decamerone*, II, novella 5.

83. As in Chaucer's Knight's Tale.

84. Vv. 1302 ff.

85. The houses at Chartres preserve a number of these.

86. See Chapter 3, n. 74.

87. Hartley and Elliot, Plate 27d.

88. *Escoufle*, vv. 5520–21.

89. Hartley and Elliot, Plate 27d.

90. Bayeux Tapestry, Nos. 28, 48, 53.

91. F.S., pp. 508–509.

92. *N.R.*, pp. 282–83.

93. Wright, pp. 109–10.

94. In Rome there is a twelfth-century house facing on the Forum Boarium which has a balcony. The house, of course, is of stone.

95. The *Grimaldi Livre d'Heures*, four centuries later, shows such construction in the picture for the month of February. A bit of the outer covering of stucco is represented as having peeled off. At Vézelay there is a capital indicating the construction of Noah's Ark. The deck-house shows a wicker framework in the process of building.—Deschamps, Plate 38c.

96. From Guiraut Riquier's *Celeis cui am. . . .* In the *Anseÿs de Mes* one finds: *Dessent li rois a son mestre perron* (v. 10416). This *perron* could stand apart from the house: *Guillelmes vient tout droit en une place, Perron i ot, entaillié de vert marbre.*—*Charroi de Nimes*, vv. 1101–1102.

97. *Lutea enim a luti fetore prius dicta fuerat.*—Rigord, ed. Delaborde, I, 54.

98. *El fist fere ung grant chemin ferré, Par ou alast a Paris la cité; Quar le pays estoit de bouays planté. . . . Par celle dame fut maint chesne coupé.*—*Aquin*, vv. 864–69.

99. L. Thorndike in *Speculum*, III (1928), 199–203, argues on the brighter side.

100. Occasionally in the heart of a city there were concerted attacks by organized bands. At times men of rank would take part in the plundering of their neighbors.—F.S., p. 92.

101. Not infrequent is the expression *tuit li gon et les verveles.*—*Conte del Graal* or *Perceval*, vv. 7680–81. It means "all the hinges and bolt-rings."

102. *Anseÿs de Mes*, vv. 9454–55.

103. Vv. 5453–54.

104. *Les Narbonnais*, vv. 1870ff.

105. This is found as Plate 23 in Aimé Champollion-Figeac's *Louis et Charles, Ducs d'Orléans* (Paris, 1844). The *Ancrene Riwle* speaks of the floodgates, of land-based mills, but this adds little to the picture: ". . . when you must needs speak a little, raise the floodgates of your mouth and do as men do at the mill, and let them down quickly" (pp. 72–73).

106. E.B., p. *lxv*.

107. This is another composite picture which I have not drawn directly from any twelfth-century source. The towing of boats on the Seine is mentioned in an act of April 22, 867: *ad ducendos*

naves et reducendos.—L. de Tisserand in *Bull. Soc. Hist. de Paris et de l'Ile de France*, IV (1877), 113. Then again, in the Truschet-Hoyau map of 1552 this process is illustrated very clearly.

108. Some way must have been used to prevent soil from slipping into the Seine. I have noted in the *Tresriches heures* of the Duc de Berry the use of willow trees for this purpose.

109. These magnificent illustrations were reproduced in *Life*, XXIV (January 5, 1948), 38–50. Louis VII had a *treillis* in his garden.—Lasteyrie, I, 156n.

110. J. McCabe, *Peter Abelard*, II, 23. Disputations were held there. I owe this reference to Miss Amy Kelly, whose book on Eleanor of Aquitaine is a monumental work.

111. Alexander's "noble" garden is a description of the kind of Spanish garden which was to be found in Cordova, Granada, and Valencia. Probably this is not just a chance comparison. These Spanish gardens had lemons, oranges, peaches, and pomegranates which had been imported into the country by the Arabs, and apples, dates, plums, and quinces which were there in Roman days. Clapham and Power, p. 354.

112. *N.R.*, pp. 274–75.

113. F.-G. de Pachtère, *Paris à l'époque gallo-romaine*, pp. 143–44.

114. The Norse custom of dueling on a small island was called *hólmgang*. It persisted into Old French literary tradition. One of the small islands in the Seine, any one, would have been ideal for this. *Brut*, vv. 10017–21.

115. In the *Charroi de Nimes* the body of Aymon le vieill is tossed from a window of the King's hall directly into the garden, at Paris (vv. 749–50). The steps before this palace are also mentioned (vv. 52–53). In the *Quatre fils Aymon* there is a mention of the *perron* (v. 1735). Philip Augustus was able to see the river from the window in this hall: *Quod Rex in aula deambularet, veniens ad palatii fenestras, unde fluvium Sequani pro recreatione animi quandoque inspicere consueverat. . . .*—Rigord, ed. Bouquet, I, 54. In the *Quatre fils Aymon* also we read: *Es prés par desus Saine, es les vos arotés. Charles fu as fenestres, si les a regardés* (vv. 950–51).

Chapter V

1. The cost of maintaining oneself as a student at Paris must have varied greatly. Rents could be very high. But there must have

been many who lived on next to nothing. When Abbot Samson of Bury-St. Edmund's was a student there, he was supported by a chaplain back home in England who sold holy water for this purpose.—Jocelin, p. 70. Abbot Samson remarked in later life that if he had had five or six marcs a year as steady income he would have remained as a scholar at Paris and would not have entered a monastery.—*Ibid.*, p. 57. This gives a fair idea of the total cost for a student at Paris.

2. John of Salisbury, *Metal.*, 830 c–d.

3. "Contra Curiales et Officiales Clericos" in *S.P.*, I, 164–66. See also C. H. Haskins in *American Historical Review*, X, 12 n.

4. *N.R.*, pp. 343–46. It was of just such a young man, not necessarily a cleric, however, that the Monge de Montaudo spoke: "*E enoia'm donzels qui sas cambas mira.*"—*Enueg*, v. 67.

5. Migne, *P.L.*, 199, col. 831: *solas opes ducunt esse fructum sapientiae.*

6. *O ars dialectica Numquam esses cognita Quare t faci clericos Exsules et miseros.*—*Carmina Burana*, ed. A. Hilka and O. Schumann (2 vols., Heidelberg, 1930), No. 89.

7. L. Bourgain, *La chaire française au 12e siècle*, p. 283.

8. *Galeran de Bretagne*, ed. L. Foulet (Paris, 1925), vv. 1676ff.

9. The reader will observe that a new day was thought to begin at sundown. This should explain the terms Christmas Eve and Easter Even. The Fête des Fous was not elaborately organized at so early a date as the twelfth century. The practice became more riotous in later times and was finally forbidden in 1445.

10. Giraldus, IV, 43. Giraldus mentions that the carole was taking place just after midday, on a feast day. He refers to the type of audience: *ad choream videndum et cantilenas audiendum* (IV, 44–45). Some dancing was done to instrumental music only. This was true of the *estampie.*

11. *C.U.P.*, No. 5. The cleric in question was severely censured by his students.

12. Giraldus, II, 120. At Bury-St. Edmund's the monastery servants joined with the townspeople in sporting in the cemetery on December 26. Their quarrelsome behavior was so unseemly that Abbot Samson showed his displeasure by not inviting the usual burghers to his table for the five days after Christmas.—Jocelin, pp. 145–46.

13. We have already cited the visit of Thomas Becket, then chancellor of England, to Paris, when he stopped with the Templars. See Giraldus, III, 27–31. Guernes says of Thomas in his more

secular days: *En la terre n'aveit plus large viandier. Adés vindrent a lui baron et chevalier, Puteins e lecheor, a beivre e a mangier. Ses ostels fist souvent l'ostel le roi voidier, Tant que li rois se prist vers lui a correcier.—Vie de Saint-Thomas*, stanza 84.

14. On Peter Pictor see Raby, *Secular Latin Poetry*, II, 28–30.

15. Much has been written on mediaeval dicing, particularly with reference to the *Jeu de Saint-Nicolas*. Here are same passages from the *Brut: Vous me boisiez, defors gitez Crolez la main, hociez les dez, Je l'an vi avant vostre get. Querrez denieers, metez. G'i met* (vv. 10861–64). Also: *Deus et deus gietent et puis quernes, Anbes as, et le tierz, ternes. A la foiee gietent quinnes, a la foiee gietent sinnes; Sis, cinq, trois, quatre, dui et as* (vv. 10851 ff.). This is so graphic that we feel we are witnessing a game of African golf. Jehan Bodel in his *Saisnes*, p. 180: *Cuverz, dist Baudoins, molt mal merchié en as, Com cil qui apres sines a gité ambes as.* We wonder about the games of *tresmerellum* and *ridechoh* [*sic*]. In the Charte de Saint-Omer we find: *Et quicumque ad tresmerellum vel ad ridechoh capti fuerint, dabunt 10 s. et illi 10 s. in quorum domibus ludentes inventi fuerint; et si dare non possunt, mittentur in pellori.*—Jean Gessler, *Textes diplomatiques latins du moyen-âge*, p. 65.

16. *Nos avommes tant but Que no drapel en demourront.—Jeu de Saint-Nicolas*, vv. 750–51. This tavern sells warm bread and herrings (v. 252).

17. In the Charte d'Arras: *Vel qui per vim feminam violaverit . . . eadem poena condemnabitur quanta a praedecessoribus comitis hujusmodi malefactores condemnari solent in Flandria.*—Gessler, p. 67. In the Privileges for the town of Ghent there is still another interesting clause in this connection: if the woman goes to the man willingly as he enters the room (in a scene prearranged by the *échevins*) then the man is acquitted.—*Ibid.*, p. 69. A neat description of the tastes of an "easy woman" is in *Ille et Galeron*, vv. 1285 ff.

18. The description which follows is drawn basically from Paré, Brunot, and Tremblay.

19. See Savon in the Glossary of Paul Dorveaux, *Le livre des simples médicines, tr. française du Liber* . . . Circa Instans *de Platearius* (Paris, 1913).

20 *Metal.*, 855 a.

21. Giraldus, II, 37. Giraldus says also that Mainier, a teacher in Paris, remarked: *Venient dies, et vae illis quibus leges obliterabunt scientiam literarum* (II, 349).

22. *N.R.*, pp. 283ff.

23. *Ibid.*, pp. 288–89.

24. *Rusticus in luna quem sarcina deprimit una, Monstrat per spinas nulli prodesse rapinas.* Carleton Brown in his *English Lyrics of the XIIIth Century* (Oxford, 1932), No. 89, has a similar poem.

25. The list of books given here does not follow completely the one attributed to Alexander by Haskins. See *Mediaeval Science*, pp. 357ff.

26. This is a remarkable passage, which I will cite in full: *Si enim codicem eis ad legendum a pueris, quasi theatralibus ludis subito capti obstupescunt, nihil scientes quod hujusmodo sunt instrumenta clericorum, sicut novit faber retia instrumenta esse piscatorum et piscator malleum et incudem instrumenta fabrorum, cum alter in arte alterius nihil sibi possit proprium vendicare, nisi quod scit instrumentorum nomina exprimere, cum usum aut artem eorum non habeat, tamen utilia inde provenentia plurimum concupiscat. Sic igitur sunt hodie in ecclesia clerici sine scientia litterarum sicut plerique milites sine usu et exercitio armorum qui etiam nomen habentes ex re vocantur ab aliis milites sanctae Mariae.*

27. Dame Custance gave a marc of silver (seven dollars) for a copy of the *Life of Henry I of England.*—Gaimar, *Estorie des Engleis*, vv. 6495–98. Abbot Samson paid twenty marcs (two hundred dollars) for a copy of the Scriptures which he bought in France, or possibly Italy.—Jocelin, p. 137.

28. There were *librarii* who did a flourishing business in Paris. Pierre de Blois gives us amusing data on the behavior of one of them. This fellow had agreed to sell a set of law books to Peter. Later he was offered a higher price and he sold to this new purchaser. Peter wrote a letter in which he outlined how the book-dealer should be brought to law.—*C.U.P.*, No. 28.

29. A book chest is featured in *De arca libraria* in *S.P.*, II, 544. Gaimar mentions the chaining of a book.—*Estorie des Engleis*, vv. 6495–98.

30. The Archpoet says that he has learned the *Ars dictaminis* and is now ready for a secretarial job.—*Carmina Burana*, No. 162.

31. R. L. Poole, *The Papal Chancery*, p. 78.

32. Giraldus, I, 410.

33. *S.P.*, I, 82–95.

34. John of Salisbury, ed. Migne, *P.L.*, 199, col. 830: *Metal.*, I, 4. Alexander Neckam, *De vita monachorum*, in *S.P.*, II, 175–200. Giraldus is very bitter in his *Gemma ecclesiastica* and elsewhere.

35. *Anseÿs*, vv. 5034-43.

36. *Yvain*, vv. 2875–87.

37. We should add to these the position of *infirmarius*. I assume that the guestmaster and the *sacerdos de hospitali* were the same; they might be separate posts. Jocelin is our authority for these facts, to which must be added the *Cronica de electione Hugonis* which continues the narrative in Jocelin's chronicle. This continuation is published in T. Arnould's *Memorials of St. Edmund's Abbey* (Rolls Series). These monastic officials are given there in II, 75–76.

There were many lay servitors in such an abbey: *Ainc n'i remest moines ne enclostriers Prieurs ne abes, prevos ne ceneliers (celeriers), Ne cambrelens ne vallés ne huissiers, Tout s'en fuirent, et keu et boutillier.—Moniage Guillaume*, Redaction II, ed. W. Cloetta (2 vols. SATF, Paris, 1906–11), vv. 148ff.

The sacristan could serve as a kind of banker for the people of the nearby town.—Jocelin, p. 15.

38. *Moniage Guillaume*, II, vv. 257ff., 268. Nigel Wireker comments on the fact that the Cistercians did not wear *braies: Ergo quid facerem, veniens si ventus ab Austro Nudaret subito posteriora mea?—S.P.*, I, vv. 2139–40.

39. Marie de France, *Yonec*, vv. 459–98.

40. James Rorimer, *The Cloisters. The Building and the Collection of Mediaeval Art in Fort Tryon Park* (New York, 1938), *passim*.

41. Jocelin, p. 23.

42. *Ibid.*, p. 72.

43. *Ibid.*, pp. 44, 163.

44. Haskins, *Renaissance*, pp. 40ff.

45. Jocelin, p. 21. See n. 19, Chapter 6.

46. Peter the Venerable, Migne, *P.L.*, 189, col. 882.

47. *Ibid.*, col. 885.

48. Jocelin, p. 152.

49. Peter the Venerable, col. 114.

Chapter VI

1. For phantasmata in the early morning see *Carmina Burana*, No. 193.

2. These and many other street calls are in the *Cries des rues de Paris*.

3. *Conte del Graal*, vv. 5765ff.

4. *Quatre fils Aymon*, vv. 4203 ff. For what was meant by India at this time see *El Cavallero Zifar*, ed. C. P. Wagner (Ann Arbor, 1929), p. 36.

5. E.B., p. *xlix*.

6. Boileau does not include whale oil; but the whaling industry was flourishing at this time and previously. See Aelfric's *Colloquy* in Wright, I, pp. 88–103.

7. All these herbs and more are listed in *Platearius*. See n. 19, Chapter 5.

8. I have at hand a number of treatises on mediaeval medicine. Among these are *La Chirurgie de Roger de Salerne*, *Comment le medicin doit se comporter aupres du malade*, and *L'ordenance de medicine et de diete*. These transcriptions are unpublished. I am making free use of them here.

9. Yvain is given skillful care by the two daughters of his host, and he gets well.—*Yvain*, vv. 4698–99. The two sisters of Guivret attend Erec.—*Erec et Enide*, vv. 5196ff. In Chrétien's *Conte del Graal*, vv. 4340–41, a *mire* sets a bone, aided by three damsels *de s'escole*. This is the next best thing to our modern system of trained nurses. Some of the clerical doctors were doubtless empirics without benefit of Galen. Giraldus comments unfavorably upon the Cistercians and the monks of Clairvaux who wander about practicing medicine. He adds: *non speciebus recentibus, non electuariis electis nec medicinis artificiose confectis, sed herbis campestribus solum, quatrinis aliquid fieri videretur curiose collectis et congestis.* —Giraldus, IV, 173–74. Later he mentions a Cistercian who has a *pixidem potu plenam.*—*Ibid.*, p. 175. John of Salisbury expresses similar disapproval in Migne, *P.L.*, 199, col. 836. William of Malmesbury, on the other hand, thinks that the monks are good physicians.—*Gesta Pontificum* (Rolls Series), pp. 150, 438.

10. *La vie d'Edouard le confesseur*, vv. 6412–13.

11. *Ibid.*, vv. 2295 ff., 5360 ff.

12. *Truevent sor un trossel de glés Un eschacier* [one-legged man] *tot seul seant, Qui avoit eschace d'arjant; A neel estoit bien doree, Et fu de leus an leus bandee D'or et de pierres precieuses.*—*Conte del Graal*, vv. 7650–55. I doubt seriously that a silver leg (wooden with silver plates nailed on?) would be encountered very often, if ever. This one-legged man was a mysterious character. He is using a *qanivet*, or small knife, to smooth off a stick of ash wood, which indicates that whittling was in favor at the time. See also the *Chanson de Guillaume*, vv. 2196–98.

13. There were many simple remedies, some more simple than

others. Cold water would assuage grief.—*La veuve*, v. 47. Kissing on the lips would bring someone out of a fainting fit.—*Des deus vilains*, v. 93. Hot bathing, even of a single spot on the body, would relieve dysentery.—*N.R.*, p. 432.

14. *Apres mengier fait mal aler, Ce nous font acroire li mire.*—*Rou*, II, vv. 349–50.

15. *N.R.*, p. 401.

16. Joseph Ben Meir Zabara, *The Book of Delight* (New York, 1932), Chapter 1.

17. *Ibid.*, p. 77.

18. *Ancrene Riwle*, pp. 422–23.

19. *Bires li mires lor fet boire et mangier une tele herbe qui moult lor puet aidier.*—*Anseÿs*, vv. 3187–88. See also Marie de France's *Les deus amanz.*

20. *Brut*, vv. 8977–78.

21. *Roman de Renart*, II, v. 966; *Erec et Enide*, v. 5208.

22. *Ille et Galeron*, v. 4014.

23. *La destre main li manoia soef, N'i senti voine batre ne remuer.*—*Mort Aymeri*, vv. 175–76. *Puis li taste, qu'il n'i arreste, Au pous du bras, puis li arreste, Puis a regardee s'orine.*—*Blonde d'Oxford*, vv. 673–75.

24. Gerins thrust a corner of his *bliaut* into a wound so that the blood would not come forth.—*Anseÿs*, vv. 1653–55. Erec and Guivret tear cloth for bandages from their own shirts.—*Erec et Enide*, vv. 3926–30. The physicians move about among the wounded, who are laid on beds, and they give them herbs to drink.—*Anseÿs*, vv. 2878–86.

25. Full treatment is described in *Erec et Enide*, vv. 5200–5208. The plaster is indicated in Thomas's *Tristan*, v. 2335.

26. A urologist has described this operation for me. The patient was laid back on a table, or in a large chair. An assistant pressed down on the bladder from the abdomen side; the operator inserted a finger into the patient's rectum and felt the stone from that side. These two pressures brought the stone and the bladder hard against the perineal tissue. A quick incision cutting through to the bladder was then made, applying the knife midway between the anus and the urether. After the stone had been pushed out, the legs were strapped together to minimize bleeding. The perineal tissue has a natural tendency not to become infected. On early lithotomists consult J. S. Joly, *Stone and Calculus Disease of the Urinary Organs* (St. Louis, 1931), p. 12. A cataract operation is pictured in Hartley and Elliot, Plate 37b.

27. Usamah, pp. 162–63. We have said nothing about leprosy. The leper was allowed to wander about alone, or in groups of his fellows. He carried a cup or bowl, a *flavel* (clicking apparatus), and often a crutch or staff.—*Wistasce li moines*, vv. 1398–1414. Lepers were called *transportani* because when gathered into special hospitals they were obliged to live outside the walls of the town.—*N.R.*, p. 223. The sexes were kept separate in a leper house.—Lambert d'Ardres, p. 594.

28. *Erec et Enide*, vv. 3615, 3629, 3660–61.

29. *Ille et Galeron*, vv. 1803 ff.

30. Excellent observations on the conditions of pregnancy were common. Take, for instance, the fabliau *Richeut*, vv. 152–53, 403, where the symptoms are described. It was customary for friends to call on the mother after the *gesine*.—*Roman de Renart*, II, vv. 1670–79.

31. Marie's *Milon* and the *Galeran de Bretagne* illustrate this care. See also *Richeut*, vv. 411–14.

32. *Coetum autem puellarum quibus custodia pueruli filii militis deputata fuit.*—*N.R.*, II, p. 157.

33. Gay and Stein, p. 625; Bayeux Tapestry, No. 31.

34. Bayeux Tapestry, No. 31; *Anseÿs*, v. 2032.

35. The sarcophagus of King Alfonso X at Las Huelgas in Burgos is still in place, in the chapel. There is burial before the altar in *Anseÿs*, vv. 2036–41.

36. See Marie's *Yonec*, also Roger de Hoveden, *Chronica* (Rolls Series), III, 167–68.

37. *Yvain*, vv. 1166 ff. Two boys with bells in hand go before.—Bayeux Tapestry, No. 31.

38. Jocelin, p. 145.

39. Vv. 3907–3909. The bowels were sometimes removed, as in *Anseÿs*, vv. 573–78.

40. Theophilus mentions anvils of various shapes: flat, horned, rounded on top, etc.—Theophilus, pp. 211 ff.

41. Solder was kept in goose quills; the same was true of niello. The part to be soldered or nielloed was first anointed with parabus gum and then the quill was rubbed over it.—*Ibid.*, pp. 238–39.

42. Wright, p. 104.

43. Formulae for making all sorts of artificial gems are in Theophilus, pp. 175 ff.

44. The stones were glued first on the proper place with a flour paste.—*Ibid.*, p. 275.

45. Gilding of lesser metals was accomplished with a wash of

mercury, salt, vinegar, and aluminum.—Gay and Stein, p. 561.

46. Wright, p. 123. The *Fabliau du mercier* has a still more remarkable list of merchant's wares.

47. *Extraneus mercator vel aliquis transiens per regnum non habens certam mansionem infra vicecomitatum, sed vagans, qui vocatur Piepowdrous, hoc est anglice dustifote.—Leg. Quat. Burg. Scot.*, XXIX (Stat. Scot. 1.361).

48. Vv. 1145–51.

49. In Aelfric's *Colloquy*, much earlier, we find a merchant selling gems, gold, purple garments, silk raiment, spices, wine, oil, ivory, brass, copper, tin, sulphur, and glass.—Wright, pp. 88ff.

50. *N.R.*, p. 239. *Subtrahe plumbum suppositum vitro, jam nulla resultabit imago inspicientis.*

51. Theophilus, pp. 119ff.

52. *S.P.*, II, 567.

53. Lambert d'Ardres, p. 590.

54. Mortar was from river mud, mixed with sand and water. Wace says that strong vinegar also was used.—*Rou,* III, v. 3841. According to Fitzstephen, the Tower of London was built with mortar mixed with animal blood.

55. The cost of living at this time is something to consider. The best statement is made by Chrétien de Troyes. He says of a merchant: *Qui gaigne la semaine vint solz* [$10.00] *n'est mie fors de paine.—Yvain,* vv. 5314–15. That is to say, $40.00 a month is a poor wage. The index figure which I have estimated for calculating over-all purchasing power between modern United States money and the money of the twelfth century is four. This being true, we arrive at $160.00 a month as the sum which would barely support a middle-class person in modern times. The pay of a skilled workman, under these circumstances, was very low in the twelfth century—about $2.25 a week in modern currency value. However, it must be remembered that a workman received a great deal extra in food and clothing. Chrétien, in the passage just quoted, adds that 1,500 sous ($750.00) per week would be a fortune for a duke. This multiplied by four would indeed be a fortune. The cheapest barley in Chrétien's time was at $1.25 a bushel.—*Yvain,* vv. 2846–49.

56. Hartley and Elliot, Plate 18d.

57. The walls of Winchester Cathedral were filled with rubble in this way. Repairs were made there with liquid cement in 1920–21.

58. Wright, p. 106; *N.R.*, p. 281.

59. A sketch of a thirteenth-century loom is reproduced in

Hartley and Elliot, Plate 22b. A vertical loom, without treadles, on which the warp threads were separated by sticks only, and not by heddles, is also portrayed (Plate 22a). In that same illustration certain figures are warping threads between an upright of the shed and a forked stick.

60. The precise meaning of "scarlet" is not known. It seems to have designated a kind of silk which was frequently *vermeille* or red—*escarlate vermeille.*—*Conte del Graal,* v. 7917. Perhaps there is some clue in this passage from Gaimar: *Vindrent .iiij. signes el pais, Vermeilles s'en vont demustrant, Tels ne vist ainz nul home vivant, Cum escarlates s'estendeient, Prof de la terre s'apareient* (vv. 2145–49). Chrétien mentions an *escarlate peonace,* "peacock-colored scarlet."—*Yvain,* v. 233.

Alexander knew about the production of silk from the silkworm, although silk was not cultivated in France in his time.—*N.R.*, pp. 272, 492.

61. Gay describes a lovely bit of silk material of which he owned a small piece. It was of dark purple with gold figures and the inscription (in Arabic) "Victory to the possessor." This came from a twelfth-century tomb at Saint-Germain-des-Prés.—Gay and Stein, p. 585.

62. E.B., pp. 126–30.

63. John of Garland says that the fuller worked naked in his trough.—Wright, p. 131.

64. Caesarius von Heisterbach, *Dialogus Miraculorum,* ed. Strange, 1.3.

65. *La vie d'Edouard le confesseur,* vv. 6086–6155.

66. John of Garland, in Wright, p. 125.

67. *Ibid.*, p. 131.

68. *Roman de Renart,* I, vv. 2236–94.

69. Some of this information on the miner and the blacksmith is drawn from L. F. Salzman, *English Industries of the Middle Ages* (Oxford, 1923). A few facts come from Theophilus. The anvil is placed on a tree stump in the fabliau *Connebert.*

70. Gilles d'Orval narrates how in 1196 a supernatural being came to a smith who could not afford to buy charcoal and said to him: "*Invenies negras venas terre patentes, que terra est igniendum ferrum.*"—MGH, *Scriptores,* XXV, 115.

71. Alexander mentioned that a whetstone was required to distinguish steel from iron. See Chapter 4, n. 77, above.

72. Theophilus, p. 215.

73. *Ibid.*, p. 209.

74. *Ibid.*, p. 223.
75. Wright, p. 129.
76. *Rou*, III, vv. 6533–49.
77. Theophilus, p. 24.
78. *Ibid.*, p. 221.
79. *Ibid.*, p. 21.
80. *Rou*, III, vv. 6356–59.
81. Wright, p. 129.
82. *Grandes chroniques de France*, ed. Viard, VI, 89–94.
83. *Girard de Roussillon*, pp. 531–32.
84. *La vie d'Edouard le confesseur*, vv. 3506–25.
85. Jocelin, pp. 113–14.
86. Emil Hannover, *Pottery and Porcelain*, ed. Bernard Rackham (London, 1925), I.
87. See Salzman, n. 69, above.
88. Giraldus, II, 45–46.
89. *C.U.P.*, No. 4. A new teacher was no longer required to pay a fee of one marc to the chancellor of Notre Dame. It was lamented by a cleric in the period 1192–1203 that beardless youths were now teachers: *Conscribunt et ipsi summulos suos omissis artium abiectisque libris autenticis.—C.U.P.*, No. 48.
90. The Archpoet speaks. *Oxford Book of Mediaeval Latin Verse*, No. 66, vv. 41–44.

Chapter VII

1. Giraldus, I, 50. From an illumination of later date I should judge that such a target was of straw, the size of a man's trunk, raised on a pole to the height of a man sitting on horseback. The pole rested in a stand. In other cases a large ring was certainly used, suspended from a crosspiece. The squires were expected to catch this ring on their lances.
2. Wright, pp. 99–100.
3. *Et avuec ce met del suen Chemise et braies deliees.—Yvain*, vv. 2978–79. For an expensive *braiel* see *Moniage Guillaume*, II, vv. 362 ff.
4. Texts describing such a dressing procedure are numerous. Further from the *Yvain: Chemise risdee li tret Fors de son cofre, et braies blanches, Et fil et aguille a ses manches* (vv. 5422–24). In the *Lai du Trot*, v. 28: *sorcot de chiere escarlate sanguine foree d'une pene ermine*.
5. Thomas, *Tristan*, Sneyd MS, v. 390; *Huon de Bordeaux*, vv.

3621–23. Observe the jongleur represented on the Limoges casket, Dalton, p. 51. He shows no linen at the neck or sleeves. Many illustrations of costume are reproduced in Camille Enlart, *Le costume.* The *Cid* offers further details (vv. 3085–99).

6. *Hist. Archb. Th. Becket,* VII, 28 ff.

7. *Ancrene Riwle,* pp. 396–97.

8. The Winchester Bible sheet in the Morgan Library gives details. Soft boots are quite visible there. Enlart gives an illustration of a typical shoe, having a small slit at the top, over the ankle, and a narrow edging or border around the top. At Vézelay (*Vézelay. Editions TEL,* Plate 33) a capital shows a shoe with a Y-shaped slash at the top and no edging. The soles were obviously soft. There was no tendency toward long, pointed toes at this time. There are numerous representations of shoes in Webster, also.

9. An excellent picture of a gentleman with his mantle gathered over both shoulders is on the tympanum of Saint-Ursin at Bourges. See Webster, Plate 42 (March). For some reason that is not clear, Webster suggests that the figure is of a cleric or monk. The tonsure is very conspicuous by its absence.

10. *Capam quam novam et optimam de scarleta et grysio indutus erat.—Hist. Archb. Th. Becket,* III, 25. The exact design of vair is seen on the mantles worn in the Winchester Bible sheet of the Morgan Library. Usamah speaks of "squirrel fur" as a lining material (p. 35). The *pellice* or *pelliçon* had a very narrow neck opening.—*Roman de Renart,* II, vv. 148–50.

11. If the hair was quite long in front, the man was considered to have a forelock *(toupet).* In the *Prise d'Orange,* vv. 120, 222, a man is seized by the *toupet* as a preliminary to having his neck broken. Such forelocks are visible in the Bayeux Tapestry.

12. On hats see Enlart, *Le costume,* pp. 161 ff., and the plates in Webster.

13. *N.R.,* p. 210.

14. Vv. 2145 ff.

15. A pleated *chainse* is visible in Deschamps, Plate 50.

16. Enlart, *Le costume,* pp. 33–37. The jongleresse, or dancer, on the Limoges casket shows no linen. Dalton, p. 51.

17. Marie de France, *Lanval,* vv. 565–68: *Que tuit li costé li paroient, Qui de deus parz lacies erent.* The long ties of the belt were called *pendant.—Piramus et Tisbé,* ed. C. de Boer (Paris, 1921), v. 330.

18. Marie de France, *Yonec,* v. 345. The dying knight hastens to give his beloved a *bliaut* to cover her *chainse.*

19. This could be short or long: *A tant vint l'autre suer a cort*

Afublee d'un mantel cort D'escarlate forré d'ermine.—Yvain, vv. 4737–39. The lady's mantle was pinned at the breast, and never over the right shoulder as the man's usually was.

20. *Oxford Book of Mediaeval Latin Verse*, No. 71, vv. 21–26. Bracelets are mentioned by Geoffroi de Vinsauf (No. 68).

21. The knight in Marie's *Guigemar* remarks that women tend to look alike (vv. 779ff.).

22. Giraldus, IV, 86.

23. *Roman de la Rose*, vv. 2170–72.

24. *Poésies*, ed. A. Jeanroy (Paris, 1922), II, v. 19. The best place to find this and other Provençal lyrics to which we refer is in K. Bartsch, *Chrestomathie provençale* (Marburg, 1904) and subsequent editions, or in C. L. E. Appel, *Provenzalische Chrestomathie* (Leipzig, 1930).

25. Such a young man is pictured on the Duomo at Ferrara. See Webster, Plate 26. The author wrongly thinks that this is the figure of a woman.

26. K. Bartsch, *Altfranzösische Romanzen und Pastourellen* (Leipzig, 1870), I, 7, 28.

27. *Poésies complètes*, ed. J.-M.-L. Dejeanne (Toulouse, 1909). The lyric is "L'autrier jost una sebissa."

28. *Charroi de Nimes*, vv. 1037ff.

29. *La folie Tristan*, ed. J. Bédier (SATF, 1907), Version I, vv. 189–94.

In the Annunciation sculpture preserved in the Romanesque Room at the Louvre, the peasant men have *gonnes* like the ones described. Each wears a short *chape* with a hood and without sleeves. One of them wears the hood over his head. The other has the hood down, and his head is covered by a flat, round hat with a large brim. Shoes and leg coverings are not very distinct, but they resemble what we have already described. The typical peasant *gonne* can be seen in many places, as on fol. 42b of Br. Mus. Add. MS 39943. It is high at the neck with sleeves extending to the wrist. There is a belt or cord around the waist. The habit of a Franciscan friar in the early thirteenth century, like other monastic dress, resembled very closely the ordinary lay peasant dress.

30. Rutebeuf, *Disputoison de Charlot le Juif*. The razor of this century is pictured on a Romanesque capital of Royat (Puy-de-Dome).—Emile Mâle, *L'art religieux du XIIe siècle* (Paris, 1924), p. 24. The equipment of the barber is listed also in the *Roman de Renart*, XVI, vv. 375–78, 393. The fox and Primaus the wolf find

a closet which holds a razor, a brass basin, and scissors. Specific mention is made that the first act in shaving is to wet the hair thoroughly. See also *Roman de Renart*, II, vv. 119, 374.

31. Once-a-week shaving is mentioned in the *Conte del Graal*, vv. 7570–71. Samuel Pepys, in the seventeenth century, used pumice stone to keep the hair down, as in his *Diary* for May 31, 1662.

32. Once more we refer the reader to the Winchester Bible sheet at the Morgan Library.

33. Criticism is implied in *C'est costume as Danois, car sovent sunt baignié.—Quatre fils Aymon*, v. 7957.

34. There is a picture of two individuals, in the thirteenth century, bathing together in Br. Mus. Sloane MS 2435, fol. 8b. There is a fabliau dealing with the lover who was hidden under the tub.

35. Vv. 1881–82.

36. *Ibid.*, vv. 3134–35. Aelis makes a living for a time washing heads and doing needlework. Her shampoo is much in demand among the knights.—*Escoufle*, vv. 5508–11.

37. *Aquin*, vv. 2315–16.

38. Ysengrim wore mittens while cutting at the King's table. See Chapter 3, n. 42, above. *Pèl. de Charl.*, v. 292. The glove could be used as a pocket for small coins: *Mieus aim avoir un besant Que riens trover en un want.—Recueil général des jeu-partis*, ed. A. Langfors (SATF, 1926), LVII, vv. 63–64.

At this point we will say a few words about the "possibility" of the pocket handkerchief in the mediaeval period. The man of the twelfth century resembled the ancients in that he was accustomed to wiping sweat from his face with a cloth *(suaire)* which, we assume, was as large as a towel, but of finer linen. Furs could be used, most unsuitably, for this purpose.—*Chanson de Roland*, v. 3940. Surely the use of the *suaire* was extended to the nose also. The earliest mention that I have seen of a handkerchief for weeping is in the *Libro de Buen Amor*, ed. Cejador y Frauca, 1179 d. The date is mid-fourteenth century. In Deschamps, Plate 49b, the corner of a mantle is used in this way.

39. *Erec et Enide*, vv. 2628ff. See also *An mi leu de sa tante fu .i. pailes gitez; Desus s'est li vassax gentement conreez. Chauces de fer chauca et esperons dorez, Hauberc ot en son dos, qui fu tresbien dorez.—Saisnes*, II, 3.

40. These remarks are from actual observation and handling of fifteenth-century mail coats. Unfortunately, no *haubercs* from the twelfth century are extant.

41. The details are from Usamah, pp. 129–30: "The jerkin en-

closed a Frankish coat of mail extending to the bottom of it, with another coat of mail on top of it reaching as far as the middle. Both were equipped with the proper linings, felt pads, rough silk and rabbit's hair." Usamah says also (p. 104): "There came out to meet him from the tower . . . a Frank wearing double-linked mail. . . ." In the *Prise de Cordres et Sebille*, ed. O. Densusianu (SATF, 1896), v. 2693: *Et par desore .i. blanc hauberc doblier.* Giraldus says: "A heavy and complex armour made of cloth and iron both protects and decorates the knight."—Giraldus, II, 8.

42. In the Winchester Bible sheet of the Morgan Library the puttees are quite visible to me. Mail *chauces* are mentioned in almost every text. They opened down the back of the calf. See *Brut*, vv. 9510–11, and *Yvain*, vv. 598–99: *Sont vostre panel anborré Et voz chauces de fer froiees.* The mailed gloves (manicles?) can be seen in illustrations reproduced by Enlart, *Le costume*, pp. 465 ff.

43. A *sorcot* of green and yellow silk completely hid the armor of a Frank.—Usamah, p. 90.

44. *Et pardesos la coiffe frema le capeler De plus tres dur achier que on peut trover, Desus le capel fist un vert elme fremer.*—*Fierabras*, ed. A. Kroeber and E. Servois (Paris, 1860), vv. 612 ff. *Ainz deslaça son vert elme gemé Aprés la quoife del blanc auberc safré Sor ses espaulles l'a laissiee coler.*—*Mort Aymeri*, vv. 2330 ff.

In the *Chaitivel* of Marie de France, vv. 137–38, the *ventaille* is unlaced and the beards are then pulled out. Cf. *Ille et Galeron*, vv. 701, 714–15. A nasal was good for holding a captive: *Par le nasel du heaume ala penre son pere, si le rendi le roi; ce est chose provee.*—*Doön de la Roche*, vv. 2539–40. The use of the adjective white to denote the *hauberc* may have reference to a silver color, as well as to a white lacquer.—*Blonde d'Oxford*, v. 310.

45. *Aspremont*, v. 10488. See also *Griés fais est de porter hauberz, heaumes aguz.*—*Saisnes*, II, 5.

46. For this innovation see Enlart, *Le costume*, pp. 471–72.

47. It is just possible that the *broigne* designates a coat made of canvas or leather with the rings or plates sewed on, as opposed to the *hauberc* or mail coat. For rust see *Fergus*, ed. E. Martin (Halle, 1872), vv. 1527 ff: *Li haubers estoit si vermaus Tout autresi con li solaus Quant il lieve vers Ethiope, Mais ce n'ert mie de sinople Ne de bresil, bien le sachiés, Ains estoit un poi ruilliés.* For red lacquer cf.: *Ses armes sont vermeilles et li tains fu tos frois.*—*Chétifs*, ed. Lucy Wenhold (Chapel Hill, 1927), v. 1207. *Les armes de sinople taintes.*—*Conte del Graal*, v. 2413.

48. Layamon's *Brut*, v. 22288.

49. Wace, *Brut*, vv. 10503–508. For the ladies, vv. 10509–10.

50. *Cote de fer ont li ceval en son, Hauberc et brogne pendant tresqu'al talon.—Aspremont*, vv. 6864–65. *Son cheval tot covert de fer.—Rou*, III, v. 7512. Also in *Chevalerie Ogier le Danois*, vv. 7357–58.

51. "All of a sudden I saw him spur his horse, and as the horse began to wave its tail, I knew that it was already exhausted."—Usamah, p. 68. "So I turned against a horseman in their vanguard, who had taken off his coat of mail in order to be light enough to pass before us, and thrust my lance into his chest" (v. 41).

52. *Prise de Cordres et de Sebille*, vv. 2698 ff.

53. Texts are numerous on this detail. Thomas, *Tristan*, vv. 910–12. *Li baron orent gonfanons; li chevalier orent penons.—Rou*, III, vv. 6529–30.

54. Usamah, pp. 69–70. The handle, or *arestuel*, of the lance was of leather: *Tant que par les quamois les tindrent.—Yvain*, v. 2249. The shaft was of ash wood: *Qui grosses erent et de fresne.—Yvain*, v. 6111. It could be painted, as well as the shield: *Monte et prent l'escu et la lance qi estoit granz et roide et peinte.—Karrenritter*, vv. 2391–92. When lances were not in use, they were stored in a *hantier*, or lance rack, while the shield was hung up on a hook.—*Karrenritter*, vv. 1000–1003.

55. *Lance levee sor le fautre.—Yvain*, v. 6086. *Richement vint lance sor fautre.—Escoufle*, v. 1138. *Le feutre od la sele del destrer suiurnez.—Pèl. de Charl.*, v. 461. Also *Ille et Galeron*, v. 1061.

56. Again the texts describing such equipment are extremely numerous. See Enlart, *Le costume*, and similar references. *Il tint traite Plorance, dont li poins fu letrés.—Queste del Saint Graal*, ed. Albert Pauphilet (Paris, 1923), p. 5. There are many occurrences of *mangon* in the *Chanson de Roland* and the *Quatre fils Aymon*.

57. *As dens en detrençoit les fors ais joins a glus.—Les Chetifs*, v. 4045. For information on the casein glue we are indebted to Theophilus, p. 21. Fine shields were made in Toulouse, Lyons, and London.—*Karrenritter*, vv. 5794–5844. On shield decoration see *Erec et Enide*, vv. 2153–55, 3613; *Huon de Bordeaux*, v. 1778; and *Aquin*, vv. 741–42.

58. Giraldus, VIII, 320–21.

59. So used in Marie de France's *Chaitivel*, v. 140: *Sor un escu fu mis chascuns.*

60. *Giete a son col une targe florie, .ix. boucles d'or ot anviron assisses.—Prise de Cordres et de Sebille*, vv. 2740–41.

61. Examples of this routine are to be found in almost every *chanson de geste* and romance.

62. Usamah, p. 82.

63. Usamah, p. 104. Two dinars would be equivalent to about ten dollars.

64. Is this what is meant by the term *broigne*, opposed to *hauberc?* The expression *haubers jazerans* probably meant nothing more than a *hauberc* made in Algiers. See *Quatre fils Aymon*, v. 759.

65. Cf. the description of the *fil de netun* and their arms in the *Yvain: N'i a nul d'aus qui n'ait un Baston cornu de cornelier Qu'il orent fez apareillier De cuivre et puis lier d'archal. Des les espaules contreval Furent armé jus qu'aus genolz, Mes les chiés orent et les volz Desarmés et les jambes nues* (vv. 5516–23). For the weapons see *Cligés*, vv. 1994ff.: *guisarmes*, Danish axes, lances, Turkish swords, quarrels, darts, and javelins. In the *Rou*, III, vv. 7691ff., the dress is described as iron cap, leather jacket, and quilted jacket girded with a belt. In *Blonde d'Oxford* a *serjant* wears quilted doublet, steel cap, and dagger (vv. 4010ff.).

66. See Guisarme in Gay and Stein.

67. *N'out en la terre chevalier, Ne bon serjant ne boen archier.* ...—*Rou*, III, vv. 6365ff.

68. *E por les haies les archiers.—Rou*, III, v. 1524.

69. I am describing a crossbow in my possession—of a later date, to be sure. But in the thirteenth century John of Garland speaks of *balistas trocleatas.*—Wright, p. 130.

70. See Sexton T. Pope, *University of California Publications in American Archaeology and Ethnology*, XIII (1917–23), 329–414, where he gives the result of his study of the early European bow and arrow.

71. Notably *Fergus* and the fabliau *Li vilains mire.*

72. Poole, p. 35, remarks that the amount of ceremony depended upon the young man's position in society.

73. This is the case in *Flamenca*, vv. 900–904; *Ille et Galeron*, v. 170; and elsewhere.

74. As at the close of Chrétien de Troyes' *Conte del Graal.* For an estimate of the true meaning of chivalry see Sidney Painter, *French Chivalry* (Baltimore, 1940).

75. Jocelin, p. 135.

76. A knight's fee could demand the personal service of the knight himself, and it could also demand the service of a number of additional knights. Such service was apt to consist of forty days

a year, mostly in August and September. Garrison duty could also be demanded. If a knight wished to avoid some of this, he was obliged to pay scutage; but an adventurous young man liked to serve where there was a promise of excitement. A mercenary knight or *soudoiier* was one who kept looking for service most of the year. See Marie de France's *Eliduc*. Mercenaries could be hired with the scutage fees exacted from less daring knights.—Poole, pp. 5, 38–39. At the beginning of Marie's *Lanval* there is a passing around of fiefs and wives. Consult also the beginning of the *Charroi de Nimes*. In Marie's *Milon* we have an experienced knight who follows the tourneys consistently.

Poole remarks that in England the wards of the king, including widows, were "sold" to prospective husbands. There is still extant the famous "Role of ladies, boys, and girls in the King's gift, for the year 1185."—Poole, p. 88.

77. There were exceptions. Yonec, in Marie's lai of that name, was raised by his "parents" and even knighted by them (vv. 469–70).

78. *N'i aura prevost ne voiier Qui volantiers ne vos convoit.*—*Yvain*, vv. 606–607.

79. A *serjant* was a man who held land in return for special services. He could be a mounted soldier, a footman, a falconer, a forester, a jailer, and so on. It was possible for him to have his service commuted into payment of rent, but most *serjanz* with special talents must have preferred to use them. By the thirteenth century special services of the kind were apt to be paid for in money and keep, rather than with a fief of land.—Poole, pp. 57–76. The heralds, along with the minstrels, are the recipients of clothing in *Le Comte de Poitiers*, ed. V. F. Koenig (Paris, 1937), vv. 1365–67. This would indicate that their social position was not high.

80. *Hist. G. le M.*, vv. 3426–3562.

81. The Third Lateran Council of March 5–19, 1179, re-emphasized that it was forbidden by the Church to use arms from sundown Friday till sunrise on Monday, and throughout Advent to the Octave of Epiphany, as well as from Septuagesima Sunday to the Octave of Easter.—*Chronicles* (Rolls Series, No. 82), p. 220.

82. This historical information can be checked in Lavisse, *Histoire de France*, and elsewhere.

83. The donjon at Quidallet (Brittany) had four stories and was fifty-six feet high. Its walls were five feet thick.—*Aquin*, vv. 219ff.

84. The various siege engines, catapults, battering-rams, and wooden towers were ordinarily manufactured when occasion demanded, before a town or castle that was being besieged. The master carpenters who superintended the work were called *engigneors*. However, some catapults were kept in the courtyard and on the wall. The principle of these stone-hurling machines is surely known to our readers. Their effect is well described by the Moslem Usamah: "I turned away . . . but soon heard the crash of a fall. I looked around, and, behold! a mangonel stone had hit the head of the old man, crushed it, and stuck it to the wall, making the brain flow on the wall. . . . Another mangonel stone struck one of our men on his lower leg and broke it. . . ." Usamah goes on to say that the injured man was shortly killed by another stone hitting him in the head.—Usamah, pp. 143–44.

Greek fire is not given any mention by Alexander, but it was an important siege weapon. Naphtha was the principal ingredient, to which pounded resin, sulphur, and niter were added in varying proportions. This was poured out on the enemy, or it was ignited on arrows, in the form of burning tow. Usamah mentions a jar of naphtha which was hurled: "The naphtha flashed like a meteor falling upon those hard stones, while the men who were there threw themselves on the ground for fear of being burnt." Joinville says of Greek fire: It resembles *estoiles qui dou ciel cheïssent* (§ 314) and it is like *un dragon qui volast par l'aire* (§ 200).—Usamah, p. 104. At times an ordinary fire was built against a fortification. The heat caused the mortar to crumble and the wall to fire.

85. In the *Anseÿs* the noise of battle is described as "such as four hundred carpenters would not make in setting up houses" (vv. 2726–27).

86. Alexander does not speak of military strategy, but others do. In Marie's *Eliduc* the protagonist prepares an ambush. Usamah mentions ambushes prepared regularly by the Franks. In the *Chanson de Roland* there is constant mention of arranging echelons or divisions of knights effectively.

87. This riffraff could be Brabançons, Aragonese, Navarrese, and Basques who were cruel and irresponsible. In the Rolls Series, No. 92, p. 209, see the decree of the Third Lateran Council.

88. Whipping was sometimes administered by a scourge which had six knots. It was considered more degrading when the punishment was administered by a deformed person such as a dwarf.—*Yvain*, vv. 4107ff.; *Erec et Enide*, vv. 218ff. For milder punishment a *balai*, or bunch of sticks, was applied.

89. These are the *soudoiiers* or mercenary knights.—Jocelin, p. 135.

90. The description of the castle in *Gawain and the Green Knight*, vv. 767–801, has resemblances to the one given by Alexander Neckam. There is a considerable discrepancy of date, however, as the English romance is of the fourteenth century. For Alexander's text see Wright, p. 103.

91. There could have been a barbican tower defending the approaches to the gate. This was a small, round blockhouse tower, usually one story high. It was supplied with all the necessities for sustaining a small siege. There are some excellent ones at Carcassonne, which are the ones that I have in mind. *Tant qu'ele aproche vers un pont Et vit d'un chastelet reont Les murs blans et la barbiquane.*—*Yvain*, vv. 4478–80.

92. This is the case with the castle of Laudine in the *Yvain*, probably where greater security was desired. However, we know from the *Conte del Graal*, vv. 1349–50, that often the drawbridge itself, when raised, formed a door for the gatehouse: *A ce que sa droiture aporte: le jor ert ponz, et la nuit porte.*

93. The gatehouse of a town or castle offers many interesting conjectures for us today. In the *Quatre fils Aymon*, vv. 2630–35, there is a description of a traitor secretly opening up the gate to the enemy: "He has lowered all the drawbridges; then he came to the gate and pulled the bolts; he came to the *bretesche* and leaned [over?] there, and with saw and file he cut the rings. The *gaubans* which hang there have fallen." I believe that *bretesche* means the projecting battlement over the gateway. The traitor leans over and cuts the drawbridge chains *(gaubans)*.

The gatehouse of the curtain wall which went around the castle at Old Sarum has been excavated and can therefore be described. There was a single door leading into the gate. There were little rooms on each side of the entrance (in the drum towers), one of them having a fireplace. The watchman on duty also had a niche, probably furnished with a wooden bench. There was, of course, a second large door leading into the courtyard or bailey. These particular doors had draw bars *(verrous?)* rather than locks and keys. Many such gates, however, did have a lock with a key. The sliding doors that we are picturing in the castle entered by Alexander are taken from the *Yvain*, where they play a prominent part in the story.

We are assuming that Alexander did not enter the courtyard through the second door, but mounted a stair within the gatehouse itself. We have in mind the small castle at Launceston, on the border of Cornwall, where such a stairway existed.

94\. . . . *et il font molt tost les chevaus delivrer Ou celier desoz terre les ont fait mener.*—*Doön de la Roche*, vv. 1666–67. *An une croute s'en antre Baufumes; .iiij. destriers a molt tost anselés.*—*Prise de Cordres et de Sebille*, vv. 1178–79. *Li cheval ont avoine et foin Et la litiere en jus qu'au vantre.*—*Yvain*, vv. 5360–61.

95\. In *Guigemar* of Marie de France the lady's room and chapel are inside such a wall. In Chrétien's *Yvain* the bedchamber of Lunete must be in the curtain wall, for she leads Yvain to it right from the gatehouse where he has been trapped.—*Yvain*, v. 1583. I suspect that the chamber of Rosemund Clifford was in such a location at Woodstock: *Infra portam castri et barbicanam . . . ab exitu Camerae Rosamundae usque ad capellam.*—See *Foedera*, IV, 629. Rosemund chamber became a common noun for some sort of room. Could it have been applied to such a bower in the curtain wall?

96\. *Yvain*, vv. 197–98.

97\. *Yvain*, v. 239; Marie de France, *Lanval*, vv. 239–42; *Anseÿs*, vv. 3714ff.

98\. *Erec et Enide*, vv. 5730–31, 5739–40. This was definitely outside.

99\. *Yvain*, vv. 5364ff.

100\. *Ja sont li mur fendu et frait Et li fossé empli d'atrait. Si ont tot ars les hordeis, Barres et lices et palis.*—*Guillaume de Palerne*, vv. 4991ff.

101\. *Sor se reube li atacoient Torques d'estrain que il faisoient Por cou ke on se gabast de lui.*—*Life of Saint Dominic*, vv. 2161–63. The gomph stick is discussed in histories of sanitation.

102\. This information is drawn from J. P. Bushe-Fox, *Old Sarum. Official Guide.*

103\. *La vie d'Edouard le confesseur*, vv. 987ff.

104\. Lambert d'Ardres, *MGH*, XXIV, 596.

105\. *As mains se prennent, el palés sont monté.*—*Charroi de Nimes*, v. 463.

106\. See the tympanum of Saint-Ursin at Bourges where there are splendid representations of boar hunting.

107\. See in particular the "Dog Genealogy" in *Life* for January 31, 1949.

108\. *Tentorium de serico magnum adeo quod ducenti milites in eo simul possint comedere.*—Benedict of Peterborough (Rolls Series), II, 133. *La ot maint tref tandu, ynde, vermoil et pers.*—

Saisnes, p. 61. *La veissiez mainte tente drecie Et maint pomel ou li ors reflambie.—Anseÿs*, vv. 10671–72. The tents are green and red in *Cligés*, v. 1263.

109. Marie de France, *Lanval*, vv. 80ff.

110. *Coronement de Loois*, ed. Langlois (Paris, 1920), vv. 2282–83.

111. V. 1779.

112. Meyer-Lübke, *REW*, 941a.

113. *Karrenritter*, vv. 5600–5603. These loges were being used as spectators' stands. I doubt that there was any railing. Compare the representation of a loge where women are weaving, in Hartley and Elliot, Plate 22b. Yet illuminations for the *Petit Jehan de Saintré* (fifteenth century) show a railing: two long beams have upright boards nailed between them.

114. *Karrenritter*, vv. 5541–43. A tourney at St. Edmund's had twenty-five knights. They were lodged at the Abbot's house and ate at his table, where they became boisterous.—Jocelin, p. 88.

115. *Aucassin et Nicolette*, §§ 19–20; Giraldus, *Descriptio Cambriae*, I, 17.

116. *Yvain*, vv. 6032–37. There are loges before the chapel at Ardres.—Lambert d'Ardres, *MGH*, XXIV, 624.

117. *Yvain*, vv. 6040–41.

118. J. Dauvillier, *Le mariage dans le droit classique de l'Eglise* (Paris, 1933). When it was believed that a previous mate was dead, although this was not confirmed, a long ban could be cried for a period of four months.—*Ille et Galeron*, vv. 3966–69.

119. This description of a wedding is combined from Marie's *Le Fresne*, vv. 384–420, and the more detailed account given in *Blonde d'Oxford*, vv. 4724ff.

120. *Yvain*, vv. 2339–2478.

121. *Brut*, vv. 10421–10590.

122. Wright, p. 106.

123. See W. H. Prior, "Notes on the Weights and Measures of Mediaeval England," *ALMA* (1924), pp. 77–97; (1925), pp. 141–70. Also C. Foulon in *Romania*, LXVIII (1944–45), 438–43.

Chapter VIII

1. "A little schedule containing the names of the knights . . . the names of the manors, and the rent which attached to each farm. Now [Abbot Samson] called this book of his his Calendar, in the

which were written down also all the debts which he had paid."—Jocelin, p. 45.

2. Hauréau, pp. 210–16. A manor house is sketched in C. W. Airne's *The Story of Saxon and Norman Britain, told in pictures* (Manchester, n.d.), p. 42.

3. Bern, *Folie Tristan*, v. 134.

4. The distinctions between knight tenure, *serjant* tenure, and free peasant were quite mixed up, particularly in England.—Poole, pp. 2ff. A serf was not supposed to bear any arms, and he had services and fees, the custom of his manor, which marked his status very clearly. The merchet or fee for the marriage of his daughter was the most distinguishing fee. Ordinarily, in case of mixed marriage a child took on the condition of the father.—Poole, p. 21.

5. Above, pp. 98–100.

6. The word is *terestrum*, which the Reichenau Glosses (No. 169) define as *ornamentum mulieris; quidam dicunt quod sit cofia vel vitta*.

7. Wright, p. 101.

8. A beehive is depicted in Hartley and Elliot, Plates 10e and f. See apiarists in Deschamps, Plate 45d.

9. Such a bucket *(saticulum)* is illustrated in Br. Mus. Add. MS 29943, fol. 42b. This container is suspended in a sling (of cloth?) which has a supporting band that goes around the neck.

10. "The sheep-fold would be moved twice a year. This was true on the Templars' estate in Gloucestershire in 1185."—Poole, p. 16.

11. The best horses and mules at this time were supposedly the Spanish breed. (This was not the same as Arabian.) The Spanish horse was sturdy, fairly low, with fine flowing mane and tail. The mule was doubtless similar in build: *Trois muls d'Espaigne et chargiez et trossez*.—*Charroi de Nimes*, v. 20. Gerald the Welshman speaks of Spanish horses in Britain: "In . . . Powys, there are most excellent studs put apart for breeding, and deriving their origin from some fine Spanish horses which Robert de Belesme, earl of Shrewsbury, brought into this country: on which account the horses sent from hence are remarkable for their majestic proportion and astonishing fleetness."—Giraldus, *Itinerarium Kambriae*, III, 12. Good horses were raised in Limousin also.

12. Alexander describes the plow further in *N.R.*, p. 280. A boy armed with goad accompanied the plowman. See Wright, pp. 88ff. Alexander forgets also to mention that the plow in his day had

two wheels on the front of it. See the plate opposite p. 134 in Clapham and Power. The earthboards, or moldboards, were planks which were set slanting to the rear on the side of the plowbeam. They widened the furrow and also piled the turned-up earth into a ridge.—Clapham and Power, pp. 134–35.

13. A harrow with large wooden teeth is mentioned by Abu Zucaria in his *Book of Agriculture.*—Clapham and Power, p. 358.

14. It was a moot question on some fiefs as to who owned the manure that was collected on the roads. The peasant owned that which he gathered before his own door. Manure was loaded into carts.—Jocelin, p. 163.

15. A cylinder was a rolling harrow, an oak cylinder provided with teeth.—Clapham and Power, p. 144.

16. Made of holly wood, wrapped in four layers of deerskin.—*Chanson de Guillaume,* vv. 3211–12.

17. A glossator has written *hortorum* over *Priapi,* not understanding the term.—Wright, p. 113.

18. Wright, pp. 110–13.

19. Webster, Plate 26.

20. Webster, Plate 34; *Erec et Enide,* vv. 3312–13.

21. Branch II, vv. 865 ff., 873 ff.

22. *Ibid.,* I, vv. 3133–34.

23. *Hali Meidenhod (EETS),* ed. Furnivall (1866) and D. Cockayne (1922), vv. 567–72.

24. *Ancrene Riwle,* pp. 314–15.

25. *Ibid.,* pp. 230–31.

26. *Ibid.,* pp. 186–87.

27. *Yvain,* vv. 2816–18.

28. *Herrod von Landsberg's Hortus deliciarum,* ed. A. Schultz (Vienna, 1888), p. 53.

29. *Hist. G. le M.,* vv. 509 ff.

30. Lambert d'Ardres, *MGH,* XXIV, 629. *Uxor autem eius Petronilla juvencula quidem Deo placita, simplex erat . . . vel inter puellas puerilibus jocis et choreis et hiis similibus ludis et poppeis sepius iuvenilem applicabat animum. Plerumque etiam in estate nimia nimium animi simplicitate et corporis levitate agitata, in vivarium usque ad solam interulam sive camisiam reiectis vestibus, non tam lavanda vel balneana quam refrigeranda vel certe spacianda, per vias et meatus aquarum hic illic prona nando, nunc supina, nunc sub aquis occultata, nunc super aquas nive nitidior vel camisia sua nitidissima sicca ostentata coram militibus nichilominus quam puellis se dimisit et descendit.*

31. Giraldus, I, 21.

32. *La Riote dou monde*, ed. J. Ulrich in *Zeit. fur Rom. Phil.*, VIII (1884), 282.

33. *Ancrene Riwle*, pp. 416–17.

34. A photograph of the group is published in *The Illustrated London News* for December 18, 1948, p. 693.

35. Clapham and Power, p. 311. Six arpents of land sell for twenty-four pounds in 1190.—*Arch.H.D.*, p. 18, No. 38.

36. Clapham and Power, p. 307.

37. *Ibid.*, pp. 263, 295–96.

38. *Ibid.*, pp. 318–19.

39. *Die Exempla des Jakob von Vitry*, No. 17.

40. Walter Map comments that the serfs are rising in arts and letters and that the barons are neglecting such studies.—W.M., p. 8. If a serf ran away and was unclaimed for a year and a day, he was automatically free.—Poole, p. 28.

41. Clapham and Power, p. 264. Such a girl had rights if she wished to press them. One of the sons of Richard Fits Drago violated a beggar girl. Abbot Samson made him pay five marks, and this sum was given to a peddler who married the girl.—Jocelin, p. 72.

42. Clapham and Power, pp. 266–67.

43. Branch I, vv. 2469–74.

44. Vv. 2415–18, 2511–17, 2563–68, 3840–3988.

45. The word is *funaculum*, which is glossed *ubi carbones ponantur*. In case the thurible or censer is meant we comment on the one made of amethyst which is mentioned in Marie's *Yonec*, v. 510. Censers had very ornate tops in the twelfth century. A bronze top, representing the tower of a Saxon church, is preserved in the British Museum. Another top in the same museum represents an assemblage of church buildings. See Dalton, pp. 34–35. It is possible that the *funaculum* may be a "chafing ball," a handwarmer which was used by a priest at Mass. One of these, preserved in the British Museum, is illustrated in Dalton, p. 112.

46. *Capitesium* is the word which I translate tentatively, after some consultations, by "silk cap." Jocelin mentions that many silk caps were pawned or pledged to Jewish moneylenders by the community of Bury-St. Edmund's, p. 47.

47. Wright, p. 172. The small reliquary contained a garment that had belonged to St. Edmund, p. 168. Abbot Samson added a pulpit in his abbey church "for the sake of those who heard him and for purposes of ornament."—Jocelin, p. 64. This furnishing

was by no means necessary. For the weathercock see Migne, *P.L.*, 156, col. 885.

48. *Eadem enim hora cecidit horologium ante horas matutinas, surgensque magister vestiarii, hoc percipiens et intuens, cucurrit quantocius et, percussa tabula tanquam pro mortuo, sublimi voce clamavit dicens feretrum esse combustum. . . . Juvenes ergo nostri propter aquam currentes, quidam ad puteum, quidam ad horologium, quidem cucullis suis impetum ignis cum magna difficultate extinxerunt. . . .—Chronica Jocelini de Brakelonda*, ed. J. G. Rokewode (London, 1840), p. 78. For translation see Jocelin, pp. 167–68.

On this type of clock I quote Jocelin in the Latin original so that the reader can form his own opinion. It is certain that the clock mentioned is a water clock, since the young men run to it to get water; yet it has some sort of falling weight which arouses the vestry warden. In the *Chronique des dus de Normandie*, II, 349, mention is also made of such a weight. This was a twelfth-century alarm clock. The *Annales regales* (ed. Kurze, pp. 123–24) mention and describe such a clock as belonging to Charlemagne.

The principle of the water clock is explained by Alfred Franklin in his *La Vie privée d'autrefois. La Mesure du temps* (Paris, 1888), pp. 22–27. The water dropped from a cone-shaped funnel and was collected in a graduated bowl. The markings on the bowl told the proper hour. The rate of the drip could be controlled by a wedge, thus allowing for a faster flow in the winter and a slower one in summer—daylight saving. For the mechanical clock, invented in 1271 or thereabouts, see L. Thorndike in *Speculum*, XVI (1941), 242–43. An important comparison to make at this point is the description of the *tabula* which was struck when a member of the community died (and which could serve as an alarm gong) with the similar *table* which was struck by the *vavassor* when Yvain (and before him, Calogrenanz) entered the enchanted forest of Bracelonde: *En mi la cort au vavasor Cui Dex doint et joie et enor Pendoit une table, ce cuit, Qu'il n'i avoit ne fer ne fust, Ne rien qui de cuivre ne fust; Sor celle table d'un martel Qui panduz ert a un postel Feri li vavasors trois cos.—Yvain*, vv. 211–19. Possibly the *vavassor* is the guardian of the entry to the Land of the Dead.

49. Migne, *P.L.*, 172, col. 915.

50. *Baudri de Bourgueil*, Nos. 213–14.

51. Jocelin, p. 168. There is a fine cupboard of this kind preserved in the cathedral at Bayeux. It has numerous compartments. Perhaps it was a vestiary for the canons, with a compartment for

each one. In the *Roman de Renart,* XIV, vv. 204–65, Renart and Primaus the wolf visit a church and find behind the altar a cupboard which contains the altar breads *(oublees)* wrapped in a fine towel. Close by is a chest which contains ordinary bread, meat, and wine, gifts received by the priest from his parishioners.

52. This material is drawn mostly from C. Wordsworth and Henry Littlehales, *The Old Service-Books of the English Church* (London, 1910).

53. There is a beautiful relief in stone (thirteenth century) in the cathedral at Rheims which shows a knight taking Communion.

54. King John offered a silk cloth (lent him for the occasion by the Sacristan) which he placed on the altar at the close of the Mass.—Jocelin, p. 182. For a special building fund a box with a slit in its top, protected by an iron bar, was placed near the church door.—Jocelin, p. 14. Prior to the Lateran Council of 1215 the Sacrament was taken in both Kinds.—Cf. *Yvain,* v. 192: *Le vin du calice beü.* A Eucharistic *chalumeau* was occasionally used.—Gay and Stein, p. 309. Jocelin says further: ". . . in many churches the sermon is delivered in French, or rather in English, for securing of the improvement of manners and not as a literary exercise."

55. Taken from the *Flamenca.* Before the crucifix one raised his eyes and then made a low obeisance.—*Vie Saint-Grégoire,* v. 1118.

56. *Home, qu'an ne puet chastiier Devroit an au mostier liier Come desvé devant les prosnes.—Yvain,* vv. 627–29.

57. *Folie Tristan,* I, vv. 210–11; also Usamah, p. 162.

58. *Atant a Renart envaï Un Benedicamus farsi A orgue, a treble et a deschant.—Roman de Renart,* XII, vv. 883–85. This branch dates from 1189–1204 according to L. Foulet, *Le Roman de Renart* (Paris, 1914), p. 115.

59. Davison and Apel, pp. 21–22.

60. Rorimer, pp. 21 ff., and *passim.*

61. Guibert de Nogent in Migne, *P.L.,* 156, col. 842; *Charroi de Nimes,* v. 843.

62. As in *Aspremont,* vv. 10972, 10995–99.

63. These facts are taken from Wordsworth and Littlehales, pp. 15, 21–22. Mass follows directly after Terce in *Flamenca,* vv. 2447, 3891–94, at the hour of Terce. In the *Roman de Renart,* XII, v. 897, Vespers is followed directly by Compline.

64. Here are a few additional notes about the Church. The *marguilliere,* or sexton, is a woman in the fabliau *Dou prestre teint,* v. 89. There is reference in some of the literature to the consecration of a church by the bishop. The procedure mentioned is still

in use, but it is not familiar to many readers. In the *Vie de Saint Edouard le confesseur*, vv. 2663–70, we read: *Les deos abécés unt truvez, Ki furent mult bien cumpassez. Les .XII. cruiz unt truvees, Ki del saint'olie uintes sunt. Des dudce cirges unt truvee La remasille as cruiz fermee. De l'evoe beneite jetee Fud l'iglise encore arusee.* The bishop with his crozier writes a Latin alphabet from one corner to the opposite one; then he writes another alphabet, the Greek one, between the other two corners. These intersect in the middle of the nave. Twelve small metal crosses are placed in the wall (today under twelve of the Fourteen Stations of the Cross). For further information consult the *Catholic Encyclopedia.*

65. It is a moot point whether a serf was free once he took holy orders.—Poole, p. 30. See Poole, p. 29, on the subject of the single day's work on the lord's land.

66. I, vv. 670–74.

67. *Ibid.*, v. 821.

68. *Si con li prestres vet au sanne Ou volantiers ou a anviz.*—*Erec et Enide*, vv. 4022–23.

69. Knights sit by the fire after supper, piling their equipment on an eating table, which has not been dismantled.—*Hist. Archb. Th. Becket*, II, 285ff. Thomas Becket himself never stayed for such amusement: *Et quand levez esteit li sainz hom de la table, N'aveit cure d'oïr de chançun ne de fable, Ne de nul' altre chose, s'ele ne fust verable.*—Guernes, vv. 3921–23. In the manor house of the family of Adam dou Petit Pont the minstrels are performing after the meal.—Hauréau, p. 203. The standard work on the jongleurs is that of Edmond Faral, *Les jongleurs en France au moyen-âge* (Paris, 1910). See further, in *Doön de la Roche*, vv. 3571–72: *Quant il orent mangié, si font traire les napes. Cil jugleor desponent lor chançuns et lor fables.*

70. *Escoufle*, vv. 7030–35.

71. I, vv. 2389ff.

72. *Flamenca*, vv. 575–701. If a jongleur noticed that his performance was not pleasing, he would shift suddenly to another song.—Migne, *P.L.*, 205, Chapter 155.

73. For this I am drawing upon an article, still unpublished, by André de Mandach, on the music of the *Chanson de Roland.*

74. In *Doön de la Roche* the jongleur stops at v. 2603 (which would require about three and a half hours to reach, by my reckoning); he then continues at the second sitting for another 2,035 verses. In *Huon de Bordeaux* the singer stops at v. 4946, at Vespers. He requests his listeners to come the next day after dinner, and he

wants each to bring a maille, or half-denier. In the *Mort Aymeri* the minstrel pauses at v. 2595. We have testimony that the jongleur Jenois de Lucca performed from after dinner until Vespers.—*Romanische Forschungen*, XXIII, 43. Walter Map says: "Only the [trifling] of mimes in vulgar rhymes celebrateth among the god-like nobility of the Charleses and the Pepins—no one speaketh of living Caesars."—W.M., p. 254. In the *Anseÿs de Mes*, vv. 289–93: *Uns jongleors ot sa viele pris qui lor viele sus le palais antis. A lui estoient li baron ententis. Un lai viele. Quant ot finement pris Doné li ont maint mantel sabelin.*

75. A minstrel might strive for comic appearance, or perhaps he was often a little crazy. In *Brut*, vv. 9336ff., a minstrel has half a mustache, half a beard, and half of his head shaved. At times the jongleur was a disgraceful glutton.—Lambert d'Ardres, *MGH*, XXIV, 622.

76. Here is an additional example of extreme *largesce: Vidimus quondam quosdam principes qui vestes diu excogitatas et variis florum picturationibus artificiosissime elaboratas, pro quibus forsan viginti vel triginta marcas argenti consumpserant, vix revolutis septem diebus, histrionibus . . . ad primam vocem dedisse. . . .*—Rigord in *Rec. Hist. Fr.*, XVII, 21.

77. I, vv. 2801–2802. Jongleur schools are discussed in Charles Beaulieux, *Histoire de l'orthographe française* (Paris, 1927), I, 32. It was at such schools that the phonemic spelling of the Old French language was developed.

78. Such was the case with Levet at the court of Raimbaut d'Aurenga. See Raimbaut's lyrics, Nos. 36 and 38.

79. On William of Longchamp consult Roger of Hoveden, *Chronica* (Rolls Series, No. 51), III, 143.

80. Lambert d'Ardres, *MGH*, XXIV, 598. To quote further: *Quis autem nisi expertum et auditum crederet Hasardum de Aldehen omnino laicum ab ipso simili modo omnino laico litteras didicisse et litteratum factum? Ipse enim quem iam diximus in Romanam linguam interpretatos et legit et intelligit.*

81. *Ibid.*, p. 607.

82. *Ibid.*, p. 627.

83. *Ibid.*, p. 603.

84. We actually know very little about the pronunciation of Latin in the Middle Ages. There are some rhymes in French verse which inform us that the ending *-um* rhymed with French *-on*. On this see *Amis et Amiles*, vv. 2812–13, and elsewhere. Probably Latin in each land was pronounced with the peculiarities of the major

tongue spoken there, but Old French pronunciation had not departed, as yet, to any great degree from that of standard Romance. French Latin was, therefore, still intelligible. There was more complaint about the ungrammatical Latin of the English clerics.

85. The dress of a pilgrim is described, only to be ridiculed, in *Roman de Renart,* I, vv. 1418ff.

86. See Holmes, *History of Old French Literature.*

87. *Roman de Renart,* I, vv. 1402–1404.

88. *Huon de Bordeaux,* v. 2564.

89. Migne, 189, col. 949.

90. This was true throughout the Middle Ages and the Renaissance. The St. Bernard Pass also was frequently used. The latter was called Mongiu, or Mons Jovis, because the Romans had constructed a temple to Jupiter there. In the Abavus Glossary the Latin word *Alpes* glosses this *Mongiu.* See Mario Roques (ed.), *Recueil général des lexiques français* (1936), p. 4. John of Salisbury made ten trips over the Alps.—*Metal.,* III, Prologue; Migne, *P.L.,* 199, col. 889.

91. See above, p. 202.

92. *Nonnulli sibi de sanguinis generositate gloriantur, qui lixarum sordidarum filii sunt.—N.R.,* p. 312.

93. *Ibid.,* p. 316.

94. *Relinquatur hoc vitium iis qui spectaculis theatralibus obnoxii sunt.—Ibid.,* p. 321. Cf. *Ille et Galeron,* vv. 239-40.

95. Alexander is one of the very few in his day who mention the tragedies of Seneca: *Tragediam ipsius et declamaciones legere non erit inutile.*—Haskins, *Mediaeval Science,* p. 373.

96. For this episode consult *Gesta Abbatum Sancti Albani* (Rolls Series), I, 72–105.

97. Giraldus, IV, pp. 40–41.

98. Alexander returned to become an Augustinian canon and was abbot of Cirencester in 1213. He died in 1217.—Dugdale, VI, 176.

Chapter IX

1. The authority on mediaeval population is Josiah C. Russell, *British Medieval Population* (Albuquerque, 1948). The information which I now give was derived largely from personal discussion with Professor Russell. In England the average man was five feet six inches; in France the average was an inch shorter. Henry II of

England was five feet seven or eight; Richard was taller than this, and John was considerably shorter.

2. This description is in many Old French texts. Geoffrey de Vinsauf phrases it in Latin.—*Oxford Book of Mediaeval Latin Verse*, No. 68. The hair was sometimes artificially curled: *flavisque capellis et arte crispatis nimis.*—Giraldus, IV, 86. The color value of *vair* is attested in an unusual way. There is a place in southern France called Roques Vaires, where the rocks are a variegated blue and brownish gray.

3. Usamah, p. 94.

4. Again I am quoting Professor Russell. Giraldus states specifically that life beyond the age of fifty is not desirable.—Giraldus, VIII, 145–46. Walter Map gives a pitiful description of the condition of an aged monk, Gregory of Gloucester.—W.M., p. 81.

5. Russell thinks that the germ diseases which carried off the most people were tuberculosis and ague.

6. The observations in this and the following paragraph are deductions on my part. There are, however, many passages which show that the mediaeval man esteemed good breath, for instance: *Vilains, car vos traites an lai, Car vostre alainne m'ocidroit.*—Bartsch, *Altfranzösische Romanzen und Pastourellen*, I, 25, 9. In *El Conde Lucanor*, ed. P. H. Ureña (Buenos Aires, 1939), Exemplar 27, both the Emperor and his wife have sores on their bodies, as a matter of course.

7. *Auzels Cassadors*, vv. 3531–32.

8. References on mediaeval education are legion. Nigel Wireker remarks how masters are too easy. They spare the rod. Boys get but little grammar and then go home and spend the rest of their days hunting.—*S.P.* "Playing hookey" existed in those days; witness: *Erat autem puer . . . pulcher quidam et nobilis sed intactum bonarum artium fugax . . . ut . . . vix in scholia, sed pene omni die dilitescens reperiretur in vineis.*—Migne, *P.L.*, 156, col. 844.

9. *Et quant a l'escole venoient, Lor tables d'yvoire prenoient. Adont lor veissiez escrire Letres et vers d'amors en cire Lor graffes sont d'or et d'argent.*—*Floire et Blancheflor*, vv. 251–55. Also, *un grafe a trait de son grafier* (vv. 787, 1408). Evidently there was a special case for the stylus which was called a *grafier.* Baudri de Bourgueil has considerable to say about his wax tablets and his styli. He received as a fine present a small handy set of tablets, with eight leaves tied together. The wax was green, which did not show dirt so easily. See above, Chapter 3, n. 33.

10. Migne, *P.L.*, 156, col. 847. The text which we are citing is from the *De vita sua* of Guibert de Nogent.

11. Haskins, *Mediaeval Science*, p. 372.

12. Guernes, *Vie de Saint-Thomas*, vv. 162 ff.

13. Giraldus, I, 356–57. He calls her Letitia.

14. *Baudri de Bourgueil*, No. 101. See also Raby, *Secular Latin Poetry*, I, 343 ff.

15. The old woman in Marie de France's *Yonec* reads her Psalter (vv. 63–64). The *Vie d'Edouard le confesseur* was written by a nun, perhaps Clemence of Barking (vv. 5313 ff.). See further Paré, Brunot, and Tremblay, p. 52.

16. Gaimar, *Estorie des Engleis*, vv. 6495–96.

17. *Yvain*, vv. 5366–72.

18. Charles Beaulieux, *Histoire de l'orthographe française*, I, 32. Many of the laymen (upper class) could read. A young knight is mentioned as reading in W.M., p. 176. Denis Piramus, in his *Vie de Sent Edmund le rei*, ed. H. Kjellman (Göteborg, 1935), vv. 1581 ff., remarks that a king should have some learning.

19. *Huon de Bordeaux*, vv. 2668 ff.

20. Marie de France, *Fables*, ed. Warnke (Halle, 1898), pp. 271–72. "Del prestre e del lu."

21. It was certainly possible for a boy and a girl to attend school together, as in *Floire et Blancheflor*. See n. 8 above. We assume, however, that they had a tutor and did not attend an organized class where there could have been a mingling of the sexes.

22. Because of the need for bilingualism a king or high noble, even if he could read French, would be obliged to pass a letter over to a clerk for interpretation. Such a missive would be dictated in French to a clerk, who would put it into Latin. When the letter was received, it had to be expanded into French again for its recipient. Take for example *Anseÿs*, v. 716: *Et le bailla a un sien clerc ouvrir*. This situation where a letter is couched in language which is not the one used by either sender or recipient in daily intercourse reminds us of the situation in modern China, where the Wen li, or cultivated written language, has to be expanded when read orally. Letters did not circulate in the French language until the middle of the thirteenth century. The same may be said about the use of French in the keeping of accounts. Probably the Kingdom of Naples and Sicily was the first one to keep its accounts in French.

23. See above, p. 41.

24. I have not given much information on the animals that were familiar to the peoples of western Europe. The wolf survived in France as late as the sixteenth century, and in England until the seventeenth. The last wolf in Scotland was killed in the eighteenth

century. Bears and monkeys were common sights, displayed by traveling minstrels and kept at the courts of nobles. The monkeys were imported, of course, and bears were very uncommon west of Germany. Giraldus says that beavers were still to be found in Wales during his day; but they were very rare south of Scandinavia, where they survive today. Lions and leopards were common beasts of prey in the Holy Land, where they had man-eating habits. The Arab chronicler Usamah gives complete information on these dreadful beasts and their habits. They frequently attacked Crusaders. Chrétien's ideas on the savagery of these beasts may have come from a returned voyager to the Holy Land, but he himself could never have seen a lion. Usamah speaks of lions and leopards in his work (pp. 97, 114, 116, 134–42). A lion, about the size of a dog, is figured in Webster, Plate 25. In *Aye d'Avignon*, ed. F. Guessard and P. Meyer (Paris, 1861), vv. 2688ff., the knights stand near the *perron* and *esgardent le gieu des ours et des lions*. Here the lion must be a figurative animal.

25. Wright, p. 100.

26. See A. H. Schutz, *The Romance of Daude de Pradas called Dels Auzels Cassadors* (Columbus, Ohio, 1945).

27. See again the tympanum of Saint-Ursin at Bourges, where the boar hunt is depicted in detail.

28. *C.U.P.*, No. 19.

29. *Le Grand Testament*, ed. A. Longnon and L. Foulet (Paris, 1932), vv. 1198–1202.

30. When a messenger was sent formally by a lord or a high ecclesiast, it was customary to make quite a ceremony out of the occasion. The lord touched the messenger with his staff, or he would give him a token to express his responsibility: a glove from the lord's hand, or a walking stick. Doubtless the tokens were returned shortly thereafter. This was a sort of dismissal. Compare the way in which Charlemagne sends Ganelon on his mission to the Saracen king. In the same symbolical manner a gift could be granted or a wife bestowed. In Gaimar's *Estorie des Engleis*, vv. 3716–18: "'Marry her, then come to me.' The king held a staff; he extended it and made the grant."

31. Davison and Apel, pp. 24–27, 218.

32. Reese, p. 299.

33. Detailed information on these instruments can be found in Reese or in the *Harvard Dictionary of Music*. The form of the *viele* was somewhat variable. I have in mind the representation on the Limoges casket.—Dalton, p. 51.

34. Three horn players perform beautifully, like swans.—Joinville, § 525.

35. There is a picture of a *rote* played by two quills in Hartley and Elliot, Plate 17e.

36. A good list of musical instruments is in *Brut*, vv. 10543–45; also in *Erec et Enide*, vv. 2035 ff.

37. For a view of it see Hartley and Elliot, Plate 15c.

38. *Ibid.*, Plate 17d.

39. *Sounant lours cors de couepvre et de leton.*—*Aquin*, vv. 38–39. The word *cor* was a generic term. Here *grailes* or *buisines* must be intended. For an ivory horn see a specimen in the Victoria and Albert Museum, London.

40. *Bondissent cil tabor, grans fu la resonee.*—*Quatre fils Aymon*, v. 1136. What are the *cors bugheres* in v. 987?

41. The construction of an organ is outlined in some detail by Theophilus, pp. 341, 351. See also Reese, p. 329. A picture of the instrument with two players will be found in Hartley and Elliot, Plates 15a and 15e. The portable organ, played with one hand and pumped with the other while resting on the player's knee, became popular in the thirteenth century.

42. *Brut*, vv. 10421–28.

43. Reese, pp. 130–31. By the close of the thirteenth century the neumes such as we have described gave way to square notes, which continued to be placed on the four-line staff. This method of notation is still retained in chant books of the Roman Catholic Church.

44. This subject matter is too complicated for a general book of the nature of this one. The reader is referred to Edgar de Bruyne's *L'esthétique du moyen-âge* (Louvain, 1947) and to his larger *Etudes d'esthétique médiévale* (Bruges, 1946), II: *L'Epoque romane.*

45. *C.U.P.*, No. 20; and *Policraticus*, II, 108–109.

46. Chabaneau, *Rev. langues romanes* (1883), p. 165.

47. I have taken this list from a later source; but it is typical. The unlucky days varied with the locality as well as with time.—Warren A. Dawson, *A Leechbook of the 15th Century* (London, 1934), p. 329.

48. I, vv. 753–59. We find *auze* with the meaning "good luck" in the *Cid*, vv. 1523, 2366, 2369.

49. For thunder and the belief about stepping out with the left foot see *Piramus et Tisbé*, vv. 633–35.

50. *N.R.*, pp. 299–300, *et al.* Friday is different from other days because of the planet Venus. When Saturn is in Aquarius there are great rains.—*N.R.*, p. 40. Mars inspires caution (p. 41). Giraldus

remarked: *Astrologi tam Toledani similiter quoque et Apuli. . . .*—Giraldus, VIII, 242. Daude de Pradas believed in the influence of planets.—*Dels Auzels Cassadors*, vv. 534–37. *De male ore est nez* (*Connebert*, v. 278) is a well-distributed expression.

51. *Enueg*, v. 25.

52. *N.R.*, pp. 466–72. On the lapidary lore of the period there are many references. For the sources themselves see Joan Evans and Paul Studer, *Anglo-Norman Lapidaries* (Paris, 1924).

53. *N.R.*, pp. 178, 179.

54. Helinand speaks of studying *Bononice codices, Salerni pyxides, Toledi daemones.*—Migne, *P.L.*, 212, col. 603. The Spaniards ascribed the same reputation to Toledo: *En Santiago habia un Dean que habia muy grant talante de saber el arte de la nigromancia, et oyo dezir que don Illan de Toledo sabia ende mas que ninguno que fuesse en aquella sazon; et por ende vinose para Toledo para aprender de aquella sciencia.*—*El Conde Lucanor*, Exemplo XI, p. 58.

55. Marie de France, *Fables:* "Del vilein et del folet."

56. W.M., pp. 98–99.

57. Gautier le Leu, *Li Sohais*, vv. 103–104.

58. W.M., p. 97.

59. *N.R.*, p. 310.

60. A ghost is called a *fantosme.*—*Yvain*, v. 1226.

61. W.M., pp. 89–98.

62. *Yvain*, vv. 1190–91, and elsewhere.

63. So in Marie de France's *Le Fresne*, and in *Elioxe* (cf. Paulin Paris in *Hist. Litt. de la France*, XXII, 350ff.).

64. The woman who lost her nose passed this deformity on to her children in Marie's *Bisclavret.*

65. *Nemo enim sanae mentis vulgi fabulosa deliramenta credit, quod pueros supponi aut transformari.*—*Hist. Archb. Th. Becket*, I, 204. In this same source (I, 157) the superstition is mentioned that a boy baptized on Whitsunday cannot drown or be burned *sicut vulgaris habet opinionem.*

66. Flemings could tell future events from the shoulders of a ram.—Giraldus, *Itinerarium Kambriae*, XI.

67. *N.R.*, p. 310.

68. *Ibid.*, p. 311; W.M., p. 179; Giraldus, VIII, 216, and III, 27.

69. This is ridiculed in *Quatre fils Aymon*, v. 6507.

70. Giraldus, *Itinerarium Kambriae*, II, 11.

71. Brunetto Latini, *Tresor*, I, 155.

72. Dalton, pp. 291–93.

73. A silver plate is used as a fan for secular purposes in the *Prise d'Orange*, v. 664. I for one believe that the admittedly difficult lines in the *Flamenca—Bels conseillers ab granz ventaillas Aportet hom davan cascu Ques anc us non failli ad u . . .* (vv. 580–82)—mean that attendants with fans were stationed by each guest.

74. Dalton, pp. 57–60.

75. *Ibid.*, p. 213.

76. There was a chalice of pewter even at Westminster.—Giraldus, III, 357.

77. I have a photograph of this from a dealer's catalogue where it was offered for sale.

78. See my article in *Speculum*, IX (1934), 195–204.

79. Dalton, pp. 73–95.

80. Ernst P. Goldschmidt, *Gothic and Renaissance Bookbindings* (London, 1928).

81. J. K. Akerman in *Archaeologia*, o. s. XXXVI (1855), 200–202, with plate. There are a sapphire ring, two rings set with glass gems, a gimmel ring, a torque ring, and one with enameled bezel.

82. I have one in my possession which came from Exeter.

83. No. 2447.

84. No. 2503.

85. This is reproduced in the Bédier and Hazard, *Histoire de la littérature française illustrée*, I, 29. It is reproduced in part in Webster, Plate 42. The frieze at Cremona (Webster, Plate 25) is remarkable.

86. Bédier and Hazard, p. 40.

87. *Religious Art in France, XIII Century* (New York, 1913), p. 52 n. The plants recognized are the plantain, arum, ranunculus, fern, clover, celandine, hepatica, columbine, cress, parsley, strawberry, ivy, snapdragon, broom, and oak leaves.

88. Rorimer, pp. 18, 22, 35, 41 ff.

89. Theophilus, p. 17.

90. Theophilus gives this "fixed" palette: pp. 3 ff.

91. *Guigemar*, vv. 233–45.

92. See above, p. 84.

93. Chapter 5, n. 14, above.

94. A twelfth-century fresco is preserved at Jelling, Denmark; see *National Geographic Magazine*, XCV (1949), 166. See also Chapter 2, n. 26.

95. *Liber de coloribus*, ed. D. V. Thompson, Jr., in *Speculum*, I (1926), 280 ff., 448–50.

96. Samuel A. Ives and Hellmut Lehmann-Haupt, *An English 13th Century Bestiary* (New York, 1942), pp. 40–41.

97. Camille Enlart, *Architecture religeuse*, I, 429.

98. Clapham and Power, p. 506n.

99. *Ibid.*, pp. 315–16.

100. Usamah, p. 94.

101. A good description of court proceedings, together with high-handedness on the part of the overlord, is in Marie's *Lanval*. See also the preliminary trial of Ganelon in the *Chanson de Roland*.

102. Many instances of ordeal are found. There is a good example in the Tristan story, both the Thomas and the Béroul versions. See Béroul, *The Romance of Tristan*, ed. A. Ewert (Oxford, 1939). The man of the twelfth century knew that this was not a good test: *Il n'a soz ciel larron tant ait avoir emblé, S'on le lait escondire qui ja soit pris provez.—Doön de la Roche*, vv. 420–21.

103. The water ordeal is described in Usamah, pp. 167-69. See also W.M., p. 65.

104. Usamah, pp. 167–68.

105. Giraldus, VIII, p. 37. Gerald says (p. 25) that capital punishment should be a last resort. A good prince forgives many offenses (p. 22).

106. W.M., p. 279.

107. For some of these horrible treatments consult *Rou*, III, 936ff., where robbers are dismembered, have their teeth drawn, eyes put out, and fists cut off; others are roasted alive or boiled in lead. *Tuz les a fait si cunreer, Hisdus furent a esgarder.* These are milder examples: *Car metez la dame en destroit, S'aucune chose vos disoit.*—Marie, *Bisclavret*, vv. 255–56. *En un tro de tarere li boutent erranment Ses deus pols, puis les coignent molt angoisseusement.*—Adenet li rois, *Berte aus grans piés*, vv. 2254–55. Eyes were put out with red-hot awls.—Usamah, p. 169. There are illustrations of the common pillory (Plate 11c) and of the gallows (Plate 11b) in Hartley and Elliot.

108. *Wistasce li moines*, vv. 695–730.

109. As in the *Chanson de Roland* (death of Ganelon), *Quatre fils Aymon* (death of Herviz), and the treatment of Lunete in the *Yvain*. For burning at the stake see J. R. Reinhardt's article in *Speculum*, XVI (1941), 186–209.

110. *Cartulaire de Notre-Dame*, I, *lxxxix*. There was considerable difference in this matter between practice and the legal codes. Murder is mentioned most severely as a capital offense to be pun-

ished by the overlord. Take, for instance, the Charte de Saint-Omer: *Si quis in villa S. Audomari hominem occiderit, si deprehensus et reus convictus fuerit, nusquam salvationis remedium habebit. . . .*—Gessler, *Textes diplomatiques latins*, p. 64.

111. *Monnaies royales et seigneuriales de France*, Rollin and Feuardent (Paris, 1891).

112. The danger of carrying cash money is expressed in the *Cid: Non duerme sin sospecha qui aver trae monedado* (v. 126). It is interesting to note how a large sum of money was paid out in Spain, and presumably in France also: *En medio del palacio tendieron una almoçalla, sobrella una savana de rançal e muy blanca* (vv. 182–83).

113. Poole, p. 78.

114. Carl Stephenson, "Les aides des villes françaises aux XIIe et XIIIe siècles," *Moyen Age*, XXIV (1922), 274ff.

115. Abbot Samson demanded twenty shillings from each knight fee when he was enthroned.—Jocelin, p. 43. The *Ancrene Riwle* speaks of the rapacious knight who likes to "plunder and pillage the church, for he is like the willow which sprouteth yet the better that it is after cropped" (pp. 86–87).

116. H. Géraud (ed.), *Paris sous Philippe le bel* (Paris, 1837). (Collection des documents inédits). One person listed, Renier le Flamenc, pays the large sum of eighty pounds (p. 116).

117. Clapham and Power, pp. 316–17. On January 1 (Feast of the Circumcision) it was customary for a lord to receive a gift from each of his vassals.—Jocelin, p. 100.

118. *Nièce, dist li evesques, ne soiez esgaree, Tenez large mesnie, donez larges sodees, Car par ce serez vos servie et honoree.—Doön de la Roche*, vv. 2593–95. On this *fole largesse* consult further p. 218 above.

119. Clapham and Power, p. 313.

120. *Arch.H.D.*, pp. 4, 5, 8, 9, 15, 16.

121. Poole, p. 5.

122. W.M., p. 76.

123. *Ibid.*, p. 72; William of Newburgh, *Hist. Rerum Anglicarum* (Rolls Series, No. 82), II, Chapter 27.

124. W.M., p. 72; *Hist. Rerum Anglicarum*, Chapter 13; Giraldus, VIII, 70.

125. Many references are available on the Albigensians. For a direct source of information see Bernard Gui, *Manuel de l'inquisiteur*, ed. G. Mollat, 2 vols. (Classiques de l'histoire de France au moyen-âge).

Index

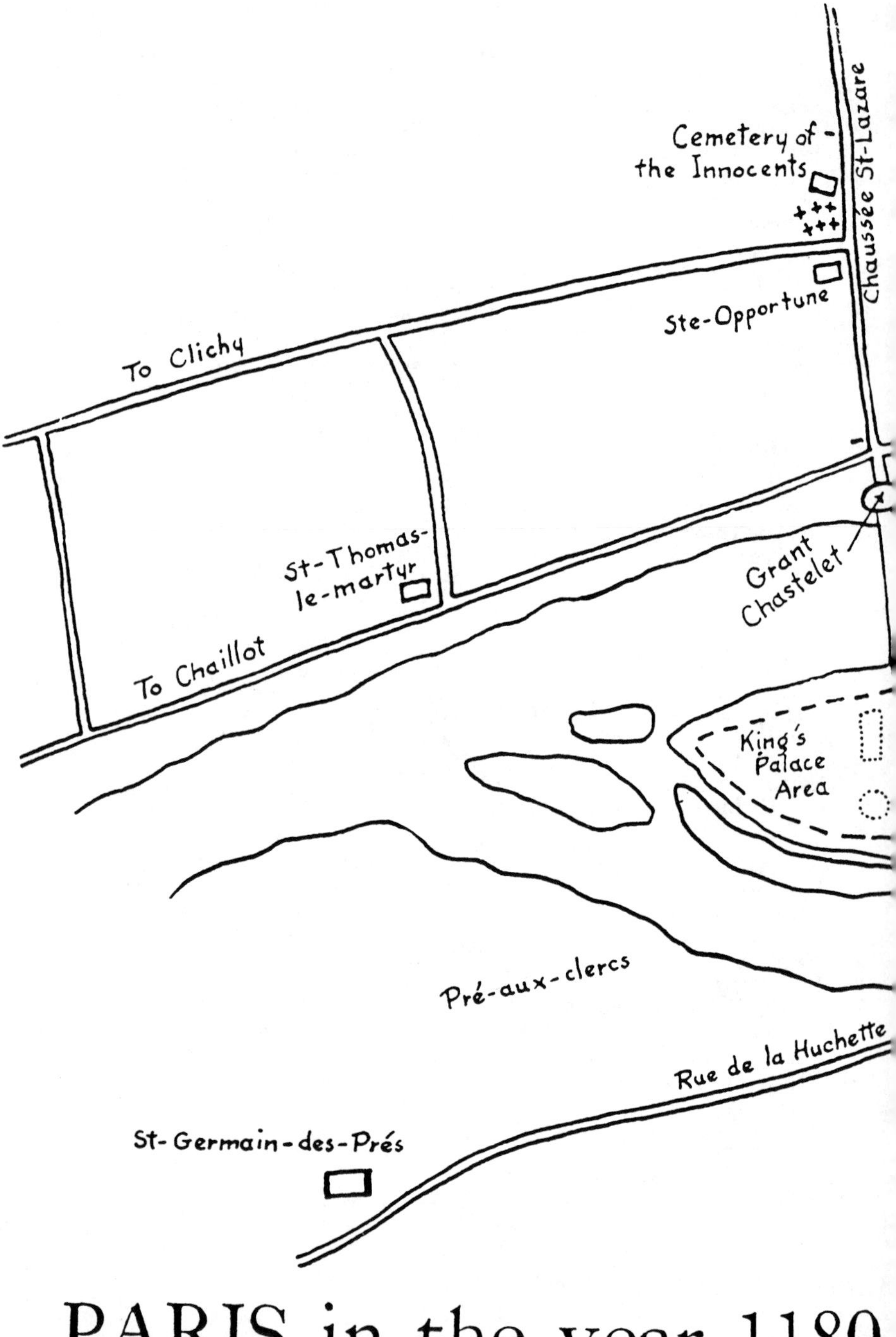

PARIS in the year 1180